THE INSPIRATION AND INTERPRETATION
OF SCRIPTURE

The Inspiration and Interpretation
of Scripture

WHAT THE EARLY CHURCH CAN TEACH US

Michael Graves

WILLIAM B. EERDMANS PUBLISHING COMPANY
GRAND RAPIDS, MICHIGAN / CAMBRIDGE, U.K.

Published 2014 by

Wm. B. Eerdmans Publishing Co.

2140 Oak Industrial Drive N.E., Grand Rapids, Michigan 49505 /

P.O. Box 163, Cambridge CB3 9PU U.K.

www.eerdmans.com

Printed in the United States of America

20 19 18 17 16 15 14   7 6 5 4 3 2 1

Library of Congress Cataloging-in-Publication Data

Graves, Michael, 1973-

The inspiration and interpretation of scripture: what the early church can teach us /

Michael Graves.

pages   cm

Includes bibliographical references and indexes.

ISBN 978-0-8028-6963-0 (pbk.: alk. paper)

1. Bible — Inspiration — History of doctrines — Early church, ca. 30-600.

2. Bible — Hermeneutics — History. 3. Bible — Criticism, interpretation, etc. —

History — Early church, ca. 30-600.   I. Title.

BS480.G73   2014

220.1'309015 — dc23

2013029794

For Ben and Nick

Contents

CHAPTER ONE

Introduction

What Is Our Topic?

Scripture has held a central place in Christianity from the origins of the church two thousand years ago up to the present day. The original message that the apostles taught about Jesus was grounded in the "Scriptures," which at that time consisted only of the "Old Testament." The apostle Paul explained the scriptural basis of his message in this way: "For I delivered to you as of first importance what I also received: that Christ died for our sins in accordance with the Scriptures, that he was buried, that he was raised on the third day in accordance with the Scriptures, and that he appeared to Cephas, then to the twelve" (1 Cor. 15:3-5). The Gospel of Matthew records numerous events in the life of Jesus that took place in order to "fulfill" what the Lord had spoken through an Old Testament prophet (Matt. 1:22; 2:15, 17, 23, etc.). The early church inherited from ancient Judaism and from the apostles the belief that God had communicated with humanity through sacred writings known as "Scripture." Over time, as the New Testament documents came to be read in the churches alongside the Old Testament, Christians began to recognize a canon of sacred writings consisting of both the holy books of ancient Israel (the "Old Testament") and the authoritative writings of the apostles (the "New Testament"). Together, these texts made up the Christian Bible, which has been read, preached, and prayed over since the first centuries of the church.[1]

What makes the Bible so special to Christians is the belief that it is uniquely inspired by God. It is true that sometimes we talk about other writings as being "inspired." A novel may be inspired by a person's life, or we may even say that an author was inspired by a sense of beauty or wonder. This kind of inspiration can be deeply profound, as great writers of the past have captured keen insights into the world we live in. Yet, this kind of inspiration is still less than what Christians typically believe to be true of the Bible. Christians believe that the scriptural writings came about because "people spoke from God as they were carried along by the Holy Spirit" (2 Pet. 1:21). When speaking of the inspiration of the Bible, most Christians imagine that God's activity in inspiring the writers was more direct, more extensive, and more uniquely purposeful than the inspiration that other writers have experienced. Saint Jerome in the early fifth century expressed his belief in the divine inspiration of Scripture succinctly: "The Scriptures were written and produced by the Holy Spirit."[2]

The present book aims to describe what Christians in the first five centuries of the church believed about the inspiration of Scripture.[3] I will do this by identifying various ideas that early Christians considered to be logical implications of biblical inspiration. In other words: What is true of Scripture as a result of its being inspired? What should divine inspiration cause us to expect from Scripture? The answers to these questions in the early church related not only to the nature of Scripture's truth claims, but also to the manner in which Scripture was to be interpreted and the possible standards by which scriptural interpretation could be measured. These dimensions of Scripture were closely interrelated in a variety of ways.

Sadly the views of the average Christian during this period are difficult to reconstruct. But we can grasp the basic shape of early Christian beliefs about Scripture through the writings of Christian intellectuals, including many bishops, known commonly as the "Church Fathers." This masculine-oriented phrase reflects the unfortunate fact that men rather than women generally had opportunities to engage in written biblical interpretation during this period. Moreover, the writings women did produce did not survive. For example, in the late fourth century Jerome exchanged letters devoted mostly to biblical topics with a woman named Marcella, an ascetic leader in Rome. Marcella studied Hebrew and is reported to have answered questions put to her by priests on scriptural matters.[4] Yet, although Jerome's letters to her survive, her letters to Jerome were not preserved.[5] This is typical of women's writings in the first several centuries of the church. As a result, the figures studied in this book will by necessity be the "Church Fathers."

I am of course writing as one who is situated in the modern world, and I cannot help but reflect my own situation in time. But my goal in describing these ancient authors will be to present their perspectives in their own terms as they formulated them within their historical contexts. Even as I seek to identify widely held beliefs, I will also take note of diversity in viewpoint where it existed. In fact, some of the major conceptual categories that I will discuss are in tension with one another, revealing differences of opinion as to the implications of inspiration. What I am trying to describe is not a coherent, systematic doctrine of biblical inspiration that was shared by all early Christians, but rather the network of ideas about inspiration reflected in early Christian writings. This network has identifiable benchmarks but also diverse trajectories.

In the course of describing what ancient Christians thought about biblical inspiration, I will try to identify some important insights that may be helpful for Christians today. I believe that the Church Fathers have much to teach us about how to understand Scripture. At the same time, there are many ideas found in their writings that reflect their ancient context; these ideas may no longer seem credible or meaningful today, at least not as they were originally formulated. But when proper account is taken of the intellectual environment within which the Church Fathers lived, many of their beliefs about Scripture prove to be not only helpful but even essential for contemporary Christians who want to read Scripture and hear its divine message. Early Christian ideas about inspiration illuminate the various ways that Scripture is meaningful for Christian readers. It is the ever-present Christian significance of Scripture that takes center stage with the Church Fathers. In the Conclusion to this book, I will suggest some ways that Christians today might be able to learn from the early church while at the same time respecting the differences between the ancient and modern contexts.

In the remainder of the Introduction I will describe some of the major conceptual and scriptural challenges that confront us in defining the nature of inspiration, provide some historical context for ancient thinking about sacred texts, and briefly introduce the major Christian figures to be discussed in the chapters to follow.

Possible Entailments of Inspiration

In logic the term "entailment" refers to the relationship between two statements, where the second is necessarily true in logical consequence of the first being true. Consider these two sentences: (1) Marcus has been hired as commander of the army. (2) Marcus has a job. If Marcus has been hired to serve as commander of the army, then it logically follows that he has a job. Provided that we are using these words in their most commonly accepted senses, the second statement is necessarily true if the first is true. Not only can the word "entailment" be used to describe the relationship between such statements, but the second, logically necessary statement can be called an "entailment" of the first. For example, if the above statements about Marcus were true, then the fact that Marcus has a job is an entailment of the fact that he has been hired as commander of the army. Thus, an entailment is some proposition or quality that necessarily accompanies another proposition or quality.

In this book, I will be considering various affirmations that could be seen as entailments of biblical inspiration. All Christians in the early church believed that Scripture was inspired by God. It seems that believing in the inspiration of Scripture was an entailment of believing in Christianity. The next question I want to ask is this: What were the entailments of believing in inspiration? If it is granted that Scripture is inspired, what must be true of Scripture as a result? Some of the perspectives that the Church Fathers offered on this question might be surprising to modern Christians. It is therefore important to point out that this question is not simple to answer.

If one were working within the framework of biblical and early Christian thought, it would be possible to come up with many attributes that could potentially be true of Scripture as a result of inspiration. But this does not mean that these attributes *necessarily* belong to Scripture. For example, there are many Christians who believe that as a consequence of divine inspiration Scripture must be unique in its ethical teachings. Since God's ways and thoughts are different from ours (see Isa. 55:8-9), they expect that what God says in the Bible should be totally different from what human beings devise by their own ingenuity.

These Christians are often surprised to learn, for example, that the *Code of Hammurabi*, written before the time of Moses, already permitted debt slaves to go free in the fourth year, which is earlier than the seventh year indicated by Exodus 21.[6] Similarly, Greek writers prior to Jesus expressed the idea that you should act toward others as you would want others to act toward you.[7] Scripture and non-biblical writings sometimes even share general ideas about how gods work in history. An example is the idea that a national deity becomes angry with his people and punishes them by handing them over to a foreign oppressor. This idea is found both in the ninth-century BCE *Mesha Stela* (with Chemosh, God of Moab) and in the biblical book of Judges (with YHWH, God of Israel).[8] Examples such as these are numerous.

The simplest theological answer to questions raised by these parallels is that the uniqueness of every part of the Bible is not a *necessary* corollary to its inspiration. In fact, it is not uncommon for Christian scholars with training in ancient history to use literary and archaeological parallels from the world of the Bible to illuminate biblical texts in church settings. For such scholars, the notion that uniqueness is an entailment of inspiration is simply a misunderstanding of the doctrine of inspiration. Nevertheless, I think it is worthwhile to reflect on this particular misunderstanding, not only because it is common, but also because there is nothing necessarily illogical about it.

If we did not possess any information about the ancient world outside the Bible, it would be possible to assume that the ideas revealed to sinful humanity by God would be entirely different from what human beings invent on their own. As it turns out, however, non-biblical writers have indeed expressed ideas that are also found in the Bible. This is likely because even fallen people bear the image of God and are capable of feeling their way toward God (see Gen. 1:27; Acts 17:26-31) and because God inspired biblical writers to make use of elements in their cultures. Christians have traditionally regarded the Bible as "true" (see below), but that does not necessarily mean that it must be unique. All of this suggests that it would be helpful for us to differentiate between what must be true of Scripture and what might be true of Scripture in consequence of its inspiration.

This observation helps us make better sense of many complex biblical issues, such as differences in details between parallel passages of Scripture. For example, in Matthew's Gospel the fig tree cursed by Jesus withers immediately (Matt. 21:19), whereas in Mark's Gospel the fig tree withers the next day (Mark 11:13-14, 20-25). Similarly, in Matthew's Gospel one angel appears at the empty tomb (Matt. 28:2-7), whereas in Luke's Gospel there are two angels (Luke 24:4-7). Such differences in detail have not traditionally been taken as evidence that the Gospel accounts are untrue. The particular message of each Gospel is expressed through its distinctive presentation of such details (for example, see section 14 below). It might have been expected that divinely inspired texts would not contain such differences. Such an expectation would not be unreasonable, but it is not a necessary entailment of divine inspiration.

These thoughts serve to illustrate what a difficult task it is to define what is necessarily true of Scripture as a result of inspiration. In fact, rather than asking what qualities *must* belong to Scripture in view of divine inspiration, a better way to approach this topic is to ask simply what *is* true of Scripture because it is inspired. Asking the question in this way allows for more flexibility in balancing our theological expectations with the actual biblical texts we possess. From today's standpoint, we can appreciate what various Church Fathers believed to be logical implications of inspiration without committing ourselves to the idea that these beliefs are logically *necessary*. Each possible entailment may be seen as open to evaluation and refinement-in light of continuing theological reflection and study of Scripture's contents.

Testimonies within Scripture about Inspiration

What Scripture says about its own inspiration was obviously important to the Church Fathers. Every Christian interpreter discussed in this book thought of himself as following the understanding of inspiration set forth in Scripture. What biblical books do and do not say about scriptural inspiration was instrumental in determining what directions the early church would take in developing its own ideas about Scripture.

In terms of defining the nature of textual revelation, the Old Testament on its own did not play a significant role in shaping the Church Fathers' beliefs about scriptural inspiration. To be sure, the Old Testament portrays God speaking to individuals such as Abraham and Jacob, and large sections of Exodus, Leviticus, and Numbers represent words that God spoke to the community (Exod. 20) or to Moses (for example, Exod. 21–24). Furthermore, the prophetic books are filled with phrases such as "says the LORD" or "The word of the LORD that came" (to the prophet), which give testimony to the fact that God spoke. But within the Old Testament itself, the overall narratives of most books do not explain how the compositions as a whole were inspired by God, and poetic books such as Proverbs, Ecclesiastes, Song of Songs, and Psalms — although clearly intending to offer instruction about God — do not make the explicit claim to be revelation. Early Christian interpreters did not find instructions within these Old Testament books as to how to read them as inspired.

The legal portions of the Pentateuch are particularly complex as revelation. The "law of Moses" was certainly known as an authoritative text during the period when the Old Testament was written.[9] This provides the most secure basis within the Old Testament for developing a doctrine of *written* revelation. Yet, in spite of their great admiration for Moses, the Church Fathers uniformly regarded the Mosaic Law as no longer relevant for them, at least at the literal level. Many early Christians believed that Old Testament laws conveyed symbolic meanings. There were also Christians who regarded the law as a punishment on Israel, or as a concession granted to Israel after they learned animal sacrifice in Egypt.[10] But in any case, Christians did not regard the rules revealed in the Pentateuch as binding in their literal sense. As a result, the legal material in the Pentateuch received only modest attention among the Church Fathers, and the revelation at Sinai did not contribute substantially to the early church's understanding of inspiration.

It is the concept of "Scripture" as found in the New Testament and located conceptually in the Greco-Roman world that became the paradigm for the Church Fathers' views. Although New Testament writers do not generally seem aware that they themselves are writing "Scripture,"[11] they nevertheless express ideas about Scripture in relation to the Old Testament that are clearly relevant for formulating a doctrine of inspiration. New Testament texts such as Luke 24:44; 2 Peter 1:20-21; and 2 Timothy 3:16 show that Jesus and the apostles viewed Old Testament compositions as a whole as Scripture. This way of thinking is evident throughout the New Testament.[12] Based on texts such as John 10:35, "Scripture cannot be broken," it is clear why the early church took such a lofty view of Scripture.

New Testament writers provide several guideposts for understanding the inspiration of the Old Testament. Two important guideposts are as follows: (1) Old Testament texts speak of major events in the ministry of Jesus, including his death and resurrection (1 Cor. 15:3-5; Luke 24:44-47; Acts 17:2-3); and (2) the Scriptures are "profitable" for "teaching, reproof, correction, and training in righteousness" (2 Tim. 3:16). Both of these are key components of the traditional Christian understanding of the Old Testament, as found in the New Testament and carried forward by the Church Fathers. But they also raise questions, and it is only fair to address these questions with regard to the New Testament before moving on to discuss the Church Fathers.

First, we may note that many Old Testament texts cited by New Testament writers as proving some aspect of Jesus' ministry do not seem to be talking directly about Jesus in their original contexts. For example, Psalm 16:10, "For you will not abandon my soul to Sheol, or let your holy one see corruption," is cited as a proof for Jesus' resurrection in Acts 2:22-32 and 13:35. In its Old Testament context, however, this verse appears to be an expression of confidence on the part of the Psalmist that God will not let him die as a result of his present calamity. Yet, Peter argues in Acts that it cannot be about David because David died and did not rise again from the grave, whereas Jesus rose from the dead (Acts 2:29-32; 13:36-37). Likewise, Matthew 2:15 states that Hosea 11:1, "Out of Egypt I called my son," was "fulfilled" when Jesus was brought out of Egypt by Joseph and Mary after the death of Herod. But in its original context in Hosea, it refers to a past event, the nation of Israel coming out of Egypt in the exodus. And again: the apostle Paul argues in Galatians 3:16 that the singular word "seed" (Hebrew *zera'*, Greek *sperma*) is singular because it points to Jesus, whereas in its Old Testament context this collective noun points in its immediate sense to multiple descendants (see Gen. 13:15-16).

Second, we may take note of how the Scriptures are actually used as "profitable" in the New Testament. For example, Paul applies the law from Deuteronomy 25:4, "You shall not muzzle an ox when it is treading out the grain," to his own situation as an apostle laboring spiritually on behalf of the Corinthians (1 Cor. 9:8-12). In fact, Paul argues that the Law of Moses was speaking "entirely" (Greek *pantōs*) for the sake of people (v. 10), that is, not for the sake of oxen.[13] In contrast to this, modern scholars who study Old Testament laws in their original context generally hold that this law was first intended in its most basic sense to address the treatment of oxen. As another example, the writer of Hebrews mentions Barak, Samson, and Jephthah as examples of faith (Heb. 11:32), whereas commentators today generally recognize that the author of Judges portrayed these characters as flawed leaders who represented the downward fall of Israel's religious ideals.[14]

As is clear, finding the proper significance of the guideposts left by the New Testament is not a straightforward process. The key to reading the signpost correctly is to find the theological link that connects the Old Testament citation with the point that the New Testament writer is trying to make. For example, when Paul makes his "seed" argument in Galatians 3:16, he wants to show that Jesus brought to fulfillment the great promises made to Abraham, including the promise that all families of the earth would be blessed in his "seed" (Gen. 22:18). There is a genuine thematic connection; the text was not chosen at random. As we will see, the Church Fathers often serve as helpful guides in seeing the theological connections that make the New Testament citations of the Old Testament work.

But even if one affirms that Jesus' ministry was "according to the Scriptures" and that the Scriptures profit by what they teach, it must be acknowledged that most of those who teach or preach from the Old Testament today do not appeal to the Old Testament in precisely the same way as the New Testament writers did. In fact, some modern Christian writers have explicitly stated that we should *not* interpret the Old Testament in the same way that New Testament writers did. They interpreted Scripture in a special and unrepeatable way — it is argued — because they themselves were inspired, whereas we who are not inspired must try to interpret according to the original intention of the biblical writers.[15]

This returns us to our opening question: What should we expect of Scripture if we believe in inspiration? Although the idea that we should *not* interpret Scripture exactly as the New Testament did is a viable Christian point of view, it is certainly not the only possible position, or even the most self-evident one. It was certainly not self-evident to the Church Fathers. One could argue that precisely because the New Testament authors were inspired we should interpret the Old Testament exactly as they did, because through inspiration they showed us the proper way to interpret. This is generally how the Church Fathers thought, and it explains much of what might seem unusual to modern readers about their biblical interpretation.

If one were to speak a word in defense of the modern perspective, it should be said that following the "method" of the New Testament, however appealing it may sound, comes with many complications, too. For one thing, if modern Christians were to adopt the same interpretive stance toward Scripture as the New Testament writers did toward the Old Testament, the results might be more subjective than many interpreters wish to allow. Another concern of modern biblical scholarship is that ancient methods of reading do not pay enough attention to the historical context and literal meaning of the text, with the result that readers cannot fully appreciate the individual qualities of each biblical book.[16] As we will see below, some of the Church Fathers attempted to address these concerns.

Ancient Readers of Sacred Texts

While certain uses of the Old Testament by early Christian writers may seem unusual to modern readers of the Bible, it is helpful to consider that the interpretive practices of these early Christians seem very much at home within the cultural context of the Greco-Roman world. When we look at how other readers in the same ancient context interpreted their sacred texts, we find striking similarities to the interpretations of the Old

Testament found not only in the Church Fathers but also in the New Testament. This shows that, however surprising they might seem to us, the appeals to the Old Testament made by early Christian writers would have been meaningful and potentially convincing for the ancient readers to whom these texts were originally addressed.

Many ancient writers believed that sacred religious texts conveyed symbolic meanings through what on the surface appeared to be straight narratives. As an example, the Neoplatonic philosopher Porphyry (died c. 304 CE), who approached the works of Homer as sacred literature, interpreted the olive tree near the Cave of the Nymphs in *Odyssey* 13 as a symbolic representation of God's wisdom in creating the world, with the cave itself standing for the world.[17] Similarly, the Jewish philosopher Philo (died c. 45 CE) interpreted the story of Abraham, Sarah, and Hagar as an allegory describing the ideal course of education starting with the liberal arts (Hagar) as preparation for the study of virtue (Sarah).[18] These examples represent the intellectual milieu within which Paul made his allegorical interpretation of Sarah and Hagar as representing two covenants (Gal. 4:21-31).

Another principle of ancient interpretation is the keen interest taken by ancient readers in peculiar linguistic details in sacred texts. These details could be seen as markers in the text left by divine inspiration to serve as jumping-off points for expositions. Thus, the famous second-century Jewish scholar Rabbi Akiba once gave an exposition based on the singular form of the word "frog" *(tsphrd')* in Exodus 8:6 to the effect that it was from a single frog that all the frogs of the second plague arose.[19] This may be likened to Paul's argument about the singular "seed" in Galatians 3:16.

Ancient interpreters also saw significance in the etymologies of proper names. This may be illustrated by the Stoic Philosopher Cornutus (first century CE), who explained the names of Zeus and Hera as "life" *(zōsa)* and "air" *(aēr)*.[20] This perspective is also represented by the etymologies of Melchizedek as "king of righteousness" and Salem as "peace" that are interpreted in Hebrews 7:2. Section 10 below is devoted to this dimension of ancient interpretation.

As a final illustration of the interpretive environment of early Christianity, the *Commentary on Habakkuk* found among the Qumran Scrolls shows how statements made in prophetic books could be applied to situations of the commentator's immediate present.[21] "For the wicked surround the righteous" (Hab. 1:4) is interpreted so that "the wicked" is identified as the "Wicked Priest," a figure contemporaneous with the community, and "the righteous" is identified as the "Teacher of Righteousness," who was the founder of the Qumran community. Similarly, the sentence "For behold, I am raising up the Chaldeans, that bitter and hasty nation" (Hab. 1:6) is said to refer to the Romans.[22] Even though this section of Habakkuk appears to refer to events of Habakkuk's day, the Qumran interpreters perceive the meaningfulness of the text by seeing in it references to events of their own time. This approach is similar to what Jesus says about those who did not comprehend his parables: "In them the prophecy of Isaiah is fulfilled that says, 'You will indeed hear but never understand, and you will indeed see but never perceive . . .'" (Matt. 13:14-15). Jesus quotes Isaiah 6:9-10, which originally spoke of Isaiah's contemporaries but is said to be "fulfilled" in those who similarly do not hear the word of the Lord spoken by Jesus. This was a recognized way to handle Old Testament predictions.

New Testament writers interpreted the Old Testament in a manner suited to the cultural context in which they lived. The Church Fathers generally followed along these lines and even tried to formulate concrete ideas about inspiration out of what they perceived in the New Testament. How does the contextual nature of early Christian interpretation relate to our understanding of inspiration? Let me suggest two major conclusions that I draw from this discussion:

First, because the early Church Fathers were closer in time and place than we are to the Greco-Roman cultural environment of the New Testament, they are likely to have useful insights for us as we try to wrap our minds around what it meant in the ancient world for New Testament writers to claim that Scripture was inspired by God. We will explore numerous angles taken on this topic by a variety of Church Fathers, and not all the views fit together neatly. But this fact does not detract in any way from their importance. On the contrary, the variety of beliefs about biblical inspiration reflected in the Church Fathers provides a full picture of the options that were available. However diverse or extreme the views of these Church Fathers might sometimes appear today, their cultural proximity to the New Testament renders their views on biblical inspiration worthy of careful consideration.

Second, since the ideas about inspiration found in the Church Fathers reflect concepts about "Scripture" prevalent in the ancient world, we are led to ask if we might express our beliefs about the nature of Scripture differently today. This kind of thinking is not uncommon for modern Christian readers even in relation to Scripture itself. For example, many Christians are comfortable accepting the theological claims and the fundamental perspective on reality found in the early chapters of Genesis, without feeling the need to adopt as scientifically accurate the ancient cosmology presented in those chapters. This same line of reasoning can be applied to the whole way in which the Church Fathers envisioned "Scripture." One could accept their theological vision of Scripture and their belief in Scripture's complete truthfulness, without needing to adopt the entire set of assumptions that were held in the ancient world about Scripture.

I hope that this book will encourage fresh and faithful thinking about inspiration. Some of what the Church Fathers say about Scripture is credible and potentially useful for Christians today. Readers may find their own appreciation of the Bible enhanced through their insights. At the same time, as we recognize the historically conditioned nature of some of their ideas, I hope that readers will consider for themselves how best to understand biblical inspiration in our context.

Of particular importance is the connection in the early church between inspiration and interpretation. If the God who was revealed in Jesus Christ inspired the sacred Scriptures to instruct humankind, then Scripture must be interpreted in such a way that people living "today" (whenever that may be) can encounter Christ and learn how God wants them to live. Early Christians read Scripture with a view toward its contemporary Christian significance. Each possible entailment of inspiration discussed in this book relates in some way to this larger concern. An important task for today's church is to understand how Christians in the modern world can best appropriate this theological vision for scriptural interpretation.

The Church Fathers and the Inspiration of Scripture

My final task in this chapter is to introduce the Church Fathers whose views I will be describing, and explain briefly how the following chapters are organized.

In the second century CE, Christian writers by and large did not yet write commentaries or tractates on biblical books. Many of the earliest Christian writings outside the New Testament, such as the letters of Ignatius and the *Martyrdom of Polycarp* (part of a corpus referred to as the "Apostolic Fathers"), are practical or devotional, and do not engage explicitly in textual interpretation. Even as the second century progressed, Scripture was read in the churches and quoted in written documents, but most of the literature that was produced focused on defending the faith against outsiders or addressing theological controversies within the church. Important works written in defense of the faith include three by Justin Martyr (died c. 165), a *First Apology,* a *Second Apology,* and the *Dialogue with Trypho,* which is presented as a dialogue between Justin and a Jew named Trypho;[23] a work by Tatian (second century) called *Oration to the Greeks;* and an *Apology* written in 197 by Tertullian. The first major Christian figure to write in Latin, Tertullian also produced many works aimed at interpreting and defending what he considered to be true Christianity. Late in his life, Tertullian joined a Christian splinter group called the "Montanists," who emphasized moral rigor and fresh revelations from the Holy Spirit. Also in the second half of the second century, Irenaeus, bishop of Lyons, wrote his important *Against Heresies,* which was composed in Greek but is preserved in a Latin translation. A final major figure from this early period is Clement of Alexandria (died c. 215), a deeply learned Greek-speaking intellectual who tried to conceptualize Christianity as a philosophically sound way of life. These are some of the most important Church Fathers of the second century.

Beginning in the third century, Christians began to write commentaries on biblical books, and we begin to have homilies preserved that treat scriptural texts somewhat systematically. Hippolytus of Rome (died c. 236), author of a work called *Refutation of All Heresies,* produced one of the first works of biblical exegesis, his *Commentary on Daniel.* The first great Bible commentator of the early church was Origen (died c. 257), who was also a philosopher and apologist for the faith. Origen's commentaries were widely read throughout the Christian world and were deeply influential on most of the later writers on Scripture. He was known for his extensive use of allegory and creative theological speculations, both of which came under criticism later on. In the Latin-speaking world, the third century saw Cyprian (died 258), bishop of Carthage, who wrote numerous letters and theological treatises and also compiled a collection of biblical prooftexts, the *Testimonies to Quirinus,* aimed at showing the truth of various facets of Christianity. Also noteworthy were two pagan rhetoricians of North Africa who turned to Christianity, Arnobius (died c. 327), author of *The Case Against the Pagans,* and Lactantius (died c. 325), who also wrote an apologetic work, *The Divine Institutes.*

After Constantine made Christianity legal in 313, opportunity was found to cultivate many intellectual pursuits, including scriptural interpretation. Eusebius of Caesarea (died c. 339), who wrote a well-known *Ecclesi-*

astical History and also apologetic works called *The Preparation for the Gospel* and *The Proof of the Gospel*, also composed a *Commentary on Isaiah* and a study of place-names in Scripture *(Onomasticon)*, both of which followed courses set by Origen. A significant writer in Palestine at this time was Cyril of Jerusalem (died 386), who is known for his *Catechetical Lectures*. The early fourth century also saw the two first major writers in Syriac (a dialect of Aramaic), Aphrahat "the Persian sage," who composed *Demonstrations* on a variety of theological topics, and Ephrem (died c. 373), who wrote beautiful hymns and also straightforward commentaries on several biblical books. Also important for this period was Athanasius (died c. 373), bishop of Alexandria, who wrote extensively on the person of Christ against the "Arians" (who regarded Jesus as a created being), and also Basil the Great (died c. 379) and Gregory of Nazianzus (died 390), who were instrumental in the development of Trinitarian theology in the fourth century, together with Basil's younger brother, Gregory of Nyssa (died c. 395). In terms of scriptural interpretation, Basil has left an important exegetical work on *The Six Days of Creation*, and Gregory of Nyssa wrote his own work on Genesis 1, a commentary on the Song of Songs, a book on the Psalms, and an important treatise on the *Life of Moses*. One last Greek writer to be mentioned here is Didymus of Alexandria (died c. 398), also known as "Didymus the Blind" (he was blind from his youth), who wrote commentaries on Genesis and Zechariah that followed Origen closely in method.

Also in the fourth century, Hilary of Poitiers (died c. 367) and Ambrose of Milan (died c. 397) played important roles in making Greek theology and exegesis known in the Latin world. In addition to his important theological treatises, Hilary also wrote commentaries on the Psalms and Matthew. Among his many works on various topics, Ambrose wrote expositions of the early chapters of Genesis and on the lives of the patriarchs (Abraham, Isaac, Jacob, and Joseph). The most capable linguistic scholar of the early church was the Latin-speaking Jerome (died 419), who not only learned Greek fluently but also learned to read Hebrew. Jerome wrote biblical reference works on proper names, published a series of homilies on the Psalms, wrote short exegetical works on the Psalms, Daniel, and Genesis, and published large commentaries on Isaiah, Jeremiah, Ezekiel, and the Minor Prophets. Jerome also composed numerous letters devoted to scriptural interpretation, and he translated into Latin the Old Testament from the original Hebrew and the Gospels from the original Greek. Another major Latin figure that belongs in this period is Augustine of Hippo (died 430). Augustine was a prodigious author, and significant comments on Scripture can be found in many of his pastoral and controversial writings. Of particular note for our purposes are his multiple commentaries on the early chapters of Genesis and his detailed exposition of the Psalms, as well as his short treatise on scriptural interpretation, *On Christian Teaching*. A contemporary of Augustine, John Cassian (died c. 433), wrote on the spiritual life and, like Augustine, was important for the development of monastic communities. Cassian's *Conferences* contains advice on the spiritual senses of Scripture that was influential in the Latin Middle Ages.

In the fourth century there was a reaction against some of Origen's ideas among a group of commentators usually grouped together as "Antiochenes," especially Diodore of Tarsus (died c. 390), Theodore of Mopsuestia (died 428), and Theodoret of Cyrus (died c. 460). These Antiochene interpreters, like Origen, searched the Scriptures for a "higher" sense, which they called *theōria* ("vision"), but they emphasized that the higher sense should be based on the literal meaning *(lexis)* and subject matter *(historia)* of the text. Most of Diodore's literary output is lost, but for Theodore commentaries are preserved on the Psalms, the Minor Prophets, and the Gospel of John; and even more of Theodoret's works are preserved. Antiochene ideas came into the Latin world through writers such as Julian of Eclanum (died 455), and they also influenced the eclectic Jerome. By the fifth century, the more extreme spiritual leanings of Origen and the more extreme Antiochene notions of Theodore had been moderated, such that the commentaries of Cyril of Alexandria (died 444) reflect certain Antiochene tendencies (for example, explaining the historical settings of prophets), and Theodoret of Cyrus reflects some "Alexandrian" tendencies (for example, the spiritual reading of the Song of Songs). One of the most prolific writers of the early church was the "Antiochene" interpreter and bishop of Constantinople John Chrysostom (died 407), whose many homilies and commentaries on biblical texts survive among his numerous compositions.

The task of compiling the exegetical tradition of the patristic period and transmitting it to the Middle Ages took place in the Latin west through figures such as Cassiodorus (died 583) and Isidore of Seville (died 636). In the Greek east, compilations of exegetical literature drawn from various authors were already being compiled in the sixth century by figures such as Procopius of Gaza (died c. 538). It is through such compilations that many readers in the following centuries encountered quotations from earlier exegetical works.

In the course of their writings — defending the faith, identifying proper Christian belief, and explaining the Scriptures — these Christians reflected on the divine inspiration of Scripture and how we should read Scripture in light of its inspiration. It is primarily from the writings of these Church Fathers that I have assembled the historical perspectives on biblical inspiration presented in the following chapters. At points, I have introduced the views of other ancient writers on their own sacred texts, Jewish writers on the Scriptures of Israel, "pagan" authors on ancient poetry (mostly Homer), and occasionally Muslim writers on the Qur'an. I do this not to suggest that these readers are all doing precisely the same thing, but to provide some frame of reference other than the modern one for understanding what these ancient writers might be trying to accomplish.

Instead of describing the perspectives on inspiration found in the various individual authors one by one, I have attempted to identify specific beliefs about inspiration that can be found in the writings of some or all of the ancient authors under discussion. Some of these beliefs were held by most ancient readers of Scripture, whereas other views, although noteworthy, are exceptional. In some cases, explicit statements can be found that express the given belief in a clear and theoretical manner. In other cases, the belief about Scripture is not stated as a principle as such, but it comes out clearly in the way certain figures handle the biblical text. The beliefs that I will be describing may be thought of as possible entailments of biblical inspiration: for example, "If Scripture is inspired by God, it must be useful for teaching," or "If Scripture is inspired by God, it cannot be deceptive." Where the Church Fathers developed their ideas from the New Testament, I try to point that out.

I have identified twenty possible entailments of the inspiration of Scripture. Obviously, there are overlaps among them, and no doubt there are other ways to organize them. I have tried to list and describe them as seemed most natural to me in light of the ancient sources. I have also grouped them into clusters, which form the major chapters of this book.

Given that differing views existed in the early church regarding these possible entailments of inspiration, it is clear that no single, systematic doctrine of biblical inspiration will emerge from these sources. Moreover, it is only reasonable when assessing these early Christians to expect that certain aspects of their beliefs will seem more useful than others for the modern world. I attempt in each section to identify at least some insight from the early church that is meaningful for today, either as a point of continuity or discontinuity. I hope that readers of this book will find broad themes and patterns, as well as particular readings and insights, that enhance their own theological reflection on Scripture.

CHAPTER TWO

Usefulness

A logical place to begin our discussion on the inspiration of Scripture is with what is probably the best-known passage in the New Testament that addresses this topic. According to 2 Timothy 3:16-17, "All Scripture is breathed out by God and profitable for teaching, for reproof, for correction, and for training in righteousness, that the man of God may be competent, equipped for every good work." The concept of Scripture as "God-breathed" was as important to the Church Fathers as it is to Christians today. It is interesting to note, however, that early Christian interpreters did not invest as much energy as modern Christians have in working out a precise definition of the term "God-breathed" *(theopneustos)*. Rather, for the Church Fathers the most important term in this passage is *ōphelimos*, which means "profitable" or "useful."

1. Scripture Is Useful for Instruction

Against the opinion of those who thought that the Homeric poems were meant simply as entertainment, the ancient Greek geographer and Stoic thinker Strabo (c. 64 BCE-24 CE) insisted that Homer composed his works not only for pleasure but also "to teach" *(didaskein)* and "to be useful/beneficial" *(ōphelein)*. Homer is said to have taught many subjects, including morals, citizenship, geography, rhetoric, the proper methods of farming, and how to be a general. This didactic view, Strabo claimed, was the traditional position, as attested by the universal and ancient practice of educating young people on the poets.[1] Whether biblical texts possess the artistic qualities necessary to give pleasure will be discussed below (see section 12), but there is no doubt whatsoever that the Church Fathers took a decidedly didactic approach to the Bible, believing 2 Timothy 3:16 that all Scripture is "useful *(ōphelimos)* for teaching *(didaskalia)."*

The general view of the Church Fathers on the profitableness of Scripture is captured well by this statement of Basil the Great introducing the Psalms:

> All Scripture is inspired by God and is useful, composed by the Spirit for this reason, namely, that we men, each and all of us, as if in a general hospital for souls, may select the remedy for his own condition. For, it says, "the remedy will make the greatest sin to cease" (Eccl. 10:4). Now, the prophets teach one thing, historians another, the law something else, and the form of advice found in the proverbs something different still. But, the Book of Psalms has taken over what is profitable from all.[2]

In Basil's understanding all Scripture was composed by the Spirit, with the Psalms being an excellent summary of the whole. Basil emphasizes the divine authorship of Scripture because he has in view the divine purpose of Scripture. Human souls are sick with sin (see Mark 2:17), and they need healing. God intends the diverse categories of Scripture to serve as healing agents for the various sins that afflict people. Healing the pain and sickness of human sin is central to Christian faith, and it is significant that Basil understands the usefulness of Scripture as primarily addressing the problem of sin. Basil is especially representative of early Christian thinking in his assertion that God inspired Scripture with the specific goal of benefiting humankind.

This belief in the profitableness of Scripture had profound implications for how the Church Fathers read the Bible. This point may be illustrated by looking at Gregory of Nyssa's treatment of the book of Exodus in his work *The Life of Moses.* Gregory concedes that no one can attain perfection in this life, but he insists that we must take seriously Jesus' command, "Be perfect, just as your heavenly Father is perfect" (Matt. 5:48). Therefore, Gregory promises to set forth the life of Moses as an example, to help his readers grow in goodness and virtue.[3] Gregory describes his procedure as follows:

> First we shall go through in outline his [that is, Moses'] life as we have learned it from divine Scriptures. Then we shall seek out the

18

spiritual understanding which corresponds to the history in order
to obtain suggestions of virtue. Through such understanding we
may come to know the perfect life for men.[4]

In order to appreciate Gregory's approach to this biblical text, let us
consider two problems that he faces. First, the book of Exodus, on which
Gregory is basing his work, contains a narrative description of events that
happened to the ancient Israelite people from the time of their oppression
in Egypt to their arrival at Mount Sinai. One could simply read this narrative as a record of the past, without any notion that it was meant to "teach"
anything. But because Gregory believes that Scripture is meant for instruction, he does not take this approach; rather, he insists that the story of Moses has something significant to teach.

Second, the most obvious way to perceive an instructional element in
the book of Exodus would be to follow the laws that it commands to Israel.
Thus, Gregory could require Christians to slaughter a Passover lamb
(which is called an eternal statute for Israel: Exod. 12:21-28), keep the laws
in Exodus 21–23, and construct a Tabernacle as described in Exodus 25–31.
Yet, for Gregory and his Christian readers, the whole basis of their identification with "Israel" in the book of Exodus is faith in Jesus Christ, and,
since the life, death, and resurrection of Jesus have transformed the way in
which they relate to the regulations of the "Old Covenant," Gregory does
not suggest that the meaningfulness of the book of Exodus for Christians
lies in the literal sense of the regulations that it prescribes. Thus, Gregory
insists not only that this biblical text is useful for instruction, but also that
it has a particular usefulness for Christians, who approach the book from a
distinctively Christian and spiritual point of view.

Gregory believes that Christians should read and contemplate the literal history of Moses in such a way that they derive benefit for the virtuous
life.[5] Gregory, of course, knows that Christians cannot repeat the same
events as Moses: "Those who emulate their lives, however, cannot experience the identical literal events."[6] How could anyone today live to see Israel
multiplying in Egypt or enslaved by a tyrant? Does the usefulness of the
book require that we live out the exact same experiences? Of course not,
argues Gregory. "Because therefore it has been shown to be impossible to
imitate the marvels of these blessed men in these exact events, one might
substitute a moral teaching for the literal sequence in those things which
admit of such an approach."[7] Gregory therefore expounds the story of Moses in Exodus in order to show Christians how they might leave wickedness

and "the passions" behind, advance toward virtue and purity of soul, and eventually ascend toward the ineffable knowledge of God. Gregory's treatment is well worth reading, both for its penetrating insights into some major themes in Exodus and also for its creative synthesis of biblical imagery with Greek Christian ethics. By the end, his exposition has traveled far beyond the historical sense of the book of Exodus. But if Gregory were to defend his approach before modern-day critics, he would probably say that Exodus is inspired Christian Scripture and therefore "profitable for teaching," and so some such exposition is required.[8]

For most Church Fathers, especially those who wrote biblical commentaries, it was axiomatic that God intended whatever scriptural text they encountered to benefit them and their readers. That this manner of thinking was grounded in concrete ideas about inspiration is expressed well by Origen in a passage cited by Basil the Great and Gregory of Nazianzus in their collection of key texts of Origen on Scripture, the *Philocalia* of Origen. Origen explains:

> Let us not then weary when we hear Scriptures which we do not understand; but let it be unto us according to our faith, by which we believe that all Scripture being inspired by God is profitable. For as regards these Scriptures, you must admit one of two things: either that they are not inspired because they are not profitable, as an unbeliever might suppose; or, as a believer, you must allow that because they are inspired they are profitable. We must, however, know that we often profit without perceiving it, just as frequently happens when we diet ourselves to improve our eyesight; we do not, I suppose, while we are eating perceive that our eyesight is better, but after two or three days, when the food is assimilated which benefits the eye, we are convinced of the fact by experience; and the same remark applies to other foods which benefit other parts of the body. Well, then, have the like faith with regard to Divine Scripture; believe that your soul is profited by the mere reading, even though your understanding does not receive the fruit of profiting by these passages.[9]

According to Origen, only an unbeliever would suggest that any part of Scripture is not profitable. If we believe in the inspiration of Scripture, it is incumbent on us to trust that *all* Scripture (as 2 Tim. 3:16 says) is profitable for us, even if we do not immediately perceive the gain that we are receiving. Origen makes his point clear through his comparison with those who take special food to improve their eyesight. The Scriptures are helping us whether we realize it or not, just as an improved diet may work slowly over days to improve our eyesight, even though we cannot perceive or register the improvement. One can imagine a list of names from the Old Testament (in this specific case, Josh. 15:20-62) being read out in Origen's church and Origen insisting that the congregation is profiting even if they cannot describe how. As he explains,

> Charms have a certain natural force; and any who come under the influence of the charm, even if he does not understand it, gets something from it, according to the nature of the sounds thereof, either to the injury or to the healing of his body, or his soul. Just so, pray observe, it is with the giving of names in the Divine Scriptures, only they are stronger than any charm.[10]

In other early Christian writers we find statements that travel along these same lines and that spell out in more detail what profit we should gain from Scripture. For example, Augustine tells us that "anything in the divine discourse that cannot be related either to good morals or to the true faith should be taken as figurative" of some higher truth.[11] This thinking is grounded in Augustine's belief in the usefulness of Scripture, as Augustine cannot accept that there is any passage in the Bible that is not profitable for instruction in at least one of the two areas mentioned (good morals or true faith). The Church Fathers generally saw a strong connection between the inspiration of Scripture and its usefulness for God's purposes.

As Strabo made clear, not everyone in the ancient world was willing to accept that the Homeric poems were intended to instruct and benefit readers. But early Christians consistently read Scripture with the guiding belief that God intended the sacred texts to be spiritually profitable for humankind. This belief was encouraged by 2 Timothy 3:16 and also made good theological sense out of the fact that God had chosen to communicate with humanity. Why else would God "speak" through human language unless the ultimate goal was the benefit of the human audience? The Church Fathers may be particularly helpful for today's readers when they reflect on specific ways that God intends Scripture to profit Christians (for example, curing sin, teaching wisdom, or healing souls). The idea that Scripture is "useful" for specific purposes might help us to focus the questions we bring to the text. In some form, at least, the didactic view of Scripture as expressed by the Church Fathers is an ancient idea well worth transferring to our own context.

Still, several potential problems arise out of this approach to Scripture. Many of these problems will be discussed in the sections below. I will mention two major issues here: first, given that Scripture contains a variety of genres (for example, narrative, poetry, visions) and not simply expository literature, it is clear that sophisticated methods of interpretation are needed in order for all Scripture to yield explicit Christian teaching; second, if one were to insist on the equal usefulness of every passage of Scripture (for example, genealogies, Psalm titles), this could potentially require complex and even convoluted reading strategies, depending on how hard the idea was pressed. But in spite of such potential problems, the "usefulness" of Scripture for communicating divine benefit to humanity is a leading idea from the Church Fathers that still has much to teach.

2. Every Detail of Scripture Is Meaningful

An idea held in common by many ancient interpreters is that every detail of the wording of Scripture is meaningful. Because God inspired the Scriptures and does nothing idly, it follows that every identifiable feature of the sacred text was placed there by God in order to teach us something. As faithful readers of Scripture, we should take up the responsibility to find out what each detail is meant to convey. I will first illustrate this idea through a pair of examples from ancient Judaism.

Philo (c. 20 BCE–50 CE), the Jewish Greek philosopher, makes the following observation before his comments on Leviticus 8:29 and 9:14: "Do not let any subtle point escape your notice, for you will not find a single pointless expression."[12] He proceeds to point out that Moses removes the breast of the sacrificial animal (Lev. 8:29), but the "belly" of the animal he washes (9:14).[13] There must be some point to this, reckons Philo, and the point is as follows: by renouncing anger, the perfect sage can successfully remove from within himself the spirit of rage, represented by the "breast," but even the most advanced wise man cannot totally extinguish his need for food, represented by the "belly." Thus, Philo shows that these details of the Mosaic Law were not given without good reason. They were meant to teach important principles for living a morally upright life.[14]

Our second example comes from the second-century CE Jewish teacher Rabbi Akiba, whose interpretation of the singular "frog" in Exodus

8:6 was discussed above (see p. 10). Our text in this instance is Genesis 1:1, "In the beginning, God created the heavens and the earth." In the Hebrew language, the direct object of a verb is often indicated by a particle, *'et*. This is particularly so when the direct object has the definite article, as is the case for the words "heavens" and "earth" in Genesis 1:1. Thus, in Hebrew, the verse reads, "In the beginning, God created *'et*-the heavens and *'et*-the earth," with the *'et* in each case introducing the definite direct objects of the verb "created." It is the interpretation of this particle, *'et,* that is addressed by R. Akiba.

There is another Hebrew word *'et* that means "together with," which is spelled just like the particle *'et* that introduces a direct object. On the basis of the similarity between these two words (which was seen not as coincidence but as divinely planned), an interpretive rule developed among ancient rabbis that wherever *'et* appears, the text intends to include ("together with") something else within its view beyond what is explicitly stated.[15] This rule could potentially be used with any form of *'et*, whether the particle or the preposition. R. Akiba was known to have made use of this rule, and in one ancient text he is challenged by another rabbi to explain how this rule would apply to Genesis 1:1.[16]

Akiba's answer is creative and illuminating. First, he says that, without the particles *'et* to mark "heavens" and "earth" as direct objects, we might have (wrongly) supposed that the heavens and the earth are deities who helped God create. But since the object markers are present, the text clearly proves that God alone is the creator and that "heavens and earth" are what was created. In other words, Akiba begins by defending these particles in their literal sense, as direct object markers.

Next, Akiba quotes Deuteronomy 32:47, "For it is no empty word for you." Here is where he shows his belief in the meaningfulness of every detail. As he explains, "It is no empty word for you, and if it is empty, then that is your fault, because you do not know how to interpret!" No, the two occurrences of *'et* in Genesis 1:1 are not there *simply* to make the point that God alone is creator, since the singular verb "created" could have made this point by itself. But then why the two occurrences of *'et?* They must be in the text for a reason, namely: the *'et* before "heavens" is meant to include the sun, moon, stars, and planets, and the *'et* before "earth" is meant to include trees, grass, and the Garden of Eden. In this way Akiba proves that not a single word of Scripture is "empty" for us, but each detail has meaning for the one who knows how to interpret correctly.

Although not every Church Father (or every rabbi) took this idea to the extreme, in general the interpretation of details was much more important for ancient interpreters than for most moderns. In fact, in addition to the examples given in this section, we will see this principle at work throughout the rest of the book.

In his work *Cain and Abel*, Ambrose of Milan comments on Genesis 4:2, "Now Abel was a keeper of sheep, and Cain a worker of the ground." The significant detail for Ambrose is this: if Cain is the older son, why does the text refer to Abel first? Ambrose explains, "Not without reason, as Scripture teaches us, is Abel mentioned first in this passage, although Cain was the first born." Abel is mentioned first, according to Ambrose, because the text does not intend to speak about the order of nature but about one's calling in life: "When it is a question of instruction in the art of living, the younger is preferred to the older because, although junior in age, he is superior in virtue."[17] Scripture, Ambrose claims, mentions Abel first to show that instruction in virtue is better than wickedness.

We see something similar in Cyril of Alexandria's comments on Isaiah 3:1. The verse states that God is taking from Judah "strength of bread" and "strength of water." The word "strength" might seem unnecessary if taken literally. Why not just say that God has taken away "bread" and "water"? Cyril comments, "Now, study closely the prophet's words: he did not simply say that the Jews lost bread and water — rather, 'strength from bread and strength from water.'" Cyril takes the "bread" and "water" spiritually, and in typical early Christian fashion he uses the passage to criticize Judaism. Cyril argues that the removal of the "strength" of bread indicates that, although the Jews may have the Scriptures ("bread"), they do not receive any benefit ("strength") from them. This is because the Jews interpret Scripture literally and not spiritually. Only through Christ can one derive spiritual benefit from the writings of Moses. Jews without Christ cannot understand Moses because a veil lies over their heart (see 2 Cor. 3:14). Cyril's spiritual interpretation is grounded in the presence of the seemingly unnecessary word "strength" in the text.[18]

As in the two cases just discussed, peculiar or apparently extraneous details were often used by early Christian interpreters as jumping-off points for allegorical interpretations. Following this approach, Genesis 12:11 does not say that Abram "descends" to Egypt but that he "enters" Egypt, in order to show that he does not actually lower himself to Egyptian vice but simply condescends to Egyptian ways for the benefit of the Egyptians (Didymus the Blind). Or again, Genesis 6:16 lists three decks for the ark, "lower, second, and third," in order to represent the three levels of Paradise: one for the repentant, a second for the righteous, and a third for the victorious (Ephrem the Syrian).[19] Examples of this kind can be found throughout the writings of the Church Fathers. It was a common assumption among early Christian commentators that the inspiration of Scripture ensured that every detail of the text would be meaningful.

For many modern readers of the Bible, the strangest aspect of the Church Fathers' emphasis on scriptural details was the widespread practice of allegorizing numbers. This is found already in the early-second-century Christian work called the *Epistle of Barnabas*. In chapter nine of this epistle, the author interprets the "18 and 300" men of Abraham in Genesis 14:14 as Jesus and the cross, since the Greek abbreviation for "18" is the same as the first two letters of "Jesus" in Greek, and the abbreviation for "300" is the letter *tau*, which is shaped like a cross. For Ambrose, the reference to the "third day" in Genesis 22:4 reminds us to remember God in the threefold elements of time, "past, present, and future," and also teaches us to believe in the Trinity.[20] According to Didymus the Blind, the "twenty-fourth day" in Zechariah 1:7 shows the order and harmony of God's actions, since the "parts" of twenty-four (its half is 12, its third is 8, and so on, yielding 6, 4, 3, 2, and 1) add up to thirty-six, which is a perfect square: 6×6.[21]

Augustine frequently employed this style of exegesis. The 6 jars of water turned to wine in John 2:6 represent the 6 ages of the world.[22] The 46 years that it took to build the Temple according to John 2:20 is derived by adding together the numbers represented by the Greek letters for "Adam": $a = 1$, $d = 4$, $a = 1$, and $m = 40$.[23] Later in the same work, Augustine explains that the 153 fish caught by Peter in John 21:11 equal the sum total of all the numbers from 1 to 17 added together, since seventeen stands for the law ($= 10$) plus the gospel ($= 7$).[24] And elsewhere, Augustine says that there are 11 curtains in the Tabernacle (Exod. 26:7) because 11 represents "transgression," that is, the law ($= 10$) plus 1.[25] This kind of interpretation made sense to most ancient Christian readers of Scripture, but it justifiably seems forced and arbitrary to most modern readers.

On the other hand, there are times when early Christian interpreters focus on the same textual details that modern commentators discuss. For example, Augustine rightly advises the reader to examine closely the order of the verbs "walks," "stands," and "sits" in Psalm 1:1.[26] Similarly, John Chrysostom, who insists that "the mouths of the prophets are the mouth of God; such a mouth would not say anything idly,"[27] presses home the force of the word "But" in Genesis 2:20: "But for Adam there was not found a helper fit for him." Chrysostom seeks to highlight the contrast between the promise in Genesis 2:18 of a helper "fit for him" and the description of the animals in 2:20 as "not . . . fit for him." As he explains,

> let us act so as to interpret everything precisely and instruct you not to pass by even a brief phrase or a single syllable contained in the Holy Scriptures. After all, they are not simply words, but words of the Holy Spirit, and hence the treasure to be found in even a single syllable is great.[28]

Origen offers perhaps the most profound theological explanation for the ancient perspective on the significance of scriptural details. According to Origen, God showed his skill in creation by carefully crafting not only the grand things of this world — such as the sun, moon, and stars — but also the smallest creatures and commonest objects. In the same way, the Holy Spirit has so carefully inspired the sacred writings that they bear the saving truth and wisdom of God not only in the grand narrative of Scripture, but also in the details of Scripture, sometimes even to the very letter.[29] One can only imagine how emphatically Origen would have insisted on this point if he had been aware of the discoveries of molecular biology.

Modern readers of Scripture agree that there are meaningful details in biblical texts. Biblical scholars today often discuss these details through methods derived from secular literary criticism. They read the Bible as "literature" and therefore interpret significant textual details in the Bible in a manner similar to how Homer and Shakespeare are interpreted in college literature courses.[30] In contrast to this, most of the Church Fathers interpreted the details of Scripture primarily from the perspective that the Holy Spirit had purposefully and even mysteriously placed these details in the text to communicate higher truths. Sometimes the observations of ancient biblical commentators run along the same track as modern readings; in such cases the ancients often add insightful theological reflections. But in other cases the focus on details led ancient Christian readers away from the discourse of the literal sense, which is probably the greatest weakness of this approach.

3. Scripture Solves Every Problem That We Might Put to It

In the previous section we looked at the usefulness of Scripture from the perspective of Scripture as the starting point. We asked: Is *everything* that we find in Scripture useful? In the present section, we will look at the usefulness of Scripture from the perspective of the reader as the starting point. We will ask: Is *everything* that we need to know found in Scripture? Does Scripture answer *every* question that we feel we need to ask?

In this case, the maximalist position was not the most commonly held view in antiquity. There were, to be sure, currents of thought among ancient interpreters that suggested that Scripture contains the answers to all our questions. This can be seen as a potentially reasonable entailment of biblical inspiration. After all, if God knows everything and Scripture is the voice of God, then perhaps Scripture tells us everything there is to know. In reality, however, most ancient readers of the Bible did not take this extreme view. People in antiquity wrote cookbooks, medical manuals, and instructions on how to assemble buildings. By and large, Christians did not stop using books such as these and try to learn this information strictly from the Bible. But they did believe that Scripture could be used to answer any important question about religion, morals, or anything touching on the ultimate questions of life.

A famous quotation from a first-century Rabbi appears to give us an example of someone who believed that everything is found in Scripture. Ben Bag-Bag, speaking about the Torah, said: "Turn it and turn it again, for everything is in it; and contemplate it and grow grey and old over it and stir not from it, for you can have no better rule than it."[31] On the face of it, this may be taken as a declaration that everything worth knowing is found in the written Scriptures.

It is true that this kind of thinking was to be found among some early rabbinic sages. This may be illustrated by a saying of R. Ishmael. When asked by his nephew if he could study Greek wisdom, Ishmael replied, "'This book of the law shall not depart out of your mouth, but you shall meditate on it day and night.' Go then and find a time that is neither day nor night, and learn then Greek wisdom."[32] In other words, all the wisdom a person requires is in the Torah, and one does not need to supplement the Torah with outside thinking. The "everything is in it" approach can also be seen in the ancient Jewish Midrash (Bible commentaries) and Talmud (philosophical law code), where individual sages sometimes attempt to ground their answers to every imaginable question in scriptural prooftexts.[33]

On the other hand, the Jewish sages of antiquity often showed themselves to be aware that Scripture did not directly answer every important question. A major example is the Sabbath. Although observing the Sabbath is one of the most important commands in the Hebrew Scriptures, apart from a few instances (e.g., Num. 15:32-36 and Jer. 17:19-23), there is very little detail given in Scripture regarding what constitutes the "work" (Exod. 20:10) from which one must refrain on the Sabbath. Because most Christians do not literally observe the Sabbath (no work on the seventh day, Saturday), they generally do not appreciate the force of this problem. But for Jews who wanted to keep the Sabbath, it was important to make the rules for Sabbath observance clear enough for people to follow. This is partly why the early Jewish rabbis developed the "oral Torah," a restatement and explanation of the laws of the written Torah that helped Jews follow the written Torah. The earliest written collection of these oral traditions is called the *Mishnah,* which has a whole tractate devoted to explaining the practical observance of the Sabbath.

Early Christians likewise attempted to find the answers to key religious questions in and through the words of Scripture. For early Christians, the Scriptures were a guide for right living, a model for Christian rituals, and above all a source of doctrine.

For those looking to Scripture for moral guidance, laws about clean and unclean animals for food in Leviticus 11–15 did not seem very helpful. Already in the early Jewish work *The Letter of Aristeas* (second century BCE), the food laws in Leviticus were read as moral instruction. The writer explains, "Do not accept the contemptible idea that it was out of regard for 'mice' and the 'weasel' and other such creatures that Moses ordained these laws with such scrupulous care; not so, these laws have all been solemnly drawn up for the sake of justice, to promote holy contemplation and the perfecting of character."[34] As examples, the writer says that the "clean" birds (which may be eaten) are civilized and vegetarian, whereas the "unclean" birds (which may not be eaten) are meat-eaters who gain their food by force and injustice (see Lev. 11:13-19). Moreover, the permissibility of eating animals with a parted hoof (see Lev. 11:3) is explained as a symbol of the fact that we must set apart our actions for good.[35]

The fact that Christians would follow this pattern was established by the teachings of Jesus, who took a moral approach to the food laws in the Old Testament (Mark 7:14-23). In the early second century, the Christian *Epistle of Barnabas* explains the Old Testament food laws morally. According to *Barnabas,* we should not eat animals whose behavior is reprehensible, such as swine, who forget God when they have plenty; or eagles, who gain their food by plundering others; or rabbits, who corrupt their young; or hyenas, who (we are told) change their gender and thus promote adultery; and so forth.[36] Christians looked to the Old Testament for moral guidance, not ritual laws, and they found what they were looking for. Regarding the commands about food and clothing in Exodus 12, Gregory of Nyssa confidently affirms:

> From all this it is evident that the letter looks to some higher understanding, since the law does not instruct us how to eat. (Nature which implants a desire for food in us is a sufficient lawgiver with regard to these things.) The account rather signifies something different. For what does it matter to virtue or vice to eat your food this way or that, to have the belt loose or tight, to have your feet bare or covered with shoes, to have your staff in your hand or laid aside? It is clear what the traveler's equipment figuratively stands for: It commands us to recognize that our present life is transient. . . . So that the thorns of this life (the thorns would be sins) may not hurt our naked and unprotected feet, let us cover them with shoes. . . . The tunic, accordingly, would be seen as the full enjoyment of the pursuits of this life, which the prudent reason, like a traveler's belt, draws in as tightly as possible. . . .[37]

Gregory's approach is typical of early Christian interpreters of the Old Testament. Before giving his own moral interpretation of Leviticus 13–14, Jerome asks: "If we were to take all of this literally, what benefits would we derive from such reading?"[38] The moral reading of the Old Testament was partly grounded in the fact that Christians expected all Scripture to be useful, even the details of the laws (see section 2 above). But the fact that Christians extracted moral guidance from the Old Testament, using their own categories of "virtues" and "vices," also reflects their belief that Scripture must speak to these questions. If the philosophers had "canonical" works (the writings of Plato, Aristotle, Chrysippus the Stoic, etc.) that showed them the noblest way to live, then the divine Scriptures must also teach principles like these, only better. If one looked hard enough, one could find these higher principles in the writings of the greatest philosopher of all time, Moses (see section 15 below).

Religious ritual was another topic on which early Christians thought the Bible should speak. Early Christians practiced several religious rites, the most important of which were water baptism and the Eucharist. The origins of these rites are to be found in the New Testament itself (e.g., Matt. 28:19 and 1 Pet. 3:21 for baptism and Luke 22:14-23 and 1 Cor. 11:17-34 for the Lord's Supper). But early Christians also looked to less obvious parts of Scripture to fill out their understanding of how these rites were to be conducted. As one example, we may cite Tertullian's explanation for why baptism in water precedes unction (anointing with oil). According to Tertullian, just as John the Baptist baptized people *in preparation* for the coming of the Lord Jesus, so also in Christian baptism the waters *prepare* for the coming of the Spirit (associated with the unction). For Tertullian, the biblical narrative serves as a "type" (or "model") for the Christian rite.[39]

As another example, we may consider Cyprian's advice to the church at Assurae (in North Africa) regarding their former bishop, Fortu-natianus.[40] This former bishop had lapsed from the faith during persecu-tion, escaping death by offering a sacrifice to the emperor, and now he wanted to return and serve as bishop. Cyprian urges the church not to per-mit Fortunatianus to resume his position, citing Old and New Testament texts against idolatry (Isa. 57:6; Exod. 22:20; Isa. 2:8-9; and Rev. 14:9-11). Cyprian also argues that Fortunatianus cannot oversee the Eucharist, be-cause Leviticus 21:17 forbids blemished priests from making offerings to God. As was true of Tertullian's instructions on baptism, Cyprian's belief that Scripture should answer the church's questions on ritual matters al-lowed scriptural paradigms to influence how these rituals were enacted.

The most important questions for which Christians sought answers from the Bible were questions of doctrine. Above everything else, early Christians believed that Scripture spoke definitively to questions of "or-thodoxy," or "right belief." In keeping with the importance of "faith" and "belief" in Christianity, Christian writers looked to Scripture to define the content of "the faith," that is, the content of what Christians were sup-posed to believe. During the golden era of the Church Fathers (c. 150-600 CE), the major questions of dogma that arose centered on the doctrine of God: the divinity of Jesus, the Trinity, and the relationship between the hu-man and divine "natures" of Christ.

It is not surprising that the New Testament played a key role in ad-dressing matters that pertained to Christ and the Holy Spirit. Even here, however, New Testament texts sometimes had to be pressed into service to answer questions that may not have been in the mind of the original writ-ers. One thinks of the role of John 1:14 ("the Word became flesh") and Colossians 2:9 ("in him all the fullness of deity dwells bodily") in the de-bates about the humanity and divinity of Jesus in the fifth century. Some groups cited John 1:14 to prove that the divinity and humanity of Jesus were united in one *hypostasis* (something like "essence"), whereas others cited Colossians 2:9 to prove that the divinity of Jesus indwelled the person of Jesus to form a single *prosōpon* (something like "person").[41] It is difficult for us today to grasp the precise shades of meaning attached to these technical terms of fifth-century Greek theology. It is likewise difficult to know what the writers of the New Testament would have thought about these later questions that their writings were used to answer.

While the use of the New Testament to address issues of Christology comes as no surprise, it is worthy of special note that Old Testament texts also played crucial roles in debates about Christ and the Trinity. An extremely important text in the debates about the deity of Jesus was Proverbs 8. In this passage, "wisdom" is introduced as the speaker, and the text says that the world was created through "wisdom" (Prov. 8:22-31). Since Jesus is the "wisdom of God" (1 Cor. 1:24), and the world was made through Jesus (Col. 1:16), early Christians read Proverbs 8 as if Jesus were the speaker. It was used as a Christological text by numerous early Christian thinkers, including Justin Martyr, Tertullian, Athenagoras, Theophilus of Antioch, Origen, Hilary of Poitiers, Athanasius, and many others.[42]

For most Christians, this text showed that Jesus was "before eternity" (Prov. 8:23 in Greek) and with God in the beginning (as in John 1:1), and therefore divine. Around the turn of the fourth century, however, a Christian presbyter in Alexandria named Arius used Proverbs 8:22 ("The Lord created me . . ." in Greek) to argue that Jesus was a created being. This gave rise to the "Arian" controversy of the fourth century, during which time the divinity of Jesus was debated furiously. Proverbs 8 was the single most important biblical text in this controversy.[43] The interpretation of Proverbs 8:22-31 was central to the argument of both sides. It is interesting from a modern perspective to notice that no one on either side attempted to argue that Proverbs 8 did not speak about Jesus. The Christological reading of Proverbs 8 had become ingrained in Christian thinking.

In sum, most ancient readers of Scripture looked to the sacred text not for the answer to everything, but for the answers to what they deemed most important. For most early Jewish readers, the Torah was read as a source for ethical and religious truth, focused particularly on divine law. Early Christians looked to the Bible to instruct them in virtue, in ritual practice, and above all in theology. These same concerns can be seen among modern readers of the Bible. If anything, the expectations placed on the Bible in view of its inspiration have only increased in modern times. Among American Christians today, for example, it is easy to find books written to explain what the Bible has to say about dating, losing weight, and financial planning. This reflects a strong belief in the usefulness of the Bible and also shows what many American Christians deem to be most important.

It was wise on the part of early Christian interpreters that they did not believe the answer to every imaginable question could be found directly in Scripture. It is still an important challenge facing the church today to identify what kinds of information we should ask Scripture to provide. For example, it is debated among modern Christians to what degree Scripture was intended by God to address questions that we approach today through natural sciences. Moreover, it is increasingly being recognized that significant questions pertaining even to ethics and theology are not necessarily addressed "directly" in Scripture, whether because new issues have arisen (for example, human cloning) or because old topics must be addressed in new contexts (for example, questions about gender in modern societies). This recognition is fostering helpful discussion in the church today regarding how to employ Scripture faithfully to deal with the questions we ask that are beyond the horizon of what biblical texts actually spoke about in their literal sense.[44]

4. Biblical Characters Are Examples for Us to Follow

The Church Fathers believed that the most important dimension of the Old Testament was the fact that it predicted or foreshadowed the coming of Jesus (see section 8 below). Next to this Christological approach, perhaps the most common method used by the Church Fathers for explaining the significance of Old Testament narratives was to set forth biblical characters as models for Christians to imitate. At least three factors contributed to this practice. First, Old Testament narratives often focus on key characters, and frequently the narrative highlights the greatness of an individual; thus, Abraham gained blessing for his descendants by obeying God (Gen. 22), Moses is identified as both the humblest and the greatest of people (Num. 12:3; Deut. 34:10-12), and king David is said to have administered justice and equity to Israel (2 Sam. 8:15).

Second, the classical Greek and Roman culture dominant at the time of the early church already possessed a catalog of noble figures of the past, such as Odysseus and Socrates. Their nobility illustrated the greatness of Greco-Roman culture. It was common for orators in this culture to encourage people to imitate the virtues of these individuals or to praise those who had imitated them. Because Christians wanted to establish their own distinct culture and values, it made sense for them to replace the catalog of Greco-Roman heroes with a catalog of their own heroes, namely, biblical heroes. Eusebius of Caesarea, in his work *Preparation for the Gospel,* begins with a long critique of early Greek culture and then introduces Abraham and Moses as ancestors truly worthy of praise: "Observe then further to what a degree of godly virtue these men are said to have advanced. . . . Such are the examples of the excellence of the Hebrews contained in the much celebrated and truly divine oracles, which we have preferred to the fables and the follies of the Greeks."[45] Christians could learn to identify with scriptural values by following scriptural models. Ambrose speaks of his listeners becoming "Hebrews" as they become companions of Jacob and imitate him.[46] Introducing his narrative on Joseph, Ambrose explains, "The lives of the saints are for the rest of men a pattern of how to live. . . . as we come to know Abraham, Isaac, and Jacob and the other just men by our reading, we may, as it were, follow in their shining footsteps along a kind of path of blamelessness opened up to us by their virtue."[47]

Third, early Christians believed that God had inspired the Bible so as to be profitable for them. Interpreting Old Testament characters as positive examples was a straightforward way to actualize this dimension of Scripture. Furthermore, the New Testament seemed to show the validity of this approach.[48] The apostle Paul had said that the events described in Numbers 14 had "happened to them as an example, but they were written down for our instruction" (1 Cor. 10:11). Abraham is a model of faith in Galatians 3:1-9, Job is a model of patience and perseverance in James 5:10-11, and Hebrews 11 gives a long list of characters whose lives demonstrated the power of faith. The early Christian epistle of *1 Clement,* written in the late first century, continues this trajectory by using biblical characters to illustrate repentance (chs. 7–8), obedience (chs. 9–10), hospitality (chs. 11–12), and many other positive attributes.[49] This kind of exposition was not merely a response to Greco-Roman culture. The early church had theological reasons to think that Scripture presented characters whose positive qualities could be imitated.

John Chrysostom's homily on Genesis 22 provides an illustration of the "ethical example" approach to expounding Scripture. According to Chrysostom, even the fact that God "tests" Abraham (Gen. 22:1) shows that "Sacred Scripture intends already at this point to reveal to us the good man's virtue."[50] Chrysostom consistently refers to Abraham as the "good man" throughout the homily, and periodically praises Abraham with phrases such as, "It strikes me as remarkable how the good man was even able to bear to hear it!"[51] Abraham demonstrated the iron-like strength of his resolve by not inquiring into the reasons for God's command, but simply obeying without question.[52] Chrysostom makes the scene vivid for his listeners with numerous asides, such as "How was his hand able to hold the fire and the sword?"[53] and "Consider, I ask you, the torture in this for the good man."[54] But despite such difficulties, in the end Abraham's obedience reveals his virtue.[55] Chrysostom wraps up the "ethical example" section of his exposition by asking why God would need to "test" Abraham in the first place. Did God not already know Abraham's faith? Of course, Chrysostom concludes, God knew the good man's virtue before the test, but God tested Abraham in order to instruct other people, including those living in later generations.[56]

The treatment of Abraham as an ethical model takes up nearly three-fourths of Chrysostom's homily on this text. In the final portion he turns to a Christological reading of the narrative: "All of this, however, happened as a type of the cross."[57] I will discuss the directly Christological element of patristic biblical interpretation later on. But it may be noted here that the bulk of Chrysostom's exposition follows along ethical lines, and the Christological section comes only at the end.

Ambrose of Milan offers another illustration of this kind of exposition in his *Jacob and the Happy Life*.[58] Jacob is presented as an example of one who attains true happiness through virtue. As Ambrose tells the narrative, Jacob received his brother's clothing because he exceeded his brother in wisdom. Furthermore, Jacob's parents Rebekah and Isaac did not favor one child over the other; they simply recognized that Jacob should rule because he was a man of moderation.[59] Isaac smelled Jacob's garments and blessed him (Gen. 27:27) because Jacob wore the old garments of Esau (= the Old Testament) imbued with the pleasing fragrance of the church.[60] When Esau tried to kill him, Jacob fled to his uncle Laban. But Jacob accepted the hardships of this exile willingly, because he wanted to help Esau; Jacob knew that only by fleeing could he prevent Esau from committing fratricide.[61] Jacob slept when he came to Bethel (Gen. 28) because he had tranquility of spirit.[62] When Jacob finally reached Laban's home he became the shepherd of his uncle's flock, because "wisdom does not forsake its task of government."[63] As a shepherd, Jacob preached the gospel and gathered to himself a flock speckled with many virtues (see Gen. 30:32).[64] During his stay with Laban, Jacob acquired two wives, showing himself to be a man of both law and grace.[65]

As Ambrose continues: Jacob willingly agreed to return to the land of his fathers, because he knew that as long as God was with him (Gen. 31:3) he would lack nothing, since "nothing is lacking to the man who has the fullness of all things."[66] Laban pursued Jacob and searched his tent, but he found nothing of his own in Jacob's possession. This is because Jacob did not need Laban's things to be happy. "The wise man is never empty but always has the garment of prudence."[67] Ambrose drives this point home for his readers: "Do not be afraid of those who can plunder treasures of gold and silver; such men take nothing from you." No matter what he lost, Jacob was filled with the fruit of justice.[68]

The climax of the story, as Ambrose tells it, unfolds as follows: In keeping with his perfection in virtue, Jacob sought reconciliation with his brother.[69] But before this reconciliation took place, Jacob slept once again, once more showing his virtuous tranquility.[70] That evening Jacob sent away all his possessions (Gen. 32:23) — forsaking all worldly things — and took up the struggle for virtue.[71] As a result of Jacob's faith and devotion, the Lord revealed his hidden mysteries to Jacob by touching his loins. This action symbolized that Jesus would descend from him ("loins" stands for descendants), and the numbness that Jacob felt in his thigh (Gen. 32:31) symbolized the cross of Christ.[72] Ambrose wraps up his account of Jacob by emphasizing Jacob's happiness in spite of all hardships. Even when very old and nearly blind, Jacob was happy, as shown by the blessings he bestowed on his sons (see Gen. 49).[73]

In contrast to Chrysostom, Ambrose does not leave Christological observations to the end. Rather, Ambrose weaves Christological symbolism into the narrative throughout his exposition. This reflects Ambrose's place in the "Alexandrian" stream of thought.[74] But although Ambrose and Chrysostom reach the Christological sense in slightly different ways, they share the same goal of setting forth their biblical hero as a model for Christians to follow. This was a common approach among many of the Church Fathers.

What is a modern reader to make of Ambrose's exposition? Most readers today would observe that Ambrose seems to have both more and less in his exposition than what is present in the text. First, Ambrose sees a system of virtues communicated through the story of Jacob that does not always appear to be well grounded in the narrative. Some of the content is borrowed from Greek philosophy. For example, the Stoic paradox that "the wise person alone is free/happy" seems to underlie Ambrose's point that Jacob is happy regardless of his circumstances in life.[75] Second, Ambrose regularly skips over or explains away elements in the narrative that might cast his hero in a bad light. Most modern readers see Jacob, at least early on, as a trickster. Likewise, most readers today perceive clear evidence in the text that Isaac and Rebekah favored one child over the other on grounds that were other than moral (see Gen. 25:28). Throughout the narrative, Ambrose chooses to rationalize or gloss over elements of the story that do not reflect favorably on Jacob. Few informed readers of Scripture today would find Ambrose's interpretation of the story of Jacob convincing.

At times, the Christological dimension of the Church Fathers' expositions allowed the figure of Jesus to function as a theological control on what in the narrative should be imitated. One thinks in this connection of the statement of Paul, "Be imitators of me, as I am of Christ" (1 Cor. 11:1). In the preface to his *Commentary on Jonah*, Cyril of Alexandria makes some astute observations about how only certain dimensions of biblical characters foreshadow Christ. Cyril cites Aaron as an example: Aaron is a type of Christ in that he served faithfully as high priest (Lev. 16), but he was not like Christ when he made the golden calf (Exod. 32:4). Especially with those interpreters who wove Christological interpretations into the fabric of their expositions throughout, the search for parallels with Jesus gave them at least a theological standard to use in ascertaining what to highlight in the actions of characters.

Augustine offered another significant qualification to the general rule of reading biblical characters as ethical examples. In certain cases, as with the polygamy of Abraham and Jacob, Augustine says that their behavior is not acceptable today, even though it was acceptable in their time.[76] In fact, even if Scripture praises someone's deeds, if these deeds do not agree with the practices of good people who have lived since the Lord's coming, a figurative meaning should be sought for the passage, and the deeds should not be emulated.[77] Augustine raises the question of whether the diversity of social practices in different times and places makes the teaching of all Scripture culturally relative. He answers that the dictum "Do not do to another what you would not wish to be done to yourself" (Tobit 4:15) is an absolute standard to govern everyone's behavior.[78]

Such qualifications, however, were exceptions to the general rule. In practice, the Church Fathers regularly interpreted biblical characters as positive role models. They generally felt compelled to defend these characters from charges of wrongdoing;[79] and when "good" characters in the Bible misbehaved, it was often considered proof that the literal sense was untenable and an allegorical interpretation must be in view.[80] There were select occasions, to be sure, when the Church Fathers allowed "good" characters to make mistakes.[81] But in a way that is not true for most Bible readers today, the Church Fathers expected that there were "good" characters in Scripture whose actions teach us how to live.

Modern literary approaches to the Bible emphasize that most Old Testament narratives present complex characters, not heroes of virtue or villains of vice.[82] Readers are probably meant to make evaluations of these characters, but few well-developed characters are either all good or all bad. From a modern literary perspective, the moralizing approach common among the Church Fathers misses out on the literary crafting of the narratives. From the perspective of the Church Fathers, however, the literary approach would probably not seem sufficiently "useful." All Scripture is inspired by God to be profitable for teaching, reproof, correction, and training in righteousness (2 Tim. 3:16). While a literary reading of Genesis may invite moral reflection on the part of the reader, it is not likely to issue any clear commands for the reader to follow. Since the Church Fathers were looking for such commands and had the precedent of the New Testament in mind, it is easy to see why they so often chose to expound the biblical text by pointing to the perceived virtues of its vividly drawn characters.

Although it is impossible to know for certain what biblical authors were thinking, it is likely that some desire to set forth models for emulation motivated the idealized and even heroic character portrayals found in certain Old Testament narratives. Examples of such narratives include the stories of Joseph and Potiphar (Gen. 39), David and Goliath (1 Sam. 17), and Daniel (Dan. 1–6). Each of these stories makes statements about the greatness of God, but each does so through the actions of human characters, and it seems obvious, for example, that Jews living under foreign domination and trying to live rightly before God would see in Daniel a model for how to remain true to God while still attempting to prosper (compare this to Jer. 29:4-7). Some controls, however, are clearly necessary for discovering the meaningfulness of these narratives. Theologically, the person of Jesus — and the Christian understanding of God generally — serves as an important hermeneutical paradigm. But in terms of staying in contact with the text itself, the modern literary approach to the Bible makes a valuable contribution to contemporary Christian interpretation. Of course, the literary approach still does not address the question of how to take the actual content of the narratives with all their literary crafting (plot, characterization, dialogue, etc.) and discover the "message" of the text for modern readers. In the end, what we are supposed to learn from biblical narratives will often not be totally clear based on a literary reading alone. Theological reasoning will need to supplement literary reading in order to find a Christian message.

5. Scripture Is the Supreme Authority
in Christian Belief and Practice

I will conclude this chapter on the "usefulness" of Scripture with a concept that touches on how Scripture is to be used in relation to other sources of knowledge. The idea here is that Scripture is the highest authority among all forms of God's revelation to humanity. Whether it be divine revelation in nature, in reason, in church traditions, or in a person's inner experience, all of these must be evaluated by the standard set by Scripture. In theory, one could argue that Christians should do nothing in the religious sphere except what is commanded by Scripture. But none of the Church Fathers made such an argument, and it would be hard to put into practice.[83] A more realistic argument would be to say that the teachings of Scripture serve as a guide for interpreting other sources of knowledge, and that Scripture overrules other sources whenever there is disagreement. It is this kind of thinking that we will consider in this section.

There are passages in the writings of many Church Fathers where Scripture is invoked as the highest authority in Christian teaching. An example is Cyril of Jerusalem's *Catechetical Lectures,* where Cyril has just finished explaining the Holy Spirit. He says:

> Always keep the thought of this sealing in your mind, according to what has now been told you, in a summary way just skimming the surface. But if the Lord permit, I will set it forth, according to my powers, with demonstration from the Scriptures. For when we are dealing with the divine and holy mysteries of the faith, we must not deliver anything whatsoever, without the sacred Scriptures, nor let ourselves be misled by mere probability, or by marshaling arguments. And do not simply credit me, when I tell you these things, unless you get proof from the Holy Scriptures of the things set forth by me. For this salvation of ours by faith is not by sophistical use of words, but by proof from the sacred Scriptures.[84]

Gregory of Nyssa gives us another statement of this idea in his treatise *On the Soul and the Resurrection.* In this passage Gregory contrasts his way of discussing the soul with the approach of pagan philosophers:

> Although some could theorize freely concerning the soul as the consequence of their reasoning led them, we have no part in this

freedom (I mean the freedom to say whatever we want), since we always use the Holy Scripture as the canon and rule of all our doctrine. So we must necessarily look towards this standard and accept only that which is congruent with the sense of the writings.[85]

I will cite one more example, this time from Basil the Great. This is a letter to a friend in which Basil defends himself against accusations of false teaching. These accusations were made by people whose custom of describing the Trinity did not include the language of "three *hypostases*," as Basil's custom did:

> We do not think that it is right to make the custom that prevails among them the law and norm of right doctrine. For, if custom is the strong point for a proof of correctness, it assuredly is also possible for us to propose in its stead the custom prevailing among us. And, if they reject this, clearly we need not follow them. Therefore, let the God-inspired Scripture be judge for us, and to those whose teachings are found to be in harmony with the divine words will belong by all means the verdict of truth.[86]

Many more examples could be cited.[87] But my interest here is to say something about the significance of this possible entailment of divine inspiration.

The notion of the "supreme authority" of Scripture has been central to Protestant churches since the beginning of the Reformation. Protestants wanted to use Scripture to challenge beliefs and practices of the Roman Catholic Church, so it was important to argue that Scripture stood as an authority over all else. In Protestant thought, the doctrine of *sola scriptura* teaches that Scripture alone contains everything necessary for human salvation and is the supreme and final authority in matters of faith and practice.[88] When disputes with the Roman Catholic Church are particularly in view, Protestants have sometimes emphasized two corollaries of the doctrine of *sola scriptura,* (1) that Scripture takes precedence over church traditions, and (2) that the Scriptures are sufficiently clear in essential matters, so that no "official" interpreter is needed.[89] I will have something specific to say below on the clarity and obscurity of Scripture (section 9). I will also address the idea among the Church Fathers that the teaching of Scripture must agree with a recognized external standard (section 19). But for now let me say something brief about the authority of Scripture in light of (1) tradition and (2) interpretation.

First, there is a stream of thought in early Christianity that favored a central role for community and tradition in the interpretation of Scripture. A quotation from Tertullian will provide an example. According to Tertullian, heretical groups have been quoting scriptural passages to prove their points, and they have succeeded in misleading some of the faithful. Tertullian believes that they are perverting Scripture, but he has decided to take the approach of not discussing Scripture with them at all. He explains:

> Appeal, therefore, must not be made to the Scriptures, nor must the contest be carried on concerning points where victory is impossible or uncertain or too little certain. For even though the discussion from the Scriptures should not so result as to place each side in an equal position, the order of things would demand that this point should first be decided — the point which alone now calls for discussion, namely: Who holds the Faith to which the Scriptures belong? From whom and through whom, and when, and to whom was the doctrinal teaching delivered whereby men are made Christians? For wherever it shall appear that the true Christian religion and faith exist, there will be found the true Scriptures and interpretations and all Christian traditions.[90]

Tertullian argues in this passage that the true interpretation of Scripture will be found in the community that possesses the church's "rule of faith." In Tertullian's day, this rule consisted of a short summary of Christian belief similar to what is known today as the "Apostles' Creed." Virtually all Christians today (Protestant, Roman Catholic, Eastern Orthodox, and Oriental Orthodox) would be comfortable with this short rule as a minimal standard for true Christianity.[91] But for the present, let us notice the significance of Tertullian's argument for the doctrine of the "supreme authority" of Scripture. Tertullian would probably have agreed to the assertion that Scripture is the supreme authority in faith and practice.[92] But for Tertullian, this did not prevent the rule of faith from serving as a standard for evaluating competing interpretations of Scripture.

Second, the topic of interpretation is crucial for thinking about the authority of Scripture in early Christianity. Most Church Fathers operated with a sense that Scripture was the supreme authority for Christian faith. But they also employed interpretive methods that allowed for a considerable amount of their own thought-world to enter into the process. Thus, many Church Fathers saw the virtues of ancient Greek philosophy taught in Scripture. Many looked for symbols of Jesus in numerous and sometimes unusual places throughout Scripture (for example, see section 9). Some Church Fathers regarded the Bible as absolutely authoritative, but insisted that Scripture cannot teach anything contrary to the current doctrines of the church (see Augustine in section 19) or contrary to our best notions of what is worthy of God (see section 20). Interpretive stances such as these complicate their ideas about Scripture's supreme authority.

In light of this, what is the best way for modern Christians to appropriate the early church's viewpoints on the authority of Scripture? One approach might be to identify a modern method of interpretation that could serve as a common basis for appealing to Scripture as supreme authority. Another approach might be to ascribe supreme authority in interpreting Scripture to one particular community. Yet another approach might be to embrace a measure of subjectivity in biblical interpretation and to assign final interpretive responsibility to the individual Christian. We will take up this topic again in the Conclusion.

All Scripture is "God-breathed" and "useful" *(ōphelimos),* as 2 Timothy 3:16-17 makes clear. The Church Fathers, like many other ancient interpreters of sacred texts, placed great confidence in the usefulness of Scripture. They believed that all of Scripture — and perhaps every detail of Scripture — is profitable for the purposes set out by God, "for teaching, for reproof, for correction, and for training in righteousness, that the man of God may be competent, equipped for every good work." That God intended the Scriptures to work for the spiritual benefit of humanity undergirds everything else that the Church Fathers had to say about the inspiration of Scripture.

CHAPTER THREE

The Spiritual and Supernatural Dimension

In this chapter I have grouped together three topics that relate to the supernatural nature of Scripture. The basic argument is as follows: If Scripture is the product of supernatural inspiration by the Spirit of God (2 Pet. 1:21), then there must be a spiritual and supernatural nature to Scripture as a result. The first section deals with the idea that divine aid is needed in order to understand the true meaning of Scripture. The second section describes the general belief that Scripture has a spiritual sense that goes beyond the straightforward literal subject matter. Finally, the third section in this chapter addresses the belief that the Old Testament supernaturally predicted major events of history, especially the coming of Jesus.

A key passage for the Church Fathers on the spiritual dimension of Scripture was 2 Corinthians 3:1-18. In this passage, Paul argues that the spiritual "letter of recommendation" written by Christ on the spiritual "tablet" of the hearts of the Corinthian Christians is superior to the physical letters of recommendation that Paul's opponents brought to Corinth in order to verify their own authority. This leads Paul to say, "For the letter kills, but the Spirit gives life." From here, Paul explains that the ministry of the Spirit through Jesus has a greater glory than does the ministry of death through Moses. Paul also makes the following criticism of the Jews of his day:

> But their minds were hardened. For to this day, when they read the old covenant, that same veil remains unlifted, because only through Christ is it taken away. Yes, to this day whenever Moses is read a veil lies over their hearts. But when one turns to the Lord, the veil is removed. Now the Lord is the Spirit, and where the Spirit of the Lord

is, there is freedom. And we all, with unveiled face, beholding the glory of the Lord, are being transformed into the same image from one degree of glory to another. For this comes from the Lord who is the Spirit. (2 Cor. 3:14-18)

From this text at least two major conclusions were commonly drawn. First, in order to understand the reading of "Moses" (= the "Old Testament") correctly, one needs the work of the Spirit through Christ. Second, the goal of interpreting the sacred texts is transformation into the image of Christ. This passage by Paul, and especially the saying "The letter kills, but the Spirit gives life," was cited frequently by early Christian writers in order to explain the supernatural and spiritual sense of Scripture.

6. Divine Illumination Is Required for Biblical Interpretation

The possible entailment of inspiration discussed in this section is that people cannot properly understand Scripture unless God supernaturally helps them. Paul suggests in 2 Corinthians 3 that only the Spirit of God through Christ can enable someone to understand the Old Testament correctly. A straightforward application of this perspective can be found in the writings of Justin Martyr in the second century. In his *Dialogue with Trypho,* Justin cites numerous Old Testament texts in order to prove that the God of Abraham had always planned to bring salvation to the nations through Jesus the Messiah. At various points throughout this work Justin expresses his belief that only through divine aid can a person recognize the true interpretation of the Old Testament passages quoted. For example, near the beginning of the work Justin depicts an old man admonishing him, "Above all, beseech God to open to you the gates of light, for no one can perceive or understand these truths unless he has been enlightened by God and His Christ."[1] Later on Justin says, "If, therefore, one were not endowed with God's great grace to understand the words and deeds of the Prophets, it would be quite useless for him to relate their words and actions, when he can give no explanation of them."[2] And following a string of Old Testament prooftexts for Jesus (including Isa. 53:8; 2 Sam. 7:14; and Ezek. 44:3), Justin asks, "'Do you, gentlemen, suppose,' I continued, 'that we could have grasped these things in the Scriptures without a special grace from Him who willed them?'"[3] Justin believes that the Old Testament Scriptures prove his case about Jesus the Messiah, but he also believes that people cannot understand the proper meaning of these Scriptures apart from God bestowing on them a special grace of wisdom.

Origen of Alexandria was another early Christian who strongly believed in the need for divine grace in order to interpret Scripture. As Origen explains, "Just as the one who was commanded these things [in this case, the prophet Ezekiel] had need of the Holy Spirit, so there is need of the same Spirit in the one who desires to explain the things that are being signified in a hidden fashion."[4]

Origen especially sought God's aid when he was trying to grasp the "allegorical" or "spiritual" meaning of the text (see section 7 below). We may cite as an example his first homily on Exodus. He starts by explaining his belief in the profundity of all Scripture: "I think each word of divine Scripture is like a seed whose nature is to multiply diffusely. . . . Its increase is proportionate to the diligent labor of the skillful farmer or the fertility of the earth."[5] Like the mustard seed of Jesus' parable (Matt. 13:31-32), a passage of Scripture may at first seem small and insignificant, but with proper spiritual cultivation "it grows into a tree and puts forth branches and foliage." Origen then announces that he is seeking this kind of spiritual cultivation in his exposition of Exodus 1:1-5, which is a list of the sons of Jacob who went down to Egypt. Origen speaks directly to his congregation:

> What then shall we do about these things which have been read to us? If the Lord design to grant me the discipline of spiritual agriculture, if he grant me the skill of cultivating a field, one word from these which have been read could be scattered far and wide to such an extent that — if your capacity to listen would permit — scarcely would a day suffice for us to treat it. . . . May you help with your prayers, that the word of God may be present with us and deign himself to be the leader of our discourse.[6]

In Origen's exposition, the sons of Jacob are souls,[7] Joseph stands for Jesus, and it is the death of Jesus that allows the sons to multiply, both in the building up of the church and in the life of the individual believer. Two important points should be made regarding the content of Origen's exposition. First, Origen believes that one of the key ways that the Holy Spirit reveals the deeper meaning of the text is by allowing the interpreter to perceive illuminating parallel passages from elsewhere in Scripture (see also sections 11 and 17 below). Thus, Origen brings in Isaiah 52:4 to illuminate the spiritual sense of the word "Egypt," explaining, "I think what the prophet says is similar to this mystery, if anyone is able to perceive it."[8] Origen also identifies the spiritual sense of "Israel" by appealing to Romans 9:1-5, insisting that we can discover the proper sense "by comparing spiritual things with spiritual things [see 1 Cor. 2:13] and putting old things together with new and new with old."[9] Second, Origen is encouraged to search for spiritual meanings in this list of names by his belief in the significance of every detail of Scripture (see section 2 above): "I, believing in the words of my Lord Jesus Christ, do not think that one 'iota or one point' in the Law and prophets is void of mysteries, nor do I think 'any of these things can pass away until all things come about'" (see Matt. 5:18).[10] Clearly Origen does not believe that he is simply reading these meanings into the text; rather, he sees himself as uncovering what God has concealed within the details of this passage as illuminated by other passages of Scripture. Still, Origen does not think that he could find this interpretation through his own ingenuity, but must ask God to give him the skill to cultivate this scriptural field.

Origen regularly searched for the spiritual sense of Scripture, and he regularly prayed for divine guidance to discover it.[11] In order to appreciate Origen's approach, we must consider his model, the apostle Paul. A text that served as a paradigm for allegorical interpretation was Galatians 4:21-26, where Paul says:

> Tell me, you who desire to be under the law, do you not listen to the law? For it is written that Abraham had two sons, one by a slave woman and one by a free woman. But the son of the slave was born according to the flesh, while the son of the free woman was born through promise — which things are said allegorically *(hatina estin allēgoroumena):* these women are two covenants. One is from Mount Sinai, bearing children for slavery; she is Hagar. Now Hagar is Mount Sinai in Arabia; she corresponds to the present Jerusalem, for she is in slavery with her children. But the Jerusalem above is free, and she is our mother.[12]

Paul interprets the story of Sarah and Hagar in Genesis as an allegorical description of two covenants: Hagar the slave represents the Old Covenant of the Law, whereas Sarah the free woman represents the New Covenant in Jesus. Based on Paul's language, especially the phrase, "which things are said allegorically," it appears that Paul thinks either that the story of Sarah and Hagar was originally written as an allegory or that the text of Scripture, "speaking" in the present tense in Paul's day, intends this as an allegory. The verb "to allegorize" was used in this way by other ancient Greek interpreters, such as Philo the Jew[13] and Porphyry the Neoplatonist philosopher.[14] The verb continued to be used positively by Christian authors after Paul, such as Clement of Alexandria and Methodius of Olympus.[15]

Much like Paul, Philo allegorized the story of Sarah and Hagar.[16] For Philo, Hagar the slave represents education, and Sarah the free woman represents virtue; one must mate with education first, before moving on to take virtue as one's wife.[17] Although Paul's meaning is different from Philo's meaning, Paul is certainly no less creative than Philo. Origen believed that God wanted him to find Christian theological meanings in the Old Testament in a manner similar to the apostle Paul. It is therefore easy to understand why Origen thought that he needed supernatural aid to arrive at the proper interpretation.

Christian authors after Origen continued to seek out the spiritual meanings of scriptural texts, and they continued to ask for God's aid. Gregory of Nyssa often spoke of his need for divine assistance in finding the deeper meaning of the text, as in the prologue to his *Life of Moses:* "We must take up the task that lies before us, taking God as our guide in our treatise."[18] In his ninth homily on the Song of Songs, Gregory reveals his sense of inadequacy and dependence on God's help in finding the spiritual interpretation of Song of Songs 4:13-15:

> But as I said before, it is those who are able to search the depth of the riches and of the wisdom and knowledge of God who would know the true account of these matters. As for us, lest we be left with absolutely no taste or enjoyment of the good things that are set before us in this text, we shall address it briefly, having taken the divine Word himself as the guide for our earnest effort.[19]

Theodoret of Cyrus similarly expresses humility and need of divine help in the preface to his *Commentary on Jeremiah:*

> I had been of the view that there was no need for a commentary on the inspired composition of the divine Jeremiah. Since, however, many studious people kept pressing me to do a commentary on the book as well by claiming that most people do not grasp the sense of the work, I shall attempt, after praying for divine grace to cooperate, to meet the demand.[20]

Theodoret's exposition consists mostly of straightforward paraphrase, with occasional comments on Christological and theological topics. But like Gregory and Origen, he asks for divine aid in his task. Few Christian authors after the time of Origen had as strong a sense as he did of the revelatory nature of biblical interpretation. But this is probably because later interpreters did not have as much to discover (or invent), since they could find in his writings a complete Christological interpretive system linking the whole Bible together.

According to John Cassian, the divine aid we need to understand the higher meanings of Scripture cannot be received unless we first become practitioners of the Christian life. In the chapter on "spiritual knowledge" in his monastic work *The Conferences,* Cassian says, "Whoever, therefore, wishes to attain to the *theōrētikē* ("theoretical") must first pursue practical knowledge with all his strength and power. For the *praktikē* ("practical") can be possessed without the theoretical, but the theoretical can never be seized without the practical."[21] For Cassian, *praktikē* consists of knowing and remedying vices, and at the same time obeying and delighting in virtues.[22] Once this *praktikē* has been seized, the Christian can move on to take hold of the *theōrētikē,* which consists of the historical and spiritual meanings of Scripture.[23] "Spiritual knowledge" is equivalent to proper understanding of Scripture. In order to possess this understanding, Christians must devote themselves to renouncing vice and embracing virtue. According to Cassian, the interpreter of Scripture becomes receptive to God's aid by practicing Christian ethics.

Cassian was not the only early Christian to think in these terms. Athanasius says much the same thing, albeit more briefly, at the end of his treatise *On the Incarnation:*

> But in addition to the study and true knowledge of the Scriptures are needed a good life and pure soul and virtue in Christ, so that the mind, journeying in this path, may be able to obtain and apprehend what it desires, in so far as human nature is able to learn about God the Word. For without a pure mind and a life modeled on the saints, no one can apprehend the words of the saints.[24]

How has the idea of divine illumination in biblical interpretation fared in the modern world? In the academic context, biblical scholars today do not seek to incorporate any notion of divine illumination into their work. This is because they are seeking to understand the historical and literal sense of the text as written by the human authors, and they desire to base their research on evidence that is available to all readers, and not on supernatural evidence that is specially revealed. Christian readers who value the literal sense of Scripture can profit greatly from this kind of research and can sometimes contribute to it. The careful identification of what biblical texts said and did not say in their original contexts can help modern Christians stay in close contact with the content of Scripture, even as they seek to go beyond the historical sense to find contemporary meaning. If there is a lesson from this section that is relevant for all who study biblical texts in their original contexts, it would be that virtues such as humility, patience, and charity in scholarship are important for understanding even the literal sense of Scripture (or of any text, for that matter).

Within the context of the church, it is common for books on theology to mention the role of the Holy Spirit and divine illumination in understanding or grasping the truth of Scripture.[25] When Christian readers look to understand the meaning of the Bible in its original context, explanations from well-researched biblical commentaries often seem more pertinent than supernatural aid (of course, humility, patience, and charity are relevant here). But when it comes to perceiving what lessons God might want an individual to learn from a passage of Scripture, the sense of inadequacy and need for divine help is probably no less for modern Christians than it was for ancient Christians. It is one thing to study a passage of Scripture to understand what it meant in the ancient context in which it was written. It is another thing to perceive the application of the text's religious truth for a specific person's life. This requires, among other things, knowledge of other passages of Scripture, Christian tradition, theological reflection, and wise counsel from other Christians. It is no wonder that many modern Christians believe that they need supernatural aid to arrive at the proper understanding of what Scripture has to teach them. This is why Christians often pray before, during, and after they read the Bible. Provided that the insights we receive are handled with the proper degree of humility, prayer for divine aid in interpreting Scripture is just as important today as it was for Origen.

7. Scripture Has Multiple Senses

In keeping with New Testament texts such as 1 Corinthians 10:1-11; Galatians 4:21-31; Ephesians 5:31-32; Hebrews 9:6-10; and 1 Peter 3:18-22, virtually all ancient Christians believed that the Old Testament had spiritual meaning beyond the literal sense. Sometimes the New Testament was also read with a spiritual signification. In his report of the church's rule of faith — a brief statement summarizing the core teaching of the church (see section 19 below) — Origen mentions the belief that "the scriptures were composed through the Spirit of God and that they have not only that meaning which is obvious, but also another which is hidden from the majority of readers. For the contents of scripture are the outward forms of certain mysteries and the images of divine things."[26] Origen is unique among the Church Fathers in identifying the hidden sense of Scripture as an explicit part of the rule of faith. He probably did so because of the important role that the higher sense of Scripture played in defending the Christian faith within the Alexandrian context. But the spirit of Origen's statement is accurate. Christians from Alexandria to Asia Minor and from Jerusalem to Rome not only practiced spiritual interpretation but also reckoned it an essential part of the faith.

Augustine gave this general advice at the beginning of his treatment of the "higher sense" in *On Christian Teaching:*

> One must take care not to interpret a figurative expression literally. What the apostle says is relevant here: "the letter kills but the spirit gives life" [2 Cor. 3:6]. . . . It is, then, a miserable kind of spiritual slavery to interpret signs as things, and to be incapable of raising the mind's eye above the physical creation so as to absorb the eternal light.[27]

For Augustine, the language of Scripture is a system of "signs" *(signa)* that point to "things" *(res),* and frequently the "things" being indicated are spiritual realities that have been indicated in the text by ambiguous expressions with figurative meanings *(signa ambigua translata).* As spelled out in the rest of book three of *On Christian Teaching,* this is Augustine's way of describing the spiritual sense. He makes the following revealing comment at the beginning of his commentary titled *The Literal Meaning of Genesis,* "No Christian will dare say that the narrative must not be taken in a figurative sense."[28] In other words, everyone agrees that the narrative has figurative meaning; the only matter of dispute is whether it has a literal sense.

To be sure, not all Christians in the early church described the spiritual sense in the same way. But it is virtually impossible to find any Christian reader of Scripture who does not believe in some kind of spiritual sense. Even Diodore of Tarsus, who criticized what he saw as the excesses of allegory as practiced by Origen and others, believed in a higher sense of Scripture. Diodore named this higher sense *theōria* ("vision"). As Diodore explained:

> While repudiating this ["allegory"] once and for all, we are not pre-vented from "theorizing" responsibly and from lifting the content into higher *anagogy*.[29] We may compare, for example, Cain and Abel to the Jewish synagogue and the church. . . . This method nei-ther sets aside history nor repudiates *theōria*. Rather, as a realistic, middle-of-the-road approach which takes into account both his-tory and *theōria*, it frees us, on the one hand, from a Hellenism which says one thing for another and introduces foreign subject matter; on the other hand, it does not yield to Judaism and choke us by forcing us to treat the literal reading of the text as the only one worthy of attention and honor, while not allowing the exploration of a higher sense beyond the letter also.[30]

Obviously Diodore did not regard likening Cain and Abel to the syna-gogue and the church as introducing "foreign subject matter." He simply saw this as avoiding the Jewish error (in his mind) of disallowing the higher sense as it relates to Christ and the church. Other interpreters, such as Gregory of Nazianzus, likewise saw themselves as "standing midway" between excessively "contemplative" interpretations on the one hand and "utterly dense" interpretations on the other.[31] But Gregory of Nazianzus was also an admirer of Origen and one of the compilers of the *Philocalia* of Origen, and he clearly approved of the passages excerpted for that work. Even Christians who regarded themselves as moderate on this issue be-lieved in some form of exegesis beyond the literal.

Belief in a higher sense for the Old Testament had practical significance for the Church Fathers. It meant that Christians were not obligated to ob-serve Old Testament laws literally. It is not logically necessary that one should draw this conclusion. Philo, for example, although he believed in the allegorical meaning of the law, nevertheless also believed that the law should be physically observed. Thus, Philo taught that the Old Testament feasts symbolized the joy of the soul and that circumcision symbolized the cutting away of the passions; but he condemned those who took this to mean that they should not literally observe the festivals or practice circumcision.[32]

For Christians, however, the higher meaning of the law took the place of literal observance. I have already discussed the allegorical reading of Old

Testament food laws in the *Epistle of Barnabas* (section 3 above). What may be noted here is that *Barnabas* firmly holds that these laws were meant by Moses to be interpreted allegorically and that it is simply a mistake on the part of Jews to follow them literally. Thus *Barnabas* 10:9 states, "Concerning meats then Moses received three decrees to this effect and uttered them in a spiritual sense; but they accepted them according to the lust of the flesh, as though they referred to eating."[33] Origen, the first Christian ever to write a systematic study of Old Testament laws, begins his first homily on Leviticus by justifying his spiritual approach with the following argument: "For if I also should follow the simple understanding . . . I, myself a man of the Church, living under the faith of Christ and placed in the midst of the Church, am compelled by the authority of the divine precept to sacrifice calves and lambs and to offer fine wheat flour with incense and oil."[34] Jerome similarly argues that those who reject the spiritual interpretation of what Jeremiah 17:21-27 says about Sabbath observance reject the teachings of Jesus (he cites John 5:18) and should submit themselves literally not only to the Sabbath but also to circumcision.[35] Virtually all Christians in antiquity believed that Old Testament laws should be understood as teaching spiritual truths instead of literal practices to be observed.

Two final points may be introduced here regarding the spiritual sense of Scripture in the early church. First, the spiritual sense could be invoked to solve problems at the literal level. Second, the spiritual sense could be used to demonstrate that Scripture teaches important truths.

On the first point, Origen explained in his work *On First Principles* that God intentionally placed difficulties in the literal sense of Scripture so that readers would know to search for a higher sense:

> But if the usefulness of the law and the sequence and ease of the narrative were at first sight clearly discernable throughout, we should be unaware that there was anything beyond the obvious meaning for us to understand in the Scriptures. Consequently the Word of God has arranged for certain stumbling blocks, as it were, and hindrances and impossibilities to be inserted in the midst of the law and the history, in order that we may not be completely drawn away by the sheer attractiveness of the language, and so either reject the true doctrines absolutely, on the grounds that we learn nothing from the scriptures worthy of God, or else by never moving away from the letter fail to learn anything of the more divine element.[36]

Some of the difficulties that Origen had in mind relate to what modern readers would simply identify as figurative expressions; for example, he noted that when Genesis 4:16 says that Cain went away "from the *face* of the LORD," this does not necessarily mean that God has a human face.[37] But for Origen this is all part of a larger program of Scripture to draw the reader's attention to the higher meaning through impossibilities. Thus, Origen observes that the Old Testament contains laws that pertain to the "goat-stag," which is a mythological creature that does not even exist (the "goat-stag" appears in some copies of the Greek Old Testament at Deut. 14:5).[38] According to Origen, God placed impossibilities such as this into the text in order to alert the reader to search for a higher meaning. Origen was not alone in interpreting difficulties in the biblical text this way.[39] Augustine testifies that the Old Testament was death to him when taken literally, but became convincing when it was interpreted according to the figurative principles of Ambrose. This was instrumental in Augustine's conversion from Manichaeism to the catholic faith.[40]

On the second point, the spiritual sense of Scripture functioned in the early church to demonstrate how Scripture addressed significant topics. Both Philo and Clement of Alexandria interpreted the Tabernacle and the priestly garments as symbols of the universe, which is God's true Temple. For Clement, the colors of the curtains in the Tabernacle signify the four elements: earth, water, air, and fire, and the high priest's robe represents the seven planets.[41] This was not due to any problem in the literal narrative, but simply shows that cosmology was an important philosophical topic for early Christians in the Greek world, and they needed to explain how the Scriptures addressed this topic (see section 3 above). Justin Martyr saw the scarlet cord of Rahab in Joshua 2:18 as foreshadowing the blood of Christ, not because of any difficulty in the literal sense, but because he expected to find reference to Jesus in a story about deliverance from death.[42] Cyril of Alexandria interpreted Zacchaeus climbing the sycamore tree in Luke 19:4 as the seeker of Jesus who must rise above the foolish things of the world (fornication, etc.), not because Cyril needed to solve a difficulty in the text but in order to promote good morals in his congregation.[43] To summarize this second point: the spiritual sense of Scripture was not simply a mechanism for dealing with textual difficulties; it was also a positive interpretive principle used to see interconnections within the text and between the text and other subjects.

The Church Fathers used a number of different terms to describe the spiritual sense of Scripture, including "allegory" ("to speak about something other"), "tropology" ("figurative expression"), "anagogy" ("elevation"), and the adjectives "mystical," "sacramental," and "spiritual." In the period of the early Church Fathers (up to the sixth century) these terms were generally used without differentiation. Any of them could be employed to indicate the "higher" sense of the text, that is, the sense above the literal level. Origen cited Proverbs 22:20 ("Record these things for yourselves triply," according to the ancient Greek translation) to suggest that Scripture had three elements: a "body" (the basic sense), a "soul" (the more advanced sense), and a "spirit" (the perfect sense, foreshadowing things to come). He often operated with only two levels of meaning, a literal and a spiritual, but sometimes identified three levels — for example, literal, "mystical" (Christological), and "moral."[44] Developing Origen's thought, John Cassian used Proverbs 22:20 to identify three senses beyond the literal sense, bringing the total number of senses to four: the "literal" sense (history — things past and visible), "tropology" (moral explanation), "allegory" (prefiguring another mystery), and "anagogy" (pointing to heavenly realities).[45] Cassian's system was passed on to the Middle Ages and ultimately became the well-known medieval "four senses of Scripture," which are summarized nicely in the following epigram quoted by Nicholas de Lyra (d. 1349): "The letter teaches events, allegory what you should believe, morality teaches what you should do, anagogy what mark you should be aiming for."[46]

The Church Fathers' belief that Scripture has more than one sense converged with numerous other beliefs that they held, such as that Scripture is useful for instruction, and that all Scripture teaches a unified message. The concept of a higher sense provided some helpful theological tools for the early church but also generated problems.

In terms of helpfulness, while the language of multiple senses reflects the distinctive Greco-Roman cultural context, the framework provided by multiple-sense thinking mapped constructively two genuine qualities of Scripture. First, biblical texts share a common historical trajectory in which later texts frequently refer back to earlier texts. This creates a great number of common themes and intertextual connections within Scripture. Early Christian thinking about higher senses served as a theological way to identify and organize these interconnections. Second, much scriptural writing, especially in the Old Testament, operates with a mode of expression that is beyond literal. For example, the taunt against the king of Babylon in Isaiah 14:4-21 deals with its subject matter figuratively when it says, "How you have fallen from heaven, O Day Star, son of Dawn. . . . You said in your heart, 'I will ascend to heaven; above the stars of God I will set my throne on high.'" This biblical text has already typologized the historical king of Babylon as a symbol for evil, so it is not surprising that later Christians applied this text to the ultimate symbol of evil, the devil.[47] Likewise, the Philistines are typologized in the Old Testament as the ultimate "other" in a manner that, even if it reflects historical realities to some extent, also places a theological overlay on top of history. The Church Fathers' belief in a higher sense gave them a framework within which to perceive such theological overlays. For reasons such as these, the interpretations that the Church Fathers identified as the spiritual sense sometimes correlate with ideas genuinely found in biblical texts.

From a Christian vantage point, belief in a higher or spiritual sense was also helpful in that it allowed the early church to appropriate Scripture through the lens of Christ. The higher sense of Scripture often amounted to the thought structure of the passage recast using the specific Christian realities that made the text meaningful to the contemporary Christian audience. The sense was "higher" in that it focused on communion with God and the virtuous life, and the fact that it was regarded as a "sense" of Scripture encouraged the best readers to stick closely to the paradigms set out in the texts. In this way belief in multiple senses contributed significantly to the Christian meaningfulness of Scripture.

At the same time, major problems accompanied the ancient Christian belief that Scripture has multiple senses. For one, without sufficient attention to the literal sense (or human discourse) of the text, readers can lose contact with the actual content and message of biblical texts. The reader may bring so much to the text that the text is not allowed to make its own points, and so it loses its capacity to challenge the reader. Emphasis on the spiritual sense in the early church sometimes undermined attention to the literal sense, and this in turn put distance between Scripture and Christian readers. As another problem, imagining one's own appropriation of Scripture as a "sense" of the text can foster an illegitimate feeling of ownership over the text's meaning. Even if the reader stays close to the paradigms and major ideas set forth in the text, the perception of the applied meaning of a scriptural passage is still very dependent on the spiritual experience of the reader. This religious encounter with the biblical text may be real, but this does not give the individual in question exclusive authority to label their personal insight as the text's "sense." Reading spiritually today requires greater self-awareness and humility than was sometimes practiced in the early church. We must be careful to avoid arrogant assertions about Scripture's meaning in our dealings both with those outside the church and also with other Christians who read Scripture differently than we do.

8. Scripture Accurately Predicted the Future, Especially about Jesus

The topic of this section is the close relationship between the inspiration of Scripture and the fact that Scripture accurately predicted major events in history, above all the coming of Jesus. Tertullian asserted that the Scriptures foretold many events taking place in his own day and that these events constituted proof that the Scriptures are divine.[48] Origen argued that the divine nature of Jesus demonstrated that the writings which had predicted his coming must be divinely inspired.[49] Eusebius, working from the other direction, started from the truthfulness of the Old Testament writings and used the predictions about Jesus contained within them to argue that Jesus and the Gospel are true.[50] Theophilus of Antioch testified that he first came to believe in Christianity because of the truth and accuracy of what Scripture predicted:

> Do not disbelieve, then, but believe. I too did not believe that resurrection would take place, but now that I have considered these matters I believe. At that time I encountered the sacred writings of the holy prophets, who through the Spirit of God foretold past events in the way that they happened, present events in the way they are happening, and future events in the order in which they will be accomplished. Because I obtained proof from the events which took place after being predicted, I do not disbelieve but believe, in obedience to God.[51]

Scripture's success at predicting the future offered proof both for the divine nature of Scripture and also for the claim that Jesus is the Son of God. Scripture and Jesus were each supported by the unfolding of events that fulfilled scriptural predictions.

Numerous Old Testament texts were cited as predictions of the advent and identity of Jesus. Cyprian wrote three books of *Testimonies to Quirinus,* which list quotations from (mostly) the Old Testament in a topical sequence aimed at proving that the Scriptures predicted various aspects of Jesus' life and ministry. The first book contains twenty-four topical headings and focuses on anti-Jewish polemic, with topics such as "That the Jews could understand nothing of the Scriptures unless they first believed in Christ."[52] Book two contains thirty topics, many of the sections being quite long, focusing on predictions of Jesus' birth, death, and resurrection, and also on his divine nature and mission. Topics include "That Christ is the First-born, and that He is the Wisdom of God, by whom all things were made," "That Christ is God," "That the Jews would fasten Christ to the cross," and "That after He had risen again He should receive from His Father all power, and His power should be everlasting." The birth of Jesus in Bethlehem in accordance with Micah 5:2 (see Matt. 2:6) was one of the most often cited Old Testament predictions about Jesus, and it receives its own section in Book two of Cyprian's *Testimonies*. Book three contains 120 shorter sections that present ethical and theological implications of the resurrection of Jesus, such as "That charity and brotherly affection are to be religiously and steadfastly practiced" and "That the grace of God ought to be without price." New Testament citations are more prevalent in Book three. Cyprian's collection of scriptural prooftexts was the most extensive list in the early church, but many other works devoted considerable attention to Old Testament testimonies; Irenaeus's *Demonstration of the Apostolic Preaching* and Eusebius's *Proof of the Gospel* are primary examples. Most of the Old Testament passages used in these works could be found quoted in the New Testament as evidence for Jesus. The Church Fathers can thus be seen as systematizing the basic approach already taken by the writers of the New Testament.

The New Testament as a whole shows deep concern to demonstrate that what Jesus accomplished was already promised in Israel's Scriptures. The New Testament contains over 250 quotations from the Old Testament. If one counts both quotations and allusions, one recent estimate suggests that ten percent of the New Testament is made up of quotations or direct allusions to the Old Testament.[53] The Gospel of Matthew explicitly states thirteen times that something occurred in the life of Jesus so that what was spoken by the prophets might be "fulfilled."[54] An example shows how concerned its author was to show the accuracy of Old Testament predictions. Zechariah 9:9 announced the coming of Israel's king in the following words:

> Rejoice greatly, O daughter of Zion!
> Shout aloud, O daughter of Jerusalem!
> Behold, your king is coming to you;
> righteous and having salvation is he,

humble and mounted on a donkey,
on a colt, the foal of a donkey.

When Jesus entered Jerusalem on what came to be known as "Palm Sunday" (the Sunday before his resurrection), he rode into the city on a colt, presumably intending to invoke the image of Zechariah 9:9, thereby proclaiming himself to be the righteous king who brings salvation. Mark, which was probably the first Gospel to be written, describes how Jesus instructed his disciples to secure the use of the colt and how Jesus rode the colt (Mark 11:1-7), but Mark does not refer to Zechariah 9:9.[55] The same may be said of the Gospel of Luke, which gives the story essentially as Mark does (Luke 19:28-35). The lack of reference to the Zechariah passage in Mark and Luke may be explained through the statement of John (the last canonical Gospel written, which does quote Zech. 9:9), that "His disciples did not understand these things at first, but when Jesus was glorified, then they remembered that these things had been written about him and had been done to him" (John 12:16). In other words, Jesus' disciples did not immediately recognize the allusion to Zechariah 9:9 implicit in Jesus' action. Only later did this allusion become clear, but it was still not pointed out either by Mark or Luke.

Matthew, on the other hand, does quote the Old Testament prooftext and is concerned to show that it was fulfilled precisely. The end of Zechariah 9:9 says literally, "humble and mounted on a donkey, *and* on a colt, the 'son' of a donkey." The quotation that I gave above (from the ESV) correctly leaves out the second "and" because only one animal is in view. Hebrew poetry is fond of giving two parallel lines in a row, connected by "and," which refer to one and the same thing. As an example, Psalm 20:2 says, "May he send you help from the sanctuary, *and* from Zion may he support you." From a poetic perspective, the two words "sanctuary" and "Zion" each contribute their own meaning to the overall sense of the line; but both words refer to one and the same object, the Temple in Jerusalem. Similarly, in the original sense of Zechariah 9:9 there is only one animal, namely, "a donkey, ("and" = "that is") a colt, the 'son' of a donkey." Nevertheless, Matthew's quotation preserves the "and" literally, with the result that two animals appear to be in view: "mounted on a donkey, *and* on a colt, the foal of a beast of burden."[56] Matthew recognizes that Jesus rode into Jerusalem in order to fulfill Zechariah 9:9, and since the text of Zechariah 9:9 could be creatively read as referring to two animals, the Gospel of Matthew uniquely has Jesus obtain and (apparently) ride two animals.

Matthew alone has Jesus tell his disciples to find "a donkey tied, and a colt with her" (Matt. 21:2). The animals are consistently referred to in the plural. An important sentence is v. 7: "They brought the donkey and the colt and put on them their cloaks, and he sat on them." It is admittedly difficult to see how Jesus could have sat on two different animals at once. For this reason, some commentators have argued that the "them" on which Jesus sat refers to the "garments." But this does not account for Matthew's reference to two animals where the other Gospel writers have only one. Even the Gospel of John, which quotes Zechariah 9:9, refers to only one animal and simply abbreviates the Zechariah quotation to avoid the difficulty ("sitting on a donkey's colt"). Furthermore, the Gospel of Mark has Jesus sitting on "it," namely the "colt" — not the "garments." So when Matthew introduces two animals and then has Jesus sit on "them," it is only natural to assume that he means the animals, not the garments. Did Matthew, then, really believe that Jesus entered Jerusalem riding on two animals?

I do not think that we can know for sure all of what Matthew was thinking about this text, but it is possible for us to appreciate Matthew's use of Zechariah 9:9 in light of ancient beliefs about Scripture. I noted above how Paul used a linguistic peculiarity of a specific Hebrew word (the collective noun "seed") in order to connect Jesus to the promises God made to Abraham (see page 8). We also have an example, preserved in the earliest Jewish Midrash on the book of Genesis, in which a sage named Rabbi Judah draws a homiletical point from the singular forms of the words "ox" and "donkey" in Genesis 32:5.[57] Based on the discussion that follows, it is clear that the sages perfectly understand the straightforward meaning of the text ("I have oxen, donkeys . . .").[58] Yet they still press the language of the text to see if it contains any clues to the continuing meaningfulness of the text for their community. The sages believed that the details of Scripture could be significant beyond the basic sense (see section 2 above).

In a similar way, but with different goals in mind, the Gospel of Matthew believes in the significance of details. The Gospel's central belief is that Jesus fulfilled the promises of the Old Testament, that Jesus so thoroughly accomplished the goals of the Old Testament that he fulfilled the sayings of the prophets with absolute accuracy. Matthew knows that Jesus entered Jerusalem on a donkey, and he knows that Jesus fulfilled Zechariah 9:9. When the Gospel writer looks at the Zechariah passage and sees the possibility of finding two animals through a hyper-literalistic reading of the text, he takes the opportunity to portray Jesus as entering on two animals — against the grain of the simple history — but precisely in keeping with the very words of the sacred text.[59] Matthew's quotation of Zechariah 9:9 is an excellent illustration of the confidence with which early Christians believed that Jesus had fulfilled the promises made in the Old Testament Scriptures.

It was clear to the Church Fathers that Jesus and the events he inaugurated were the fulfillment of predictions made by the Old Testament. As Hilary stated, "Every work that is contained in the sacred books announces in words, conveys through facts, and demonstrates by examples the coming of our Lord Jesus Christ, that he was born from the Father from a virgin through the Spirit."[60] But there was not uniformity of thought on whether or not these predictions were stated clearly enough originally to have been understood before the coming of Jesus. One line of thinking emphasized that the Old Testament had predicted Christ through "types and parables" that could not be correctly explained until after Jesus came into the world.[61] Another line of thinking insisted that the Old Testament predicted Jesus not only through allegories but also through prophecies taken in their straightforward literal sense.[62] Origen, in his defense of prophecy against the pagan critic Celsus, summarized the Christian position as follows: "Many prophets foretold in all kinds of ways the things concerning Christ, some in riddles and others by allegories or some other way, while some even use literal expressions."[63] This statement not only captures well what early Christians believed about the predictive quality of Scripture but also sets the stage for the next chapter, which deals with Scripture's mode of expression.

In this chapter I have considered three dimensions of the spiritual and supernatural nature of the Bible as seen by the early church. Each of these dimensions flowed from the early church's commitment to the inspiration of Scripture. Because the Scriptures were produced by the supernatural activity of the Spirit, it follows that they will have a spiritual sense and that illumination by the Spirit will be necessary to interpret them properly. Moreover, the church could offer as proof of Scripture's divine origin the fact that Old Testament prophets accurately predicted the major events surrounding the coming of Jesus long before these events took place.

As I will explain more fully in the Conclusion, I think the notions of a spiritual sense of Scripture and the need for divine illumination remain important today, although they require further reflection and refining. I do not think the "proof from prophecy" idea should play a role in the church today analogous to the role it played for the Church Fathers. Although Christians can and should endeavor to make convincing cases for Christian belief on the basis of the Old Testament, it is unwise and disingenuous to argue that Old Testament texts "prove" Christianity. Even if compelling theological arguments for Christian faith in Jesus can be made using Old Testament texts, these arguments will not focus on the purely predictive dimension of Scripture, and they will constitute testimony or witness rather than proof. Reading the Old Testament with a view toward Jesus remains central to Christian biblical interpretation, but I think modern Christians would do well to leave in the past the ancient Christian idea that scriptural predictions "prove" either the inspiration of Scripture or the authenticity of Jesus.

CHAPTER FOUR

Mode of Expression

What the sections in this chapter have in common is that each one deals specifically with the language of Scripture. What impact did divine inspiration have on the linguistic character of Scripture? Does Scripture express itself in any special ways because it is inspired by God? In the first two sections of this chapter (9 and 10) the possible entailment of inspiration that I describe represents the basic outlook of most early Christian thinkers. For the next two sections (11 and 12), the Church Fathers reflect significant differences in viewpoint on the nature of the divine impact and the extent of the human element in scriptural language. Still, even for these last two sections I identify a specific belief that at least some early Christians affirmed, even though other Christians qualified or challenged that belief.

9. Scripture Speaks in Riddles and Enigmas

Ancient Greeks believed that oracles from the gods were typically spoken in riddles and enigmas.[1] In his *Introduction to the Traditions of Greek Theology,* Cornutus the Stoic (first century CE) applied allegorical interpretations to Greek myths (stories of Zeus, Hercules, and so forth), explaining "that the men of antiquity were no common men, but that they were competent to understand the nature of the cosmos and were inclined to make philosophical statements about it through symbols and enigmas."[2] Heraclitus, a late-first-century CE Greek intellectual and author of the allegorical treatise *Homeric Problems,* spoke of Homer as "obscuring his philosophy by these symbolic names" and defended Homer for having philosophized in this way by arguing that even self-proclaimed philosophers spoke obscurely and through symbols.[3] In the Greek intellectual context, it was reasonable to expect that divine communication to humanity would take place through obscure and enigmatic sayings that held symbolic meaning.[4]

Similarly, many interpreters of Scripture in the Greek world expected to find symbolic meanings in the enigmatic language of biblical texts. Philo asserts that figurative meanings are concealed beneath the enigmatic expressions of the sacrificial laws in Leviticus.[5] Clement of Alexandria introduces his symbolic interpretation of the Tabernacle with this explanation:

> In a word, all who have spoken of divine things, both Barbarians and Greeks, veiled the first principles of things and delivered the truth in enigmas, symbols, and allegories, and tropes such as these. Of this kind also are the oracles among the Greeks. . . . And the spirit says by Isaiah the prophet, "I will give you treasures, hidden and dark" [Isa. 45:3 in Greek]. Now wisdom, which is hard to discover, is the treasure and unfailing riches of God. But those who are taught in theology by these prophets, the poets, expound much philosophy by way of a hidden sense.[6]

Justin Martyr says that Daniel spoke enigmatically about the birth of God as a man when Daniel said that he who received the eternal kingdom was "as a Son of Man" (Dan. 7:13).[7] Justin found many other symbols of Jesus hidden within the Old Testament. Thus, the tree of life in Genesis, Moses' staff, the stick that Moses threw into the bitter waters (Exod. 15:25), the sticks placed by Jacob in front of the goats' watering trough, Jacob's walking stick, and the ladder which Jacob saw in his dream — all these pieces of wood are symbols of the cross. Moreover, similar lists of figures pointing to Jesus could be compiled for "stones" and instances of "anointing" in the Old Testament.[8] The Church Fathers expected to find "enigmas" and "figures" in Scripture pointing to deeper realities, and they found these enigmas both in prophetic visions such as Daniel and in seemingly mundane details such as Jacob's walking stick.

Early Christian thinkers offered several explanations for why God had chosen to communicate in Scripture through riddles and enigmas. These explanations include the following:

1. God wanted to conceal the deeper truths of Scripture from those who are unworthy. Only those who put forth the effort to understand the Scriptures can grasp their truest sense.[9] To disclose the full magnificence of Scripture to all would be to cast pearls before swine.[10] The goal of Scrip-

ture is both to reveal and to conceal.[11] Only those who are willing to strive for virtue will succeed in unraveling the obscurities of Scripture.[12] In most early Christian sources, anyone who makes the effort to find the truth will find it.

2. The fact that Scripture has hidden meanings allows for different levels of teaching to reach people at different levels of spiritual receptivity. The straightforward and obvious sense benefits the multitude, whereas the hidden inner sense benefits those interested in their souls' well-being.[13] The stories of Jesus' healings are beneficial for the masses who live primarily by their physical senses; but the more spiritual readers learn from the higher meaning, which addresses the healing of the soul.[14] In fact, it can be harmful for people to take in teachings that are beyond their capacity to receive. It was wise, therefore, for God to hide these more profound realities from those who are not yet ready for them.[15]

3. God's prophets spoke obscurely in order to protect themselves from persecution. If the original audience had understood the meaning of everything that was said, they would have killed the bearers of the divine message.[16] The practice of speaking cryptically for protection's sake was followed not only by Old Testament prophets but also by Paul, who issued a concealed condemnation of the Roman Empire in 2 Thessalonians 2:5-8.[17]

4. Working hard to unpack the meanings of obscure expressions gives more satisfaction and delight than simply grasping the meaning at first glance. The spiritual truths taught in the Song of Songs can be learned more straightforwardly elsewhere in Scripture, but it is more pleasant to learn these lessons through imagery, and it is more rewarding to possess truth that has been won with difficulty.[18] The search for hidden realities in the early chapters of Genesis invokes a feeling of reverence within us.[19] The presence of hidden meanings in Scripture encourages us to become inquisitive and eager for discovery.[20]

5. Obscure and enigmatic language is an effective means of communicating profound ideas. Sacred texts speak obscurely precisely so that they may be explained in manifold ways.[21] The discourse of the prophets is always obscure, and thus filled with hidden thoughts and divine mysteries.[22] In Augustine's usage, the terms "obscurity" and "allegory" are both ways of referring to the higher sense, which is also called "figurative expression."[23] Cryptic language was seen as a fitting medium to express deep mysteries.[24]

In terms of unraveling the enigmas of Scripture, several early Christian writers explicitly mention the principle that clear passages should be used to interpret those that are unclear.[25] In principle, then, "clear" texts of

Scripture provided the entryway into the symbolic world of the hidden mysteries of Scripture. This at least provided some controls on the content that could be derived from an unclear text, although in practice interpreters still exercised considerable freedom to import material into Scripture, especially in the areas of cosmology and ethics.

The ancient belief that sacred texts communicated mysteries through obscure language did not always serve early Christian interpreters well. Many texts were unclear in the Old Testament simply because the translations into Greek (or Latin) were unclear, or because the objects or names involved were culturally foreign to Christians living in the Roman world.[26] If they had attempted to resolve these obscure expressions at the literal and historical level, they would have been better able to appreciate the surface meaning of the narrative, poem, or discourse they were reading. In general, better effort was given to untangling obscurities at the literal level among "Antiochene" interpreters and in some of Jerome's commentaries, such as his *Hebrew Questions on Genesis* and *Commentary on Jeremiah*.

At the same time, two concessions must be made to the perspective of the Church Fathers as described in this section. First, there are a fair number of passages in Scripture, such as Daniel 7 and Matthew 24, that are genuinely obscure and seemingly symbolic. Indeed, it can hardly be doubted that at least some curious details in the description of the Tabernacle had symbolic value.[27] If one came to Scripture expecting it to speak in enigmas, it is easy to see how these texts could confirm that belief.

Second, a good deal more of the language of Scripture is obscure than most modern English readers of the Bible realize. This is because most modern translations of the Bible start from the assumption that the Bible is meant to be clear and understandable, and so the translators create an English Bible that is clear and understandable for today's English readers. Yet, many texts in Scripture are genuinely unclear. For example, the Hebrew underlying the English translation "and the heir of my house is Eliezer of Damascus" (Gen. 15:2) is almost incomprehensible. Likewise the Hebrew behind the English translation "until tribute comes to him; and to him shall be the obedience of the peoples" (Gen. 49:10) is extremely difficult. A good deal of the book of Job in Hebrew is hard to untangle, although one would not know this based on most English translations. Ancient readers who encountered such difficulties, either in the original or in translations that made little effort to straighten out problems, found confirmation that the divinely inspired writers spoke in riddles and enigmas. Whereas many ancient Christian readers of Scripture started from the assumption of obscurity and mystery, most modern Christian readers expect the Bible to be straightforward and clear.

10. The Etymologies of Words in Scripture Convey Meaning

The early Greek poet Hesiod, who described the genealogical relationships of divine beings, included elements of nature ("deep-swirling Oceanus") and human experience ("Hateful Strife bore painful Toil") in his account, as if to explain the original connection between these "names" and the things they signify.[28] This connection was the topic of discussion in Plato's dialogue *Cratylus*. In this work, Plato ascribes to his character Cratylus the view that the name of a thing necessarily reflects the essence of the thing named, just as a picture reflects reality.[29] The character of Socrates in the dialogue is skeptical of this view. Among other ideas that Socrates mentions and then rejects is the notion that, because the gods bestowed the first names on things, these names must be "correct" in capturing the essence of the things.[30] Yet, Socrates' skepticism notwithstanding, belief in the divine origin and essential correctness of names became a significant part of many streams of later Greek philosophical and religious thought.

The Stoics, for example, taught that names were first given to things in imitation of the things named, and on this basis the Stoics believed that the etymological meaning of a name yielded accurate information about the thing itself.[31] The first-century Stoic Cornutus used etymology extensively to explain the true nature of the Greek gods. Thus, the name "Poseidon" is connected to "drinking" *(posis)* and "to sweat" *(idiein)*, since "Poseidon" stands for the force of nature that produces moisture.[32]

One of the major problems with the "name-essence" connection suggested in the *Cratylus* and employed by Cornutus is the fact that things have different names in different languages. How can there be a singular connection between the name and essence of a thing, if the thing — whose essence does not change — has different names in different languages? Of course, if one believed that the original language of divine speech was Greek, then it would make sense to analyze Greek etymologies in order to study the essence of a thing through its name. But if one believed that some other language or languages were older and closer to the gods, then one would obviously need to study the etymologies of names in these older languages. Such a view was taken by the Neoplatonic philosopher Iamblichus (late third century) in his work *On the Mysteries:*

Because the gods have shown that the whole dialect of sacred nations, such as those of the Egyptians and Assyrians, is adapted to sacred concerns, and because such a mode of speech is the first and
most ancient, we ought to think it necessary that our conference
with the gods should be in a language related to them. . . . For if
names existed through convention, it would be of no consequence
whether some names were used instead of others. But since names
are based on the nature of things, those names that are more
adapted to the things will also be more dear to the gods. . . . To
which may be added, that names do not entirely preserve the meaning when translated into another language. . . . And in the next
place, although it is possible to translate them, yet they no longer
preserve the same power when translated. In addition, primitive
names possess much emphasis, great conciseness, and partake of
less ambiguity, variety, and multiplicity.[33]

According to Iamblichus, the names of sacred things as found in the languages of ancient nations contain special divine insights. One must study
the names of these things in the sacred languages in order to comprehend
their truth. The beliefs of Iamblichus, as well as the whole discussion of
names and things in the ancient Greek world, provide an important back-
drop for understanding the use of proper name etymologies in early
Christian interpretation of Scripture.

The Bible itself presents names as symbolizing realities. In the Hebrew
Bible, "Adam," whose name means "human being," is formed from the
ground (Hebrew 'adamah), and the name of his wife, "Eve," resembles the
word for "living" (Gen. 2:7; 3:20). Examples of name-thing associations in
Genesis are too numerous to mention; one need only think of the three
great patriarchs Abraham ("father of a multitude," Gen. 17:5), Isaac ("he
laughs," 21:2-6), and "Jacob" the trickster ("Jacob" means "he tricks") who
becomes "Israel" ("he strives with God," 32:28). The New Testament continues to utilize the etymological meanings of names; for example, "Jesus"
is related to the Hebrew word for "he saves" (Matt. 1:21), and the name
"Immanuel" from Isaiah 7:14 is interpreted according to its etymology as
"God with us" (Matt. 1:23). Not all of the "etymologies" in the Bible necessarily reflect the historical origin of the given word;[34] thus, the connection
between "Babylon" (babel) and "confuse" (bll) is probably wordplay rather
than historical etymology. Moreover, New Testament writers could capi-
talize on Hebrew etymological meanings creatively for new contexts, as

with the interpretation of "Siloam" as "sent" (Aramaic *sheliah*) in John 9:7. But either as historical descriptions or as after-the-fact wordplay, etymologies of names in the Bible often reflect meanings that pertain to their larger contexts.

The interpretive significance of etymologies in Scripture was recognized and developed in ancient Judaism. The rabbis of antiquity made interpretive wordplays based on proper names, such as the interpretation of "Rephidim" in Exodus 17:8 as "weakness of hands" *(rephyon yadayim)* at the start of the story where Moses must keep his hands lifted to defeat the Amalekites.[35] What underlies such an approach is the belief that God inspired the very words and names in Scripture so that they contain keys to unlock the interpretation of the text. Philo shared this belief, and he employed proper name etymologies in Scripture as starting points for allegorical interpretations. Philo explains the rationale behind his method:

> Elsewhere the universal practice of men as a body is to give to things names which differ from the things, so that the objects are not the same as what we call them. But with Moses the names assigned are manifest images of the things, so that name and thing are inevitably the same from the first, and the name and that to which the name is given differ not a whit.[36]

Philo's position is not that all names in every language reflect the realities of the things named. Only the Hebrew names given by Moses in the Torah are "images of the things." Moreover, as is evident throughout Philo's writings, the significance of the etymological meaning of a proper name in Scripture is not limited to the passage where the name is introduced, but can be invoked any time the name is mentioned. Thus, if "Judah" is taken to be related to the Hebrew word "praise" (see Gen. 29:35), then the idea of "praise" is potentially in view any time the biblical text mentions Judah. For Philo, "Judah" represents the mind that blesses and praises God unceasingly.[37]

As early as the first century BCE, Greek-speaking Jews created word lists called *Onomastica* which gave biblical proper names spelled in Greek letters followed by Greek explanations of their Hebrew meanings. Such lists would have been available to the first Christian interpreters of Scripture, and in the fourth century Jerome created a Latin handbook of Hebrew etymologies which he called *The Book of Hebrew Names*.[38] Some of the "etymologies" in these lists were quite fanciful. For example, one of the meanings given for "Israel" is "the man who sees God." Not only is this meaning based on a bizarre division of the consonants, but it actually ignores the meaning of "Israel" given in Genesis 32:28. Nevertheless, "Israel" is expounded as "the man who sees God" in Philo, Origen, and Didymus the Blind.[39]

The interpretation of proper name etymologies was a common and widespread feature of biblical interpretation in the early church. It is found in early Church Fathers such as Justin Martyr and Clement of Alexandria.[40] Origen says that "divine wisdom arranged certain names of locations to be written in the Scriptures to contain a certain mystic meaning . . . these things are arranged by very particular reasons and do not happen by chance or accidentally."[41] He elsewhere explains that worthlessness reigns in "Midian" (that is, in our worldly bodies) because one of the kings of Midian in Numbers 31:8 is "Rekem," which means "worthlessness."[42] Proper name etymologies are regularly interpreted symbolically by Greek authors such as Gregory of Nyssa, Cyril of Alexandria, and Didymus the Blind.[43] For Cyril, Moses' father-in-law goes from being "superfluous" ("Jethro" in Exod. 3:1) to the "shepherding of God" ("Reuel" in Num. 10:29) as a result of his interaction with Moses.[44] For Didymus, the word "Rimmon" in Zechariah 14:10 means "lofty" and signifies that the divine word goes to the lofty and elevated mind.[45] As Didymus explicitly states, the etymologies of names in Scripture come not from convention but from nature.[46] Etymology continues to be a productive source of spiritual exposition in later Greek authors such as Maximus the Confessor (d. 662). Maximus expounds Jesus' transfiguration through the names "Simon" ("obedience") and "James" ("supplanter"); and he interprets 2 Kings 19 using the "strength of God" for Hezekiah and "loftiness of God" for Isaiah, saying that those who follow in their path may become spiritually another "Hezekiah" or "Isaiah."[47] Maximus offers the following advice to those who wish to understand Scripture: "If you want to absorb the precise spiritual sense of Holy Scripture in a way that accords with Christ's wishes, you must train yourself diligently in the interpretation of names, for in this way you can elucidate the meaning of all that is written."[48]

Proper names were also interpreted symbolically among the Latin Church Fathers. According to Ambrose, when Moses drives the flock of his father-in-law "Jethro" (= "superfluous"), this means that he compels the irrational wordiness of superfluous speech to enter into the mysteries of sound doctrine.[49] Hilary unfortunately interprets the name "Abimelek" to mean "the power of my brother" (it really means "my father is king"), but he has greater success with "Solomon" as "peace."[50] Augustine affirms that many Hebrew names "have considerable significance and much help to give in solving the mysteries of the scriptures."[51] An example is his exposition of Psalm 60:7, where Augustine draws spiritual insights from the etymologies of "Gilead," "Manasseh," and "Ephraim."[52] Even Jerome, whose knowledge of Hebrew surpassed his contemporaries and who was capable of improving the accuracy of some traditional etymologies,[53] never gave up his belief in the symbolic nature of Hebrew names. In the final section of the last commentary he wrote before he died, Jerome interpreted Jeremiah 32:42-44 spiritually through the etymological meanings of the names of Benjamin, Jerusalem, Judah, Shephelah, and Negev.[54] Jerome believed that Hebrew names were filled with divine mystery, and that to interpret them correctly is to discover the teaching of the Holy Spirit.[55] This is the perspective on Hebrew names passed on to Christians of the Latin Middle Ages, whose belief in Hebrew as the original human language and in the mystical significance of Hebrew names is reflected in the encyclopedic work of Isidore of Seville (d. 636) entitled the *Etymologies.*[56]

The symbolic exposition of Hebrew etymologies is an area where modern biblical interpretation differs significantly from ancient interpretation. Modern scholars recognize that biblical texts employ etymologies and wordplay, but they generally restrict their discussions of wordplay to passages where the text explicitly identifies the wordplay, or at least to passages where the wordplay fits convincingly into the literal and contextual sense. Ancient Christians, in contrast, inhabited an intellectual culture that regarded all sacred name etymologies as potentially symbolic at the mystical level. To some degree, they were encouraged to think of biblical etymologies as meaningful by the multitude of explained names in the Old Testament and by New Testament texts such as Hebrews 7:1-2: "Melchizedek . . . He is first, by translation of his name, king of righteousness, and then he is also king of Salem, that is, king of peace."

Furthermore, many early Christians believed on the basis of Genesis 11 that Hebrew was the original language and that the diversity of human languages resulted from the events surrounding the Tower of Babel. This belief in a single original language made it more plausible to believe that there could be an intrinsic connection between the original names of things and the essence of the things named. Modern scholars take a very different view of the development of languages. For example, Akkadian is a Semitic language thought to be considerably older than Hebrew, which is itself seen as just one of a number of languages in the Semitic language family. This modern understanding of how Hebrew fits into the history of ancient languages obviously changes the way we see etymologies in the Bible. From today's perspective, Hebrew words evolved into their biblical meanings, and many names (such as "Babylon") predate the writing of the biblical texts.

In view of today's perspective, we cannot assume that proper names in the Hebrew Bible represent the original names given by God in order to describe the essence of the things named. Moreover, attention to the literal and contextual sense of biblical texts shows that proper name etymologies are significant in far fewer instances than ancient interpreters supposed. Thus, the exposition of proper name etymologies constitutes one of the aspects of ancient biblical interpretation that is least helpful for modern Christians.

11. God Is Directly and Timelessly the Speaker in Scripture

According to one early Christian source, "the divine scriptures were spoken by the Holy Spirit."[57] The topic of the present section is whether the divine authorship of Scripture is the only voice speaking in the text. It is possible to imagine God's activity in inspiration as so dominant that the historical contexts and conceptual categories of the human writers become irrelevant. This manner of thinking had a place in early Christian approaches to Scripture. At the same time, for most of the Church Fathers the human author remained in view as part of the interpretive equation. These two tendencies, focusing on the divine element of Scripture exclusively or including the human together with the divine, are found side by side in the early church.

The first tendency was to imagine God as the sole author of Scripture, with the human writer serving merely as an instrument. Philo expresses this view of divine inspiration:

> For no pronouncement of a prophet is ever his own; he is an interpreter prompted by Another in all his utterances, when knowing not what he does he is filled with inspiration, as the reason withdraws and surrenders the citadel of the soul to a new visitor and tenant, the Divine Spirit which plays upon the vocal organism and dictates words which clearly express its prophetic message.[58]

Using similar metaphors, Athenagoras describes the process of inspiration by saying that God "moved the mouths of the prophets like instruments," and he goes on to say regarding the prophets, "Under the impulse of the divine Spirit and raised above their own thoughts, they proclaimed the things with which they were inspired. For the Spirit used them just as a flute player blows on a flute."[59] These quotations represent one line of thinking about divine inspiration in the early church.[60]

The "divine author only" perspective on inspiration impacted the reading of the biblical text in at least two different ways. First, the biblical text could be read as devoid of any historical context of its own. In classical exegesis of the Qur'an, the historical situation in the life of Muhammad to which the Qur'anic text was thought to be responding was called *sabab al-nuzūl*, the "occasion of revelation."[61] The revelation is divine, but it was sent down in order to address a specific need in a particular historical context. Applying this concept to the Christian conversation, one could suggest that the "divine only" position on inspiration would render the "occasion of revelation" irrelevant for interpreting Scripture. From this point of view, the reader of Scripture does not attempt to grasp what Amos said to the Israelites or what Paul said to the Corinthians but what God is timelessly "saying." In this mode of thought, God's voice speaks directly through Scripture without reference to the historical "occasion of revelation."

Second, the biblical text could be read as a timeless unity, where any text from anywhere in Scripture is potentially relevant for elucidating any other passage. The rabbis of antiquity had a saying to describe situations where this kind of interpretation seemed proper: "There is no earlier or later in the Torah."[62] This allowed for thematic combinations of Scripture without regard for the limitations of historical context. One interesting passage in the Midrash pictures a sage linking together words of Torah with other words of Torah and with words of the Prophets and the Writings, and, as he interprets the Scriptures, fire flashes around him.[63] Biblical texts could find new theological significance when taken out of their immediate context and placed alongside other passages of Scripture.[64] Following in this tradition, Origen and Jerome use the analogy of clouds rubbing together to produce lightning (as this was understood at the time) in order to describe the sparks that are created by bringing together diverse passages of Scripture and interpreting them in light of each other.[65] This notion that the entire Bible serves as the proper context for reading any verse is another possible implication of the "divine author only" perspective on Scripture.

An illustration of biblical interpretation that essentially ignores the historical context of the human writer can be found in the commentary of

Didymus the Blind on Zechariah 6:9-11.[66] Didymus begins his discussion by stating that the "word" that came to the prophet is God the Word, which leads into a discussion of God the Father and God the Son. After a brief comment about those who went into exile, which is the only reference to the historical setting of the passage, Didymus claims that the "useful" and "familiar" things brought out of captivity were virtues and wise thoughts (the names "Tobijah" and "Jedaiah" were translated "useful" and "familiar" in the ancient Greek translation). After this, the name "Joshua" (= "Jesus" in Greek) is interpreted as "he saves" and "Zephaniah" is interpreted as "Yahweh's long stay," such that God grants a long stay to those receiving salvation. The silver and gold are interpreted spiritually as speech and understanding. The reference to the crown is related to the spiritual victory of Christian martyrs over their persecutors. Christians receive the crown of eternal life by maintaining their steadfast faith in the Trinity. The words "son of Jehozadak, the high priest" are referred to Jesus, who is the "son of righteousness" ("Jehozadak" = "righteousness") and the true high priest. Didymus closes his discussion by stating that those who imitate Jesus can receive all the crowns of virtue.[67] Numerous New Testament prooftexts are cited throughout this discussion. The reader of the commentary gets very little sense that Zechariah was an Old Testament prophet who lived in the post-exilic period. Didymus's treatment of Zechariah 6:9-11 illustrates how the Church Fathers could interpret Scripture as if God were directly speaking, without reference to the historical situation of the human writer.[68]

Regarding the idea that Scripture is such a timeless unity that passages from all over the biblical canon can be used to illuminate one another, it is accurate to say that most biblical commentators in the early church practiced this kind of intertextual reading of Scripture to one degree or another. Origen gave the following illustration, which he borrowed from a Jewish scholar, in a passage quoted by Gregory of Nazianzus and Basil the Great in the *Philocalia*:

> That great scholar used to say that inspired Scripture taken as a whole was on account of its obscurity like many locked-up rooms in one house. Before each room he supposed a key to be placed, but not the one belonging to it; and that the keys were so dispersed all round the rooms, not fitting the locks of the several rooms before which they were placed. It would be a troublesome piece of work to discover the keys to suit the rooms they were meant for. It was, he

said, just so with the understanding of the Scriptures, because they are so obscure; the only way to begin to understand them was, he said, by means of other passages containing the explanation dispersed throughout them. The Apostle, I think, suggested such a way of coming to knowledge of the Divine words when he said, "And we impart this in words not taught by human wisdom but taught by the Spirit, comparing spiritual things with spiritual" (1 Cor. 2:13).[69]

In other words, the key to understanding a passage of Scripture is not found in the immediate literary context, but in some other passage found elsewhere in Scripture. In fairness, this analogy does not do sufficient justice to Origen's skill at interpreting the Bible at the literal level. Origen regularly prefaces his spiritual interpretation with literal exposition, which usually takes into account the immediate literary context. But for Origen, the spiritual level is where God speaks timelessly through Scripture, and the only way to grasp the spiritual sense of most passages is to locate them within their proper theological context within the whole Bible.[70]

I have tried to give a sense of what impact the "divine author only" point of view could have on biblical interpretation when taken to an extreme. But in reality, most Church Fathers paid at least some attention to the human authorship of Scripture, and a few took the human authors quite seriously.

Focus on the human element of Scripture is seen most clearly in Antiochene interpreters. For example, in his *Commentary on the Twelve Prophets,* Theodore of Mopsuestia introduces each prophet with a brief preface that describes the historical setting and overall theme of the book.[71] Theodore always tries to explain the message of the prophet in terms of the original Old Testament audience, even for passages such as Joel 2:28-32 that are quoted as having been fulfilled in the New Testament. According to Theodore, Joel's prophecy was meant to encourage the post-exilic community that God would provide for them with wealth and with his care. In terms of the original audience, the prediction that "the sun shall be turned to darkness, and the moon to blood" (Joel 2:31) came to pass only in the perception of those living at that time who saw great troubles befalling them. Theodore goes so far as to point out that, strictly speaking, the "Holy Spirit" as a person distinct from the Father and the Son was not yet known in the time of Joel.[72] Theodore showed an unusually high interest in the historical contexts of the human writers.

But such interest was not limited to the Antiochenes.[73] Cyril of Alexandria often uses information about the prophets' historical situations in his exegesis.[74] Jerome likewise interprets prophetic books in light of their historical contexts, frequently citing other biblical books (especially Kings and Chronicles) to supply the *historia* relevant for explaining specific passages.[75] Cyril and Jerome were also both regular practitioners of allegorical interpretation. Emphasis on the human context did not deter them from seeking higher meanings.

Ancient interpreters did not often discuss the human discourse of Scripture in a theoretical way, but occasional passages show their thoughts on the subject. When a particular text seemed best suited to a simple explanation following the normal rules of grammar, the rabbis would sometimes say, "The Torah (here) speaks in human language."[76] Diodore of Tarsus's comment on Psalm 45:1, "My tongue is the pen of a ready scribe," offers a Christian statement on inspiration that allows some room for the human writer: "Since he had said, 'I utter the psalm from the depths of my mind,' he says, 'I bring to bear also my tongue to the extent possible so as to serve the thought coming from grace in the way that a pen follows the lead of a writer's thought.'"[77] In this metaphor, the Holy Spirit is the writer and the human being is the pen, as the scriptural quotation requires. But according to Diodore, the Holy Spirit provides the "thought," whereas the human writer presumably supplies the words, which serve the thought "to the extent possible."

The concept of divine inspiration could easily lend itself to the idea that God was so directly the speaker in Scripture that the human writers were irrelevant for understanding the text's meaning. This kind of thinking can be found in the writings of the Church Fathers, but in general most early Christian interpreters had at least some awareness of the human authors. The modern study of the Bible in the context of other ancient sources has made it nearly impossible to read Scripture today without recognizing its human authorship. In the contemporary world, it is the divine authorship of Scripture that can be harder to conceptualize and articulate.

In my view, it is commendable that Christians today carry on the tradition of paying attention to the contexts and intentions of Scripture's human authors. Thinking about the human writers enables us to appreciate the particular content of each biblical text. At the same time, the idea that all scriptural passages potentially illuminate each other is still helpful. When the literal sense of any given text has been carefully studied, part of the process by which we perceive what the text teaches about God is that we ask how it fits with what we know about God from elsewhere. If we believe that every scriptural text has something to teach about God and that the same God stands behind every scriptural truth, then what we learn about God from one passage of Scripture can properly be brought into theological conversation with truth learned from another passage. In fact, this process of combining scriptural passages along theological lines can help us with certain difficult texts as we consider how they might best be interpreted as speaking about God. Starting with the literal and historical sense is valuable because it helps Scripture address each generation in a fresh way. But the theological teaching of Scripture must be sought by comparing Scripture with Scripture and trying to ascertain how all these texts point to the one God who as Christians we believe was made known supremely in Jesus.

12. The Scriptures Represent Stylistically Fine Literature

In Islamic thought, the Qur'an itself is the supreme miracle that validates the prophetic status of Muhammad. Muslim scholars describe the uniqueness of the Qur'an in terms of its "inimitability," that is, the fact that it cannot be imitated. The idea of the inimitability of the Qur'an (*i'jāz al-Qur'ān*) is grounded in Qur'anic texts where the Prophet's enemies charge him with inventing the Qur'an, and he is told to reply, "Then produce ten invented suras [= chapters] like it, and call in whomever you can beside God, if you are truthful."[78] The concept of inimitability pertains to both the content and the literary style of the Qur'an. The Qur'an is thought to be not only truthful above all other books but also beautiful above all other books. The artistic beauty of the Qur'an is highly regarded throughout the Arab-speaking world, where it can be appreciated in its original medium — recited aloud in Arabic.[79] According to one line of thought, just as God gave Moses magical signs to present to the Egyptians who excelled in magic, and God gave Jesus signs of healing to present to the Greeks who excelled in medicine, so also God gave Muhammad a stylistically magnificent Qur'an to present to the Arabs, who excelled in literary eloquence.[80] For Muslims, stylistic beauty is an entailment of the miraculous nature of the Qur'an.

In this section I will explore this topic as it relates to the Bible in the early church. Did Christians believe that divine inspiration had caused biblical writers to produce literature that was not only truthful in content but also beautiful in form? For the most part, the answer is "No." But starting in the fourth century, certain Christian thinkers began to work out new ways of thinking about Scripture that allowed space for the Bible to be considered stylistically fine literature.[81]

Literary style was an important component of the cultures of ancient Greece and Rome. Aristotle (384-322 BCE) had given the Greek world its first systematic discussions of style, especially in his books *Poetics* and *Rhetoric.* Later Greek authors developed further ideas on literary criticism, including Demetrius's *On Style* (perhaps first century BCE) and Longinus's *On Sublimity* (first century CE). Literary consciousness developed in the Latin world during the period of the Roman Republic through the poetry of Ennius, the plays of Terence and Plautus, and above all the oratory of Cicero (106-43 BCE). Early Latin works of literary criticism include Cicero's writings on oratory, the anonymous work *Rhetorica ad Herennium* (first century BCE), certain poems and letters of Horace, and the *Institutes of Oratory* by Quintilian (first century CE). Literary theorists discussed different levels of style for various purposes (for example, to stir up emotions or to persuade), listed figures of speech, identified virtues of style (clarity, beauty, conciseness, etc.), and tried to maintain "correct usage," described as *hellēnismos* among the Greeks and *latinitas* in Latin. Among Greek and Roman intellectuals, "classical" literary style served as a symbol of cultural prestige throughout the period of the Church Fathers, with representative figures such as Homer and Demosthenes in Greek, or Virgil and Cicero in Latin, serving as standards for great literature.

The Bible first came into the Greek world when the Hebrew Scriptures were translated into Greek in Alexandria, Egypt. This translation of the various books of the Old Testament came to be known as the "Septuagint" (see section 16 below). In the late first and second centuries CE, the New Testament documents were coming together to complete what would become the Christian Bible. The Greek style of the Christian Bible was the popular *(koinē)* style of the day, with some peculiar features of vocabulary and syntax that reflected influence from Hebrew and Aramaic. The first Latin translations, which began to appear in the second century CE in North Africa, imitated the simple style and peculiar idioms of the Greek.

The Greek and Latin versions of the Bible could be understood throughout the Greco-Roman world, but they were not stylistically very pleasing. The earliest pagan critics of Christianity, who were generally well-educated members of the upper class, scoffed at the low literary level of the Bible. As one early opponent of Christianity said, "the language [i.e., of the Scriptures] is commonplace and of low quality. . . . Your narratives

. . . are overrun with barbarisms and solecisms and vitiated by ugly faults."[82] The earliest Christians responded to these criticisms not by trying to prove that the Bible was great literature, but rather by explaining why God had inspired the Bible using simple and common language.

One reason, it was argued, that God inspired the Scriptures in a low style was to communicate the truth of Christian humility. Tatian says that he was converted to Christianity not only because of the truth of Christian doctrines and prophetic predictions, but also because of the humility of Scripture, "the lack of arrogance in the wording, the artlessness of the speakers."[83] Another explanation for the simple style of Scripture was that God wanted to give prominence to the message. As Origen explained, "Had the Scripture been embellished with elegant style and diction, like the masterpieces of Greek literature, one might perhaps have supposed that it was not the truth which got hold of men, but that the clear sequence of thought and the beauty of the language won the souls of the hearers, and caught them with guile."[84] God did not want people to follow Scripture because they were charmed by its beauty, but because they were obedient to its message. John Chrysostom made the following observations about the simple style of the Gospel of John, "We shall not see noise of words or pomposity of style, or careful ordering and artificial, foolish arrangement of nouns and verbs . . . but invincible and divine strength, irresistible power of authentic doctrines, and a wealth of good things without number."[85] It was also observed that the simple language of Scripture was well suited for reaching a wide audience.[86] Moreover, it is the common people, rather than those who are wise in their own eyes, who are most likely to receive the gospel. As Lactantius observed, "This reason is one of the first why the wise and learned people and the princes of this world do not place any sacred trust in the Scriptures; the fact that the prophets spoke the common and simple speech, as though they were speaking to the people."[87]

Most Christian leaders in the first three centuries of the church were themselves learned people who attempted in their own writings to approximate the most respected writers of Greek and Latin culture. They were educated on classical "pagan" texts and recommended them to others.[88] Some Christians even produced paraphrases of biblical books in classical forms, such as Moses in hexameters, historical books in dactylic measure, and the Gospels as Platonic dialogues.[89] It was obvious to the Church Fathers that the Bible in its Greek and Latin forms did not stylistically resemble the writings of Homer or Virgil. Instead of pretending that they did, the Fathers thought theologically about why they did not.

Nevertheless, after the persecutions were past and Christian culture became more powerful in the fourth and fifth centuries, some Christians began to explore ways of seeing the Bible as great literature. As Christian Scripture took on the status of a major cultural symbol, it was necessary to explore what literary merit it might possess. Two figures in particular, Jerome and Augustine, made significant observations about the potential literary quality of Scripture.

The first line of thought in defense of the Bible as good literature pertained to the Old Testament as a translation from Hebrew. Origen and Eusebius had already noted in passing that the Old Testament was stylistically better in the original Hebrew than it was in translation.[90] Jerome actually learned Hebrew himself and repeatedly insisted that the Old Testament was good literature in the original. He was initially unimpressed with what seemed to him the harshness of Hebrew in comparison with the smoothness of Cicero and Pliny.[91] But over time, Jerome came to realize that the Old Testament only seemed like bad literature to certain men because they were only reading it in translation. As Jerome states: "Thus it has come about that the sacred writings appear less adorned and lyrical, because the aforementioned men are unaware that they have been translated from Hebrew. . . . What is more melodious than the Psalter? What is more beautiful than the songs of Deuteronomy or Isaiah? What is more elevated than Solomon? What is more polished than Job?"[92] Jerome loved pointing out figures of speech in the Hebrew text, and he had a good eye for wordplay in Hebrew. An interesting example is his comment on Isaiah 5:7, which says, "He looked for justice *(mishpat),* but behold, bloodshed *(mishpah);* for righteousness *(tsedakah),* but behold, an outcry *(tseʿaqah)."* Jerome says, "And so with one letter being either added or altered thus, he properly mingled the similarity of the words, so that for 'mesphat' he said 'mesphaa,' and for 'sadaca' he put 'saaca,' and he produced an elegant structure and sound of the words according to the Hebrew language."[93] In spite of natural imperfections in his knowledge given his time and circumstances, Jerome attained strong competency in Hebrew and represents the high point of Hebrew scholarship in the early church.[94] His appreciation of the literary merits of the Old Testament in Hebrew was a significant contribution to early Christian thought.

A second line of thought in defense of the Bible as good literature grew out of deeper reflection on the role of convention in art. Is Homer's *Iliad* a standard for great literature because it is intrinsically artistic? Or is the *Iliad* considered great literature because it adheres to social conventions that determine what is deemed "artistic"? Or is it both? Christian writers in the first three centuries insisted that the sacred writers did not try to produce "great literature" by pagan standards. But this did not mean that they could not have produced works that had some literary merit. It simply meant that Scripture's literary quality might be different from what is found in the pagan classics. The individual who contributed most to this line of thinking was Augustine.[95]

The young Augustine, like Jerome, was turned away by the unattractive style of Scripture and focused instead on content.[96] Still, even in his early days as a Christian, Augustine sometimes used artistic terms, such as "marvelous sublimity," to describe the allegorical sense of Scripture hidden under the plain language.[97] But it was in his later years that Augustine formulated his clearest statement on Scripture, art, and convention. In the context of giving advice to preachers, Augustine asserts that we should regard the writers of Scripture as both wise and eloquent.[98] The eloquence of scriptural writers sometimes corresponds to the eloquence found in secular writers, but Scripture also has a different eloquence all its own *(alteram quandam eloquentiam suam),* which is particularly suited to its divine authority. Scriptural eloquence does not make itself too prominent, but serves the content by delighting readers and inspiring them to follow. Augustine illustrates his point by explaining certain rhetorical devices found in Romans and Amos. According to Augustine, scriptural writers did not intentionally try to follow any "rules of rhetoric," but simply wrote as they were led by divine inspiration. Yet even the pagan rules of rhetoric were not merely invented by people but represent the best practices of good speakers, whose natural ability ultimately came from God.[99] Thus, it should not be surprising if writers inspired by God should exhibit some of the stylistic qualities known from the rules of rhetoric. In the end, however, Scripture cannot be judged by these standards, because it has an eloquence all its own. This was essentially Augustine's view, and it was passed on to the Middle Ages by scholars such as Cassiodorus (d. 583), whose *Commentary on the Psalms* followed Augustine's lead in looking for rhetorical figures in the biblical text.

Modern readers familiar with the King James Version are accustomed to thinking of the Bible as a great work of literature.[100] This was obviously not how things played out in the early church. The honesty of the early Church Fathers in dealing with the low stylistic level of Scripture in Greek and Latin is refreshing. Moreover, the tendency in the early church to emphasize content over form was insightful. The Bible is a collection of books

that share a particular ideological trajectory; it was not originally compiled on the basis of stylistic criteria. Jerome's desire to appreciate the Old
Testament in Hebrew may be granted as valid. Even Augustine's argument
about the relative nature of what constitutes "fine literature" contains
some truth. But high literary style was not associated with the Christian
Bible in any way similar to how Muslims view the artistic merits of the
Qur'an. The Bible and the Qur'an had different historical origins and were
taken in different theological directions in relation to this topic.

Early Christians generally expected Scripture to speak in particular ways
because it was inspired by God. It was customary for divine oracles to
communicate through riddles and enigmas, and since scriptural language
possesses its own obscurities, it was logical to take the principle of obscurity as a general rule. Some Christians operated as if God's voice directly
spoke to them through the words of Scripture, and most Christians believed that New Testament doctrines were taught in the Old Testament,
since the same God was speaking there. Few Church Fathers knew any Hebrew, but most reckoned Hebrew to be a sacred language whose names
contained deep secrets in their etymologies. On the negative side, most
Christians recognized that the Bible in its widely authoritative Greek and
Latin forms was not great literature by the cultural standards of the day.
But in the end this did not matter, because it was the divine voice that most
Christians expected to see in Scripture. Jesus was born in a humble stable,
so why should the divine Scriptures not be humble, too? Only occasionally
did certain Church Fathers place significant emphasis on the human element in Scripture, but when they did they were capable of making percep-
tive observations about the literal sense and literary quality of the text.

CHAPTER FIVE

Historicity and Factuality

The Bible is filled with stories that appear to be set in the real world. The Old Testament refers to historical nations such as Egypt and Babylonia and even mentions specific rulers, such as Pharaoh Neco of Egypt and Nebuchadnezzar of Babylon, who are known from ancient historical sources. The Gospel of Luke places the birth of Jesus in the time of Herod the Great and Quirinius, governor of Syria, both of whom were real historical persons.[1] Innumerable facts and figures are given in Scripture, both in narrative accounts and in expository writings such as the prophetic books and Paul's letters. Thus, Isaiah 7:8 states that the city of Damascus was the capital of Syria, and Paul says in Galatians 3:16-17 that the law of Moses was given 430 years after God's promises were made to Abraham.[2] This chapter addresses from several different angles the relationship between the inspiration of Scripture and its historicity and factuality as seen by the early church. If the Bible is inspired, does it follow that its narratives are all historical? Does it follow that all its facts are correct? Belief in the inspiration of Scripture impacted how the Church Fathers approached these questions in a variety of ways.

13. Events Narrated in the Bible Actually Happened

The general tendency among early Christians was to assume that stories narrated in Scripture actually took place. We know this not because Church Fathers typically took the time to say so explicitly but because they regularly discussed the events of biblical narratives as if they had happened.[3] Occasionally one finds a direct statement on this topic. For example, Jerome affirms the historicity of various biblical figures in his *Com-*

mentary on Philemon 5, where Paul refers to "the faith that you have toward the Lord Jesus and all the saints." Jerome's question is: How can one have faith "in the saints"? His answer is as follows:

> Someone believes in the Creator God. He is not able to believe un-less he first believes that the things written about his saints are true: that Adam was formed by God; that Noah alone was saved from the shipwrecked world; that Abraham, when first commanded to de-part from his land and kinsmen, left to his descendants circumci-sion, which he had received as a sign of future offspring. . . .

Jerome goes on to mention the near sacrifice of Isaac, the story of the ten plagues in Egypt, the account in Joshua where the sun stands still, and var-ious events from the books of Judges and "Kingdoms" (1 Samuel through 2 Kings), including Elijah being taken away by a fiery chariot and Elisha raising the dead. Whereas modern commentators typically identify the "saints" in Philemon as Christian believers contemporaneous with Paul,[4] Jerome interprets them as Old Testament saints and insists that unless one believes in the things written about these saints, one cannot believe in the God of the saints.[5]

Jerome is typical of early Christians in that he believes in the historic-ity of miracles in Scripture. Even the story of Jonah being swallowed by a large fish is reckoned as historical by figures such as Theodore of Mopsuestia, Jerome, and Cyril of Alexandria. Theodore recognizes that the story is fantastic, but refuses to comment further, stating that it would be extreme folly "to think that one could grasp it by human reasoning and ex-plain how it happened in our terms."[6] Both Cyril and Jerome defend their belief in the story not only by appealing to God's power but also by point-ing out that many pagans believe in supernatural stories involving gods and heroes. If pagans can believe in absurd stories such as these, Jerome and Cyril argue, it should be no problem for Christians to believe that Jo-nah lived inside a large fish for three days.[7] Early Christian intellectuals might acknowledge the fantastic nature of miracle stories in Scripture, but they generally affirmed them nonetheless.

It is important to point out that ancient people did not simply believe in the complete historicity of any and all narratives they read. An excellent illustration of this can be found in the fourth-century BCE writer Palaephatus, whose work *On Unbelievable Tales* was devoted to giving his-torical explanations for Greek myths. For example:

82

They say that Europa, the daughter of Phoenix, was carried across the sea on the back of a bull from Tyre to Crete. But in my opinion neither a bull nor a horse would traverse so great an expanse of open water, nor would a girl climb on the back of a wild bull. As for Zeus — if he wanted Europa to go to Crete, he would have found a better way for her to travel. Here is the truth. There was a man from Cnossus by the name of Taurus ("bull") who was making war on the territory of Tyre. He ended up by carrying off from Tyre quite a number of girls, including the king's daughter, Europa. So people said: "Bull has gone off with Europa, the king's daughter." It was from this that the myth was fashioned.[8]

Palaephatus does not question the existence of Zeus — although his conception of "Zeus" might be strictly philosophical — but he does doubt the historicity of elements in the narrative that seem unlikely or insensible. He thus represents a broad trend in Greek thought that approached traditional narratives with at least a measure of skepticism as to their historicity. This trend can be seen not only in philosophical critiques of traditional myths but also in historians such as Herodotus and Thucydides.[9]

Early Jewish sources typically treat biblical narratives as historical in much the same way as Christian sources do. It was certainly in the interest of the Jewish historian Josephus to accept biblical narratives as historical, although he shows a tendency to downplay the supernatural elements in the stories.[10] For a strongly philosophical commentator such as Philo, however, historicity was not always an essential part of the scriptural text. For example, he tells his readers that they should not regard the story of Sarah and Hagar as just a customary story of women's jealousy, because "It is not women that are spoken of here; it is minds — on the one hand the mind which exercises itself in the preliminary learning, on the other, the mind which strives to win the palm of virtue and ceases not until it is won."[11] Elsewhere, Philo is noncommittal regarding the historicity of Samuel: "Now probably there was an actual man called Samuel; but we conceive of the Samuel of the Scripture, not as a living compound of soul and body, but as a mind that rejoices in the service and worship of God and that only."[12] Even the rabbis were open to certain things in Scripture not being historical; thus, there is a tradition that Chronicles, which differs in certain details from the books of Samuel and Kings, was given simply as a midrash (interpretive retelling) on Israel's history.[13] In light of the questions raised about historicity in these and other ancient sources, it is not surprising to find that the Church Fathers also raised historical questions.

The second-century Greek philosopher Celsus disparaged the Gospels as complete fabrications that were "no better than fables." Origen responded to this charge in his widely respected apologetic work *Against Celsus*. The following passage from *Against Celsus* was quoted by Gregory of Nazianzus and Basil the Great in the *Philocalia*:

> Our answer is that to reconstruct almost any historical scene, even if true, so as to give a vivid impression of what actually occurred, is exceedingly difficult and sometimes impossible. Suppose someone asserted that there never was a Trojan war, mainly on the grounds that the impossible story of Achilles being the son of a sea goddess (Thetis) and a man (Peleus) is mixed up with it. . . . How could we dispose of such objections? Should we not be very hard pressed to explain how the blending of strange fiction into the narrative fits with the universal belief that there was a war between the Greeks and Trojans at Troy? Or let us suppose someone doubted the story of Oedipus and Jocaste, and of their sons Eteocles and Polynices, because a half-woman, the Sphinx, is mixed up with the story. How should we clear up the difficulty? Well, the prudent reader of the narratives who wishes to guard against deception will use his own judgment as to what he will allow to be historical and what he will regard as figurative; he will try to discover what the writers meant by inventing such stories; and to some things he will refuse his assent on the grounds that they were recorded to gratify certain persons. And this we have set forth, having in view the history of Jesus as a whole contained in the Gospels; for we do not invite intelligent readers to bare unreasoning faith, but we wish to show that future readers will need to exercise prudence and make careful inquiry, and, so to speak, penetrate the very heart of the writers, if the exact purport of every passage is to be discovered.[14]

As Origen explains, it is common for genuinely historical stories to have some impossible elements woven into them. But just because certain elements in a story may not be historical, this does not mean that the whole narrative is fictitious. For Origen, an example of a non-historical element in the Gospels is the story of Jesus driving the moneychangers from the Temple (John 2:13-22). This story is probably not historical, Origen thinks, because it is unlikely that the Temple officials would let someone of Jesus' social standing get away with such an act, and because the picture of Jesus hitting people with whips makes the Son of God look rash and undisciplined.[15] Other examples include discrepancies in detail between the Gospels, which will be treated in the next section. According to Origen, these are not mistakes but divine clues that some symbolic meaning is intended.[16] Origen defends the overall historicity of the Gospel accounts by pointing to details that reflect negatively on the disciples, such as Peter's denial (John 18:17, 25, 27) or places where the disciples take offense at Jesus' teaching (e.g., John 6:60-61). The Gospel writers would not have included such information, argues Origen, if they were merely inventing stories from scratch.[17]

Other early Christian interpreters likewise raised doubts about the historicity of certain aspects of Scripture. A common theme in many of these passages is that a difficulty in the biblical text indicates that a narrative should not be taken historically, but in a spiritual sense. Thus, Jerome interprets the command in Joshua 5:2 to "circumcise the sons of Israel a second time" as referring to Israelites who were already circumcised,[18] and since a man cannot literally be circumcised twice, it must have a spiritual meaning: "If we take this literally, it cannot possibly stand." Jerome says that this second circumcision is Joshua circumcising Israel spiritually with the gospel knife.[19] As another example, Gregory the Great asserts that the dimensions of the city described in Ezekiel 40–48 "cannot be literally true." After comparing the dimensions of the city gate with the dimensions of the city itself, Gregory concludes, "Obviously it is by no means possible to accept the building of this city according to the letter." But as often in Holy Scripture, that which cannot be accepted according to history should be understood spiritually.[20]

The historicity of the Garden of Eden was a matter of dispute among the Church Fathers. The word in Genesis 2–3 translated "garden" in most English Bibles was translated "Paradise" in the ancient Greek translation (the "Septuagint"). Revelation 2:7 confirms the appropriateness of this translation from a New Testament perspective. Jesus uses this same word when he tells the repentant thief on the cross, "Today you will be with me in Paradise" (Luke 23:43). Furthermore, Paul suggests that he was caught up into Paradise through a mystical experience (2 Cor. 12:3). Origen interprets the account of Paradise allegorically, finding in these chapters philosophical truths about "humanity" (which is the meaning of "Adam") and the devil (symbolized by the serpent). In defense of this reading, Origen points out that Plato himself spoke philosophically about the garden of Zeus.[21] Many other Christians, including Didymus the Blind and Ambrose, followed Origen's symbolic exposition.[22] Ambrose, for example, interprets the serpent as the devil (= enjoyment), the woman as the senses, the man as mind, and the four rivers as prudence, temperance, fortitude, and justice, that is, the four cardinal virtues of Greek philosophy.[23] None of these interpreters thinks that Paradise was ever a place in the real world.

Antiochene interpreters, on the other hand, considered the Paradise of Eden a historical place. Diodore of Tarsus acknowledges that Genesis 3 contains enigmas with symbolic meaning, but he still insists on a historical garden with a real serpent, through which the devil spoke.[24] Theodoret of Cyrus similarly believes in a real Paradise on earth and in four actual rivers, the locations of which have now been hidden by God.[25] According to Theodore of Mopsuestia, the fact that Christ cancelled Adam's sin (Rom. 5:12-21) means that the sin of Adam must have actually taken place in the historical past.[26] The Antiochenes generally accepted the symbolic significance of the story of Paradise in Genesis 2–3, but they also thought it was important to affirm its historicity. "For history is not opposed to *theōria*," Diodore states. "On the contrary, it proves to be the foundation and the basis of the higher senses."[27]

It should be noted, however, that the Antiochenes did question the historical nature of certain biblical texts. Thus, Theodore is reported to have made the following comment on the book of Job:

> The name of the blessed Job . . . was famous among all the people, and his virtuous acts as well as his ordeals were related orally among all the people and all the nations from century to century and in all the languages. Now, after the return of the Israelites from Babylon, a learned Hebrew who was especially well versed in the science of the Greeks committed in writing the history of the just, and in order to make it larger he mingled the story with exquisite utterances borrowed from the poets, because he composed his book with the purpose of making it more pleasant to the readers.[28]

Theodore later calls the Behemoth of Job "a dragon of pure fiction created by the author according to his thoroughly poetic manner; it is thus that he has also composed many speeches in the name of Job and his friends, and in the name of God, which neither agree with nor correspond to reality."[29] Diodore agrees that the book of Job contains fictitious speeches.[30] The historicizing tendency of the Antiochenes dissuaded them from accepting purely symbolic interpretations, but it also promoted critical thinking somewhat along the lines of modern biblical criticism.

When Origen likens Genesis 2–3 to Platonic myth, or when Theodore refers to the poetic manner of Job, they are invoking the category that we today call literary genre. A newspaper article is a different kind of writing from a novel, and we bring to these texts different expectations as to their historicity. The best early Christian interpreters tried to figure out what kinds of texts Scripture contains, and what expectations should be brought to these texts as a consequence. Such thinking was not considered incompatible with belief in divine inspiration. The willingness of some early Christian commentators to inquire into the literary genres of biblical texts is a commendable aspect of their approach to Scripture that is worthy of emulation by modern Christians.

14. Scripture Does Not Have Any Errors in Its Facts

The idea addressed in this section is that divine inspiration ensures that all facts reported in Scripture are correct. Philo affirmed that prophetic inspiration caused Moses to legislate without any mistakes, on the grounds that "with God nothing is in fault."[31] Augustine argued that even on such a difficult topic as the human soul nothing could be true that contradicts inspired Scripture; if any proposition appears to contradict Scripture, either the proposition is wrong or Scripture has been misinterpreted.[32] According to Cyril of Alexandria, prophecies in the book of Isaiah must be true, because "it is out of the question for God to speak falsely."[33] If there is no fault or falsehood with God, one might conclude that Scripture, which was written under divine inspiration, does not err with regard to any of the facts it contains.

Seldom did commentators take the time to quibble about facts in the text unless some specific problem presented itself. Sometimes commentators would address problems that they themselves discovered, but often they addressed problems that had been pointed out by others. Aristotle's *Poetics* 25 contains an early example of textual discussion focused on "problems and their solutions."[34] In this chapter, Aristotle describes several kinds of problems that could be raised with traditional poetry, especially Homer, and offers possible solutions. The main categories of criticism against poets are as follows: that they have said things that are impossible *(adynata)*, irrational *(aloga)*, harmful *(blabera)*, contradictory *(hypenantia)*, or contrary to artistic standards *(para tēn orthotēta tēn kata technēn)*. Aristotle suggests possible avenues of explanation, such as that the poet has introduced something impossible in order to make the work more thrilling, or that an apparent contradiction in the poem can be resolved by interpreting one of the passages in question in a different sense.[35] Many writers after Aristotle composed works with similar themes. Examples include Porphyry's *Homeric Questions,* Jerome's *Hebrew Questions on Genesis,* and Theodoret's *Questions on the Octateuch.*

Whenever the Church Fathers identify and attempt to resolve a problem in Scripture, they bear witness to their overall belief that Scripture does not make mistakes. In some cases the solution offered involves appealing to a higher sense of Scripture. But in other cases a solution is sought at the literal level.

Many ancient interpreters believed that Scripture conveys symbolic meanings through texts that are not factually correct. Leviticus 19:23 in the Septuagint states that fruit in the Holy Land "shall remain uncleansed for three years; it shall not be eaten." According to Philo, this statement does not make sense in the real world, because no gardener ever cleans fruit. Yet, Philo does not suggest that Scripture has spoken in error. Rather, Philo believes that this textual phenomenon indicates that a higher meaning is intended: "Let me say, then, that this again is one of the points to be interpreted allegorically, the literal interpretation being quite out of keeping with the facts."[36] Philo concludes that the "three years" stand for the threefold division of time — past, present, and future — and that not eating "uncleansed" fruit symbolizes the avoidance of unwholesome teaching.

Origen was deeply concerned to understand differences between the Gospels' accounts of Jesus' life. In his *Commentary on John,* Origen sets forth numerous points of apparent discrepancy between the different Gospel writers regarding the events of Jesus' ministry. For example, Origen points out that in the Gospel of Matthew, directly following his temptation in the wilderness, Jesus withdraws to Galilee and then goes to live in Capernaum after hearing that John the Baptist had been arrested,[37] but in the Gospel of John, Jesus turns water into wine in Galilee, goes down to Capernaum, makes a visit to Jerusalem to drive out the moneychangers (which does not occur until the end of Jesus' ministry in the other Gospels),[38] and still afterward John the Baptist is baptizing and preaching, not yet having been arrested.[39] Origen concludes:

On the basis of numerous other passages also, if someone should examine the Gospels carefully to check the disagreement so far as the historical sense is concerned . . . he would grow dizzy, and would either shrink from really confirming the Gospels, and would agree with one of them at random because he would not dare reject completely the faith related to our Lord, or, he would admit that there are four and would say that their truth is not in their literal features.[40]

Origen believes that each of the Gospel writers teaches something specific about Jesus and that "they have made some minor changes in what happened so far as history is concerned, with a view to the usefulness of the mystical object of these matters."[41] In other words, the Gospel writers sometimes presented details in their accounts not according to what really happened but in order to make a "mystical" point about Jesus. Thus, Origen would accept that the Gospels do occasionally contain deviations from history at the literal level, but not errors at the more important mystical level.

Augustine makes a revealing comment on the factual accuracy of Scripture while discussing the Hebrew and Greek versions of Jonah 3:4. Like most early Christians, Augustine believed in the inspiration of the ancient Greek translation of the Old Testament, the "Septuagint." Even when he became aware of the differences between the Hebrew and Greek texts of the Old Testament, Augustine was unwilling to give up the authority of the Septuagint; rather, he simply affirmed both the Hebrew and Greek texts as inspired, even at points where they differ. Just as the Holy Spirit inspired different messages through Isaiah and Jeremiah, so also the Hebrew and Greek texts of a single passage of Scripture are both inspired, even though they say different things. Thus, in the Hebrew text Jonah says, "Yet forty days, and Nineveh shall be overthrown," whereas in the Septuagint Jonah says, "Yet three days, and Nineveh shall be overthrown." Augustine remarks, "So if I am asked which of these Jonah said, I suppose that it was rather what we read in the Hebrew." Nevertheless, continues Augustine, the Spirit inspired the Greek translators to write "three days" in order to convey a symbolic meaning, namely, that Jesus rose from the dead on the third day. As far as the facts are concerned, Jonah did not say "three days," but the Holy Spirit still inspired "three days" in order to point spiritually to Jesus.[42]

Let us return to Aristotle for a moment. One thing to notice about the

"Problems and their Solutions" chapter in Aristotle's *Poetics* is that the solutions do not usually involve allegorical interpretation. There were other approaches to ancient Greek poetry that did make use of allegory (see section 20 below), but Aristotle's solutions focus more on the literal sense. Similar in this way to Aristotle, there is a stream of thought among the Church Fathers that attempted to resolve alleged factual problems in Scripture at the literal level.

Although he firmly believed that Scripture contains allegorical meanings, Jerome was one of the most adept in the early church at resolving textual difficulties on the literal plane. In the story where Jesus is anointed at Bethany, the Gospel of John portrays Judas as complaining about the wasted ointment, whereas in the Gospel of Matthew all the disciples are said to be indignant.[43] Jerome says, "I know that some criticize this passage and ask why another evangelist said that Judas alone was angry, whereas Matthew writes that *all* the apostles were indignant. These critics are unaware of a figure of speech called *syllēpsis*, which is customarily termed 'all for one and one for many.'"[44] Jerome also suggests another solution: perhaps the apostles were genuinely indignant for the sake of the poor, whereas Judas was indignant for the sake of his own profit. But what is notable is that both of Jerome's solutions defend the factual correctness of the text at the literal level without appealing to allegory.

Jerome's works furnish many examples of this kind. In his *Commentary on Matthew* 27:32, Jerome uses historical harmonization to answer the question of who carried Jesus' cross, Jesus himself (John 19:17) or Simon of Cyrene (Matt. 27:32). According to Jerome, Jesus began carrying his own cross, but then Simon of Cyrene carried it later. The Gospel of Mark begins with quotations from both Isaiah 40:3 and Malachi 3:1, but only mentions Isaiah. But this cannot be a mistake, Jerome argues, because "The utterances of the evangelists are the work of the Holy Spirit." Jerome's solution is that the words "it is written" in Mark 1:2 refer only to Isaiah 40:3, and that Mark is simply using Malachi's testimony to confirm that John the Baptist is the fulfillment of the Isaiah passage.[45] On the issue of why Mark says that Jesus was crucified at the third hour (Mark 15:25) when the other Gospel writers place the crucifixion at the sixth hour (Matt. 27:45; John 19:14), Jerome argues that the apparent mistake in Mark is the result of a scribal error: originally Mark wrote "sixth," but it was miscopied as "third."[46] Jerome was not the only early Christian interpreter to resolve difficulties in this way, but with his strong linguistic skills and creativity he was probably the ablest.

Early Christian interpreters sometimes responded to potential factual problems in Scripture by making observations that foreshadow elements of modern biblical studies. Theodoret raises the question as to why Judges 1:8 uses the name "Jerusalem" when during this period the city was called "Jebus" (see Judg. 19:10-11). Theodoret explains, "I believe the composition of this book is to be dated to a later period. In support, I note that the narrative refers to this city as Jerusalem; previously named Jebus, it was only later that it received this name."[47] Jerome says that allowance should be made for Luke to omit certain things about Paul from his account in view of Luke's "freedom as a historian." Moreover, Luke can refer to Joseph as Jesus' "father" or "parent" (see Luke 2:33, 41), even though strictly speaking he was not, because it is the custom of historians to describe things as they are commonly believed to be, not necessarily as they are.[48] Such observations look forward to discussions in modern biblical studies about the composition history and compositional practices of biblical writers.[49]

In some instances, Church Fathers were willing to concede minor discrepancies in Scripture without feeling the need to harmonize them. In refuting the views of Marcion, the leader of a schismatic group in the early church who placed sole authority for information on Jesus' life on an edited version of Luke, Tertullian says the following about the four Gospels: "It matters not that the arrangement of their narratives varies, so long as there is agreement on the essentials of the faith — and on these they show no agreement with Marcion."[50] In other words, even if the Gospels do not agree on every detail, they agree at least on the main points of Jesus' life and teaching, and this is sufficient to counter Marcion's views. John Chrysostom took the discrepancies between the Gospels as proof that they represent four independent witnesses to the life of Jesus. "For if they had agreed on all things exactly even to time and place, and to the very words," Chrysostom explains, "our enemies would have simply believed that they met together and composed what they wrote by mere human agreement. . . . But as it is, the discordance which seems to exist in small matters delivers them from all suspicion, and speaks clearly on behalf of the character of the writers."[51] As Chrysostom sees it, the Gospel writers were at least honest enough to write what they knew, without conspiring together to create a single seamless account. This helps to substantiate their testimony regarding the bigger points of the story on which they agree.

The general tendency in the early church was to see freedom from factual error as an entailment of biblical inspiration. Interpreters who made much of allegorical interpretation were sometimes willing to acknowledge certain kinds of flaws at the literal level while affirming the truth of the text's spiritual meaning. There were also Church Fathers who tried to resolve problems in Scripture working with the literal sense. One finds this especially where specific biblical texts had been attacked by critics of the church. Origen's candid admission that the Gospel narratives contain conflicting elements that cannot be reconciled at the historical level reflects the fact that he defended these narratives at a time when Christianity was a small minority in a world hostile to the church. Most intellectuals in Origen's time scoffed at Christianity. The culture at large was not willing to turn a blind eye toward problems in the Bible. Origen could not afford to rely primarily on forced historical harmonizations or simply leave matters open for future resolution.

In the end, it is not necessary that Scripture be free from all inaccuracies at the literal level in order to fulfill its inspired purpose of being profitable for teaching, reproof, correction, and training in righteousness (2 Tim. 3:16). Still, it makes sense for Christians to expect their sacred writings not to be deceptive in purpose or written out of ignorance. Christians should assess the factual accuracy of Scripture with charity, giving the text the benefit of the doubt when issues are unclear, provided that we keep in mind that biblical texts come from antiquity and will naturally reflect the literary and historical conventions of the ancient world. As for ancient Christian approaches to dealing with potential factual problems in Scripture, allegory as a purely defensive mechanism is not particularly useful today. But it seems quite realistic to posit that biblical writers sometimes presented textual details not strictly in keeping with the facts in order to make a theological point. This is undoubtedly behind many of the discrepancies in the Gospels. Furthermore, it was sensible for figures such as Tertullian and John Chrysostom to acknowledge factual problems on smaller issues while still affirming the truth of the basic picture of Jesus presented by the Gospels. The value pertaining to biblical inspiration discussed in this section is still meaningful today, but it should be explained with proper nuance.

15. Scripture Is Not in Conflict with "Pagan" Learning

Most of the Church Fathers were well educated by the standards of their day. Consequently they were in a good position to compare and contrast scriptural teaching with the teaching of the leading philosophical schools on important topics such as the nature of the physical world and the principles of ethics. Especially in the earliest centuries, this constant process of evaluation was thrust upon the church as it sought to create a Christian identity within the broader intellectual landscape. Occasionally Christians claimed that scriptural truth was in such direct opposition to "pagan falsehood" that there was no common ground between them. But more often early Christians conceded that "pagan" learning did possess some measure of truth. When this concession was in view, the Church Fathers held that Scripture and genuine philosophical learning would not be in conflict.

The classic expression of Christian opposition to "pagan" philosophy is Tertullian's series of questions, "What indeed has Athens to do with Jerusalem? What concord is there between the Academy and the Church? What between heretics and Christians?"[52] In opposition to Heraclitus, Plato, Zeno the Stoic, the Epicureans and others, Tertullian cites Colossians 2:8, "See to it that no one takes you captive by philosophy and empty deceit, according to human tradition, according to the elemental spirits of the world, and not according to Christ." As Tertullian sees it, philosophical notions are the "teachings of demons" and the source of heresy (see 1 Tim. 4:1). Even if we today might view certain aspects of Tertullian's Christianity, such as his moral rigor, as connected to the general atmosphere of Roman Stoicism, Tertullian would not have seen it that way. For Tertullian, Scripture was not in agreement with "pagan" learning because "pagan" learning was wrong and scriptural truth was right.

Lactantius, although he qualifies his position more than Tertullian, expresses the same basic sentiments often in his *Divine Institutes:* What the philosophers failed to do, the heavenly doctrine accomplishes because it alone is wisdom.[53] Likewise Origen, who imbibed much of the spirit of Greek philosophy and occasionally granted that Plato had benefited humanity, usually stressed the shortcomings of Plato's philosophy, even ascribing one of Plato's sayings to the devil.[54] Tertullian represents an extreme form of a stream of thought in early Christianity that emphasized conflict between the error of "pagan" philosophy and the truth of Christian Scripture.[55]

On the whole, however, it was common for Christians to grant some measure of credibility to the "pagan" philosophical tradition. This presented the challenge of reconciling belief in the perfect revelation of truth in Scripture with the belief that some truth was to be found in "pagan" philosophy. Starting with Greek-speaking Jews living in the second century BCE and continuing on into the early church, a common way to answer this challenge was to argue that "pagan" philosophers had borrowed their best ideas from Moses or the prophets. In his apologetic work *The Preparation for the Gospel*, Eusebius of Caesarea quotes extensively from two early Greek-speaking Jewish authors, Aristobulus and Artapanus, who attempted to show that many notable intellectual figures of the past, including Orpheus, Pythagoras, Socrates, and Plato, had relied on the writings of Moses in developing their philosophies.[56] Clement of Alexandria also argued this way and quoted earlier authors in support, including Aristobulus and the Pythagorean philosopher Numenius, who said, "What is Plato but Moses speaking Greek?"[57] That Moses was of greater antiquity than Greek thinkers and was the source of their correct doctrines was a common theme in early Christian apologetic works such as Tatian's *Address to the Greeks*, Justin Martyr's apologies, Theophilus's *To Autolycus*, and Augustine's *City of God*.[58] While these early Jews and Christians were correct to date Moses earlier than Socrates, there is of course no evidence that Socrates or Plato actually borrowed from Israel's Scriptures. But the story of how Moses founded the Greek intellectual tradition allowed early Christians to affirm elements of Greek philosophy while at the same time maintaining their belief in the unique truthfulness of Scripture.

Justin Martyr's concept of the "seminal divine Word" represents another avenue in the early church for reconciling Greek philosophy with Scripture. According to this idea, the divine Word, that is, the "Logos" of God, became flesh in the person of Jesus (John 1:1), so that Jesus represents the whole Logos in its pure form. Yet the Logos did not first enter the world in the incarnation of Jesus, nor did the Logos speak only to Moses and the prophets. Rather, "Everything that the philosophers and legislators discovered and expressed well, they accomplished through their discovery and contemplation of some part of the Logos. But, since they did not have a full knowledge of the Logos, which is Christ, they often contradict themselves."[59] Justin identifies Socrates as a good example of someone who spoke truth as a result of having received a share of the Logos. But because Socrates and others like him only had a portion of the Logos, everything they said must be verified and potentially corrected on the basis of the supreme revelation of the Logos, Jesus. Justin explains,

> I am proud to say that I strove with all my might to be known as a Christian, not because the teachings of Plato are different from those of Christ, but because they are not in every way similar; neither are those of other writers, the Stoics, the poets, and the historians. For each one of them, seeing, through his participation of the

seminal Divine Word, what was related to it, spoke very well. But, they who contradict themselves in important matters evidently did not acquire the unseen [that is, heavenly] wisdom and the indisputable knowledge. The truths which men in all lands have rightly spoken belong to us Christians. . . . Indeed, all writers, by means of the engrafted seed of the Word which was implanted in them, had a dim glimpse of the truth.[60]

With this argument, Justin was able to affirm whatever he regarded as true in any "pagan" writer and still see Jesus as the standard for truth, all without needing to argue that earlier "pagan" writers actually borrowed from Moses.

The imprint of Greek thought is evident throughout the writings of many Church Fathers.[61] Some were even willing to recommend that Christians get a "classical" education, provided that they focused only on what was useful for the Christian life. Basil the Great affirms that "pagan learning is not without usefulness for the soul" in his *Address to Young Men, On How They Might Derive Profit from Pagan Literature*,[62] and Augustine in *On Christian Teaching* encourages Christians to read Platonist philosophers.[63] Gregory of Nyssa, Augustine, and others used the analogy of the Israelites plundering the Egyptians to describe the process whereby Christians might make use of pagan learning. Just as Israel took the silver and gold that Egypt had used for idols and recast these materials to make the sacred furnishings of the Tabernacle, so also Christians could receive the plunder of "pagan learning," including moral and natural philosophy, geometry, astronomy, and dialectics, and bring these to the church as offerings to God.[64] This paradigm was especially helpful for Christians in the first five centuries, since most of those who received a classical education during this period did so in a "pagan" context.[65]

To illustrate how the Church Fathers applied the principles discussed in this section to the biblical text, we will now consider how Genesis 1 was interpreted in relation to ancient scientific thought. Some early Christian interpreters of Genesis 1 paid little attention to the claims of natural philosophy. Origen, for example, interprets Genesis 1 in purely spiritual terms. It is obvious to Origen that the text is not meant to be taken literally: "Now what man of intelligence will believe that the first and the second and the third day, and the evening and the morning existed without the sun and moon and stars?"[66] The "expanse" of Genesis 1:6 is our "outer person" (2 Cor. 4:16), and the lights that illuminate us are Christ and the church

(John 8:12), with Moses, Abraham, Isaac, Jacob, Isaiah, and so forth as stars.[67] In an exposition such as this, there is little need to reconcile Scripture with natural science. Ephrem the Syrian's treatment of Genesis 1 is concise and focuses on the literal sense. Ephrem begins by saying, "Let no one think that there is anything allegorical in the works of the six days." Ephrem affirms that everything was actually created in six days, but he does not attempt to relate any of the details to "pagan" learning.[68] John Chrysostom's exposition of Genesis 1 is neither allegorical nor simply explanatory, but is devoted primarily to moral exhortation.[69] None of these interpreters shows much interest in what natural philosophers said about the created world.

For other interpreters, however, it was a top priority to deal with "pagan" science when discussing Genesis 1. We see three different approaches to this topic in Ambrose, Basil the Great, and Augustine. For Ambrose, the story of creation in Genesis 1 confronts and corrects "pagan" theories. Ambrose begins his work *The Six Days of Creation* with a general summary of opinions about the physical world held by Plato, Aristotle, Pythagoras, and Democritus. He then moves to introduce the biblical text by saying, "Under the inspiration of the Holy Spirit, Moses, a holy man, foresaw that these errors would appear among men and perhaps had already appeared."[70] Next, Ambrose introduces Moses as the author, emphasizing that he was "learned in all the sciences of the Egyptians" and "instructed in all phases of secular learning." From here on, Ambrose weaves into his treatment of Genesis 1 numerous comments aimed at showing how Moses corrects the erroneous views of philosophers. For example, (a) the earth is not suspended in the middle of the universe as they think, but is upheld by God's will; (b) water can indeed sit above the heavenly sphere (Gen. 1:7) — despite philosophers' objections — because the heavens are only spherical inside, having a square-shaped outer roof that can hold water; (c) God, not the sun as they suppose, is the author of vegetation, because vegetation came into existence before the sun was made (Gen. 1:11-18). As Ambrose argues throughout, the opinions of the philosophers cannot withstand the words of the prophet Moses.[71]

For Basil, the teachings of Genesis 1 and the findings of natural science are essentially compatible. In *The Six Days of Creation*, Basil rejects "those who do not admit the common meaning of the Scriptures," who "say that water is not water." "When I hear 'grass,'" says Basil, "I think of grass, and in the same manner I understand everything as it is said, a plant, a fish, a wild animal, and an ox. 'Indeed, I am not ashamed of the Gospel' [Rom.

1:16]."[72] Basil thus promises to read Genesis 1 as pertaining to the physical world. Like Ambrose, he mentions the views of Greek philosophers and points out how they contradict each other and therefore cannot be trusted. But what Basil presses home as their great error is the belief that the world came about by chance.[73] Basil attempts to refute this view whenever it comes up, but he does not expend his energies in *The Six Days of Creation* trying to prove that Moses' account is superior to "pagan" philosophy. Rather, Basil weaves information about the natural world into his exposition, as if to show how up-to-date Moses was. Thus, Genesis 1:20, "Let the waters swarm with swarms of living creatures," is said to include amphibians, such as frogs, crabs, and hippopotamuses, and encompasses both the "vipara, such as seals and dolphins and rays and those like them that are called cartilaginous," and the "ovipara . . . which are, roughly speaking, all the different kinds of fish," that is, fish with or without horny scales and with or without fins.[74] Basil does not usually invoke the opinions of Greek philosophers to refute them but instead utilizes his knowledge of natural philosophy to show how successfully Genesis 1 describes the creation of the world.

Finally, in his *Literal Commentary on Genesis,* Augustine sets forth a vision for interpreting Genesis 1 that assumes coherence between what Scripture teaches and what true natural philosophy upholds. In this work, Augustine deals with the literal creation of the physical world but also allows for considerable use of figurative language.[75] Thus, "Let there be light" in Genesis 1:3 must be an immaterial utterance of God in his eternal Word, because before the creation of matter there was no possibility of sound and no human languages. The "deep" in Genesis 1:2 is a metaphor for "life which is formless unless it is turned toward its Creator," and the "waters" represent "the whole of material creation."[76] These examples give a sense of the physical yet metaphorical interpretation that Augustine pursues.

But what interests us presently is Augustine's attitude toward Genesis and natural science. First, Augustine believes that Scripture, when rightly interpreted, will never contradict what we learn from the natural world when the facts have been correctly understood. If a human theory about the natural world conflicts with a presumed teaching of Scripture, and "reason should prove that this theory is unquestionably true," then "this teaching was never in Holy Scripture but was an opinion proposed by man in his ignorance." Augustine is clear that reason and the facts of nature can redirect how Christians interpret Scripture. It may be the case that Scripture teaches precisely the same thing as natural science, but this need not be so. Scripture might be teaching something else entirely, such as a spiritual lesson, which is different from natural science but still true. But when rightly interpreted, Scripture will never be in conflict with what reason and nature tell us about the natural world.[77]

Furthermore, Augustine warns Christians not to engage in needless debates about Genesis and the natural world, lest this take away from the religious intention of the biblical text. Augustine explains:

> Usually, even a non-Christian knows something about the earth, the heavens, and the other elements of this world, about the motion and orbit of the stars and even their size and relative positions, about the predictable eclipses of the sun and moon, the cycles of the years and the seasons, about the kinds of animals, shrubs, stones, and so forth, and this knowledge he holds to as being certain from reason and experience. Now, it is a disgraceful and dangerous thing for an infidel to hear a Christian, presumably giving the meaning of Holy Scripture, talking nonsense on these topics; and we should take all means to prevent such an embarrassing situation, in which people show up vast ignorance in a Christian and laugh it to scorn. The shame is not so much that an ignorant individual is derided, but that people outside the household of the faith think our sacred writers held such opinions, and, to the great loss of those for whose salvation we toil, the writers of our Scripture are criticized and rejected as unlearned men. If they find a Christian mistaken in a field which they themselves know well and hear him maintaining his foolish opinions about our books, how are they going to believe those books in matters concerning the resurrection of the dead, the hope of eternal life, and the kingdom of heaven, when they think their pages are full of falsehoods on facts which they themselves have learnt from experience and the light of reason? Reckless and incompetent expounders of Holy Scripture bring untold trouble and sorrow on their wiser brethren when they are caught in one of their mischievous false opinions and are taken to task by those who are not bound by the authority of our sacred books.[78]

Most modern Christians would agree that we can learn significant truths about the world from non-scriptural sources. Of course, all avenues for knowing truth involve some measure of interpretation; it is not only Scripture that needs to be interpreted. But explorations into the natural sciences and fields such as psychology and anthropology show that valuable insights are to be gained from sources that do not base themselves in Christian revelation. In view of this, it remains important Christian teaching that what we learn as genuinely true from "non-Christian" sources will not be incompatible with what we learn as true from Scripture. This way of thinking is grounded in the belief that God is the single unifying element behind all truth. This belief can impact not only how we interpret the world around us but also what we take Scripture to be teaching. Obviously, it can no longer be argued that all significant knowledge ultimately derives from Moses. Yet Justin Martyr's theology of the seminal divine Word offers a constructive way to think about Christ as the source of all truth that is rightly open to the activity of the Word broadly in human history. As for the interpretation of Genesis 1, where literary form and historical context are important factors, Augustine's caution about trying to learn natural science from Genesis still has value today.

16. The Original Text of Scripture Is Authoritative

The books of the Old Testament were originally written in Hebrew, with the exception of a few chapters written in Aramaic.[79] Following the conquests of Alexander the Great in the fourth century BCE, Greek language and culture spread throughout the Mediterranean world. In the third century BCE, Greek-speaking Jews living in Alexandria, Egypt produced a Greek translation of the Pentateuch for the benefit of the many interested readers who did not know Hebrew. This translation of the Pentateuch into Greek was known as the version of the "Seventy" (translators), that is, "*Septuaginta*" in Latin, or, as it is known in English, the "Septuagint." The rest of the Hebrew Scriptures (= Old Testament) were translated into Greek over the next two hundred years, so that by the time of Jesus and the apostles all of the Old Testament was available in Greek translation. In the early centuries of the Christian era, the term Septuagint (Greek *hebdomēkonta*) was applied to the Greek translation of the whole Old Testament. Today scholars often use this term to refer to the original translations of each book of the Old Testament into Greek.

By the time of the New Testament, Greek had become the most widely known international language in the Mediterranean world. The first written language of the early church was Greek, and all the documents that make up the New Testament are in Greek. The Gospels were composed in

Greek despite the fact that Jesus spoke Aramaic.[80] Moreover, Paul wrote his letter to the Romans not in Latin but in Greek. The fact that these early Christians used Greek as their language of communication helped Christianity to spread throughout the Mediterranean world.

The Septuagint was the primary source used by New Testament writers for their quotations of the Old Testament. Still, there are many places where the New Testament quotes the Old Testament in versions that differ from the Septuagint.[81] Some of these quotations are closer to the Hebrew text as we know it, but some are not. Modern scholars have suggested that some New Testament authors may have quoted Old Testament passages from memory or made their own interpretive translations on the spot, or there may have been multiple translations of some parts of the Old Testament. In any case, the important fact that pertains to our discussion is this: the New Testament authors do not show self-conscious interest in making sure that their quotations of the Old Testament adhere precisely to the original text.

Two examples will illustrate this general lack of interest. First, Hebrews 10:5-7 quotes Psalm 40:6-8, introducing the quotation with "When Christ came into the world, he said. . . ." According to the original Hebrew, Psalm 40:6 begins, "Sacrifices and offerings you have not desired, but ears you have dug for me" — this last phrase perhaps meaning "you have given me an open ear." In Hebrews, however, the original "ears you have dug for me" becomes "a body you have prepared for me." In interpreting the verse, the author of Hebrews points out that "we will have been sanctified through the offering of the body of Jesus Christ once for all." The quotation in Hebrews agrees neither with the Hebrew nor the Septuagint, but the particular wording of the text as it appears in Hebrews, with its reference to the "body" of Jesus, is integrated into the point that the writer of Hebrews is making.

The second example is the citation of Amos 9:11-12 in Acts 15:16-17. In the original context in Amos, the text speaks of the restoration of the Davidic dynasty ("the booth of David"), with the following result: "that they may possess the remnant of Edom and all the nations who are called by my name." Several changes take place in the New Testament quotation. First, the Hebrew word "Edom" is interpreted as *adam*, that is, "humankind."[82] Second, whereas the "remnant" is the object of the verb in the Hebrew, it becomes the subject of the verb in Greek. Third, the verb "possess" (Hebrew *yarash*) is interpreted as if it were the verb "seek" (Hebrew *darash*). As a result, "that they may possess the remnant of Edom" becomes "that the remnant of humankind may seek." This transformation had already taken place in the Septuagint. The text as quoted in Acts 15:17 follows the Septuagint, except that the New Testament writer fills in the missing object of the verb, producing, "that the remnant of humankind may seek the Lord." This version of the text fits especially well with the point of Acts 15, that is, the inclusion of the Gentiles through Jesus.

Two important caveats should be made with respect to the textual form of Old Testament quotations in the New Testament. First, not every quotation of the Old Testament in the New Testament involves a textual difficulty. Many of these quotations correspond to the Hebrew in a relatively straightforward fashion. Second, even where textual problems have come into play, there is generally a clear theological connection between the Old and New Testament passages. For example, the passage in Amos 9 addresses the restoration of the Davidic monarchy and the expansion of Israel's kingdom, presumably through military conquest, so as to include other nations. The citation in Acts, while leaving aside the national and militaristic dimensions of the text, taps into the connection between David's rule and the inclusion of the nations. Thus, the presence of a textual problem does not take away from the overall thematic connection between the original text and the point the New Testament author is making.[83]

At the same time, the presence of so many free quotations of the Old Testament in the New Testament tells us something about the authors of these texts. The discipline of textual criticism had existed in Alexandria since the third century BCE. Scholars such as Aristophanes of Byzantium and Aristarchus of Samothrace produced critical editions of Greek poetic works and even used critical symbols to mark variant readings.[84] But there is no trace of such interest in the New Testament. New Testament writers make no observable effort to conform their quotations to the Hebrew text, or to the Septuagint, or to any other known text. Furthermore, they do not discuss textual variants or manuscripts. In sum, the writers of the New Testament do not seem interested in the question of the original text of the Old Testament. They give every appearance of being pragmatists, making use of whatever version is at hand in order to preach the gospel message.

The question of the text of the Old Testament was eventually addressed by the Church Fathers. The overwhelming majority of early Christians during this period ascribed canonical authority to the Septuagint.

Early Christian beliefs about the Septuagint ultimately derive from the *Letter of Aristeas,*[85] which was composed sometime in the second century BCE.[86] It describes the translation of the Law (the Pentateuch only) into Greek by seventy-two Jewish translators under the direction of Ptolemy II

Philadelphus. *Aristeas* affirms the skill of the translators, but it also hints at a divine purpose in the translation, stating that the seventy-two translators finished their work in seventy-two days, "as if this coincidence had been the result of some design."[87] This account of the Greek translation of the Law was developed through successive layers of restatement, beginning with the Greek-speaking Jews Philo and Josephus. While the version of Josephus is essentially non-supernatural,[88] Philo adds several elements, including explicit mention of the divine inspiration of the translators[89] and the assertion that God had intended the translation to profit the human race.[90]

The first Christian witness to the origin of the Septuagint is Justin Martyr, who relates that not only the "Law" in the strictest sense (the Pentateuch), but also the prophets (i.e., the entire Old Testament) were translated by order of King Ptolemy of Egypt.[91] Justin also brings the number of translators down to seventy, which became the traditional number.[92] Irenaeus was the first to popularize the legend of how each of the Septuagint translators arrived miraculously at the same translation even though they worked in different cells.[93] He claims that the apostles confirm the authority of the Septuagint, which was inspired by God to testify prophetically to the coming of the Lord.[94] The story about the translators working in separate cells is also found in the anonymous Christian treatise *Exhortation to the Greeks,* where the author claims to have visited the island of Pharos and seen the actual cells where the translation had been made.[95] Clement of Alexandria describes how the seventy translators worked separately but arrived at the same translation. According to Clement, God inspired the translators as prophets in keeping with his plan to make the Scriptures available to the Greek world.[96] In the fourth century, Eusebius of Caesarea recounts in some detail the story of the Septuagint, following the account in the *Letter of Aristeas,* agreeing that God ordained the Septuagint as an instrument for the conversion of the Greeks.[97] The inspiration and authority of the Septuagint were affirmed by many other Church Fathers, including Cyril of Jerusalem, John Chrysostom, Epiphanius of Salamis, and Augustine.[98] Moreover, it was the Septuagint that served as the basis for translating Scripture into other languages, such as Latin, Coptic, and Ethiopic. In sum, the Greek Septuagint was the most widely recognized authoritative version of the Old Testament during the period of the Church Fathers.[99]

For the most part, belief in the authority of the Septuagint coincided with a sense of complete confidence that the translators had successfully reproduced the meaning of the original. This was already the case with Philo, who insisted that the Septuagint rendered the literal and exact sense of the Hebrew.[100] Although Origen was a unique case, he likewise stayed faithful to the Septuagint. Origen compiled a multicolumn Bible called the *Hexapla* which contained the Hebrew text in one column, a transliteration of the Hebrew into Greek letters in another column, and then four Greek versions: the Septuagint and three Greek translations produced in the second century CE (by Aquila, Symmachus, and Theodotion).[101] Origen's aim in compiling this parallel Bible was not to correct the Septuagint by appealing to the Hebrew but to show Christians who debated Jews how the Septuagint differed from the Hebrew, and also to make available the other Greek translations for use in biblical interpretation.[102] When Origen did speak of correcting textual errors, he seems to have had in mind simply restoring the Septuagint to its presumed pristine state.[103] Another interesting theory was held by Hilary of Poitiers, who believed that the translators of the Septuagint possessed secret knowledge handed down orally from Moses and that they incorporated this knowledge into their translation. This made the Septuagint the best surviving witness to the original Hebrew, since the secret knowledge necessary to interpret the Hebrew text was no longer available.[104] Theodore of Mopsuestia did not defend the Septuagint on the basis of inspiration, but he stuck closely to the text of the Septuagint because he trusted in the great skill of the seventy translators.[105] Most Church Fathers did not intend to choose the Septuagint over the original Hebrew, but they assumed that the Septuagint captured the precise meaning of the original. Since most of these individuals did not know Hebrew, they were never confronted with the actual differences between the Hebrew text and the Septuagint.

Origen's rudimentary studies in Hebrew and his diligent textual work with the Greek versions in the *Hexapla* bore fruit in the person of Jerome, who followed Origen's lead and took the next step of learning enough Hebrew to read the Old Testament.[106] Jerome came to recognize the differences between the Hebrew text and the Septuagint and eventually adopted the view that the "Hebrew truth" *(hebraica veritas)* should be the standard for the Old Testament.[107] What is important for the present discussion is that Jerome's return to the Hebrew was considered radical at the time. The prefaces to Jerome's Hebrew-based translations into Latin testify to the severe criticism that he received for suggesting that the Jewish Hebrew text should be preferred to the church's Septuagint.[108]

Augustine's initial reaction to Jerome's Hebrew version was negative, and only after considerable time did he come to accept the legitimacy of the Hebrew.[109] Even then, he did not abandon his belief in the inspiration of the Septuagint, but merely accepted the Hebrew text as inspired alongside the Septuagint, as discussed in section 14 above. It was not until the seventh century that Jerome's Hebrew-based Old Testament began to displace the (Septuagint-based) Old Latin version in the west, and even this replacement was based more on Jerome's personal authority and superior Latin style than on the authority of the Hebrew text.[110] Jerome was the only figure in the early church who regarded the original text of the Old Testament as authoritative over against the Septuagint.

The situation as described in this chapter relates specifically to the Old Testament. For the New Testament, the original Greek was of course regarded as the authoritative standard.[111] Greek Christians could read the New Testament in the original, and for Christians who spoke Latin, Syriac, or any other early Christian language, it was not too difficult to find someone who could explain the meaning of the original Greek. This was not the case with Hebrew. By this time, knowledge of Hebrew was primarily confined to Jewish circles.[112] Most early Christians read the Old Testament strictly in translation. This often had a significant impact on how they interpreted the text, especially in light of their emphasis on details.[113]

Since the Renaissance there have been continuing advances in our understanding of the textual history of biblical books. These advances have been encouraged by improvements in research methods, new textual discoveries, and (for the Old Testament) the full appreciation of the Hebrew manuscript tradition as preserved by Jews. This greater insight into the earliest known forms of biblical texts has been extremely beneficial for our understanding of numerous passages of Scripture. Ancient translations of the Old Testament, such as the Septuagint, remain important witnesses to the earlier texts from which they were translated (for example, the Septuagint for any given book remains an important witness to the Hebrew text from which it was translated). Moreover, the ancient translations serve as valuable witnesses to how early Christians interpreted the Scriptures in their contexts. Nevertheless, for most modern readers it is obvious that our best reconstructions of the original texts of biblical books in their original languages provide the firmest foundation for hearing the message of Scripture today.

The Church Fathers generally assumed that the facts reported in Scripture were correct and that events narrated in Scripture took place. Occasionally, certain Church Fathers actually expressed the idea that the factuality or historicity of Scripture was an entailment of divine inspiration. For some early Christian interpreters, problems at the level of factuality or historicity signaled the presence of a spiritual level of meaning. While none of the early Christians discussed in this chapter doubted the possibility of miracles, the historicity of certain events could be questioned on grounds of implausibility, quite apart from the question of whether miracles occur. The teaching of Scripture was obviously viewed as superior to "pagan" learning, although the early chapters of Genesis could be read with the help of natural science, or with the explicit intention of not contradicting natural science. Except for Jerome and Origen, the Church Fathers did not endeavor to study the Old Testament in the original Hebrew. Christians by and large accepted the authority of the Greek Septuagint, and many believed this translation to be inspired. Early Christians had a stake in factuality and historicity, but the importance of these issues was measured in balance with other components of divine inspiration, such as the usefulness and spiritual significance of Scripture.

CHAPTER SIX

Agreement with Truth

Whereas the previous chapter dealt with the claims of Scripture in relation to the physical world (facts and history), the present chapter addresses the truthfulness of Scripture in relation to its spiritual subject matter. As a general rule, the Church Fathers considered the truthfulness of scriptural teaching to be an entailment of biblical inspiration. We have seen in earlier chapters the variety of ways that early Christians thought about the language of Scripture and how it should be interpreted. But whatever other points of diversity can be found among the Church Fathers, they all looked to Scripture for true teaching on the Christian faith. Only with reference to specific issues did complications arise. In these final sections I will discuss a few of these issues.

17. Scripture's Teaching Is Internally Consistent

If the inspiration of Scripture ensures that what it teaches is true, and all Scripture is inspired by God, it is logical to conclude that the teachings found throughout the biblical canon must be harmonious with each other. There can be no contradictions in the teaching of Scripture. At issue here is the possibility of contradictions not in facts but in message. The message of Scripture must be consistent, with no internal conflicts.

Numerous examples can be given to illustrate the Church Fathers' belief in the internal consistency of Scripture. Tertullian, commenting on the apostle Paul's discussion of remarriage in 1 Corinthians 7, says,

> This, then, is our interpretation of the passage. We must examine it
> to see whether it harmonizes with the time and occasion of writing,

with illustrations and arguments used earlier, as well as with assertions and opinions which follow later on, and — most important of
all — whether it agrees with the advice of the Apostle and his own
personal practice. Obviously, there is nothing to be more sedulously
avoided than inconsistency.[1]

The early Christian apologetic work *Exhortation to the Greeks* contrasts the
contradictory claims made by "pagan" philosophers with the harmonious
teachings of the inspired writers of Scripture: "as if by one mouth and one
tongue, without contradicting themselves or one another, they have instructed us concerning God, the origin of the world, the creation of humanity, the immortality of the soul, the future judgment, and all other
things which we should know."[2] In his *Dialogue against the Pelagians,*
Jerome takes up the question of why even the apostles could not attain
perfection, despite the fact that Jesus commanded, "You therefore must be
perfect, as your heavenly Father is perfect" (Matt. 5:48). Jerome explains
that different testimonies of Scripture will not ultimately disagree when
the specific time and place of the testimonies are considered, "lest it appear
that the Holy Spirit is contradictory." Augustine provides a clear statement
on the consistency of Scripture in replying to the arguments of a certain
man named Faustus, who argued on the basis of Romans 1:3 ("who was de-
scended from David according to the flesh") and 2 Corinthians 5:16 ("Even
though we once regarded Christ according to the flesh, we regard him thus
no more") that Paul changed his mind on whether Jesus was physically
born from David. Augustine explains the two passages in such a way that
they both teach the incarnation, justifying his procedure with the following remark:

> The books of later authors are distinct from the excellence of the
> canonical authority of the Old and New Testaments, which has
> been confirmed from the times of the apostles through the succes-
> sions of bishops and through the spread of the churches. It has been
> set on high, as if on a kind of throne, and every believing and pious
> intellect should be obedient to it. If something there strikes a per-
> son as absurd, it is not permissible to say, "The author of this book
> did not have the truth," but, "Either the manuscript is defective, or
> the translator made a mistake, or you do not understand." . . .
> Hence, whoever you are whom these texts have upset as if they were
> self-contradictory, because it is written in one place that the Son of

God is a descendant of David but in another, "And if we knew Christ according to the flesh, yet now we no longer know him in that way," even if both statements were not taken from the writings of one apostle but Paul had made one of them and Peter or Isaiah or any other apostle or prophet had made the other, they all agree with one another in canonical authority. Hence, we should believe with a most just and prudent piety that they were spoken as if by one mouth.[3]

Augustine states explicitly what most Church Fathers believed and practiced in their reading of Scripture, namely, that the teachings of different parts of Scripture will not contradict each other when they have been properly understood.

In some cases, potential conflicts between different scriptural passages were harmonized at the literal level. For example, Jerome addresses the possible contradiction between Romans 2:25 and Galatians 5:2 on the value of circumcision by pointing out the different audiences addressed by the two letters and by stating that Paul qualifies his claim in Romans 2:25 later on in the book of Romans.[4] As another example, Origen upholds the literal sense of Jeremiah 4:1-2, which affirms the swearing of oaths in the name of the LORD, and also Matthew 5:34, which forbids the taking of oaths, by suggesting that the novice Christian must swear "in truth, in justice, and in righteousness" (Jer. 4:2), while more advanced Christians will not swear at all, letting what they say simply be "Yes" or "No" (Matt. 5:37).[5]

The presence of potential conflicts could also point to a meaning beyond the literal level. Didymus the Blind explains that, when two biblical texts appear to be in conflict, it is permissible to force one of the texts into agreement with the other. This is because all inspired Scripture has a higher sense, and just as one would not tell an expert in geometry that he does not know how to draw a certain figure, so also one should not say that the Holy Spirit does not know what he is saying. According to one scenario proposed by Didymus, we may force into agreement the literal sense of a text whose concord is not clear, as the higher sense is clear and alleviates the contradiction.[6] Justin Martyr illustrates how one might resolve apparently conflicting teachings when he addresses the problem of Moses' bronze serpent in Numbers 21. Since Moses forbade the making of an image or likeness of anything in the heavens or on earth (Exod. 20:4), why then does God command Moses to make a bronze serpent to be placed on a pole for the people to see and be saved (Num. 21:8-9)? According to

Justin, the apparent contradiction is resolved when we realize that God was announcing a mystery through this action. The mystery, of course, is that God would break the power of the serpent through the cross of Jesus (see John 3:14).[7] As far as Justin is concerned, no other interpretation can explain why Moses would so blatantly violate the prohibition on images. It must be a mystery pointing to Christ.

The relationship between the Old Testament and the New Testament constituted a special problem for early Christians. Figures such as Marcion raised major controversies in the second century by claiming that they adhered to apostolic teaching while at the same time rejecting the Old Testament. In contrast to this, the mainstream church throughout the Mediterranean world and Mesopotamia followed the New Testament documents in believing that the Old Testament was in harmony with the teachings of Jesus and the apostles. Cyril of Jerusalem explains the majority Christian view in his *Catechetical Lectures:* "Let no one therefore draw a line between the Old Testament and the New. Let no one say that the Spirit in the Old Testament is not identical with the Spirit in the New. For whoever does so offends none other than that Holy Spirit who is honored with one honor together with the Father and the Son."[8] According to Origen the "Old Testament" is not really "old" for Christians, because they interpret the text in a spiritual way:

> The law becomes an "Old Testament" only for those who want to understand it in a fleshly way; and for them it has necessarily become old and aged, because it cannot maintain its strength. But for us, who understand and explain it spiritually and according to the gospel-meaning, it is always new. Indeed, both are "New Testaments" for us, not by the age of time but by the newness of understanding.[9]

Belief in the harmony between the testaments allowed Christians to see New Testament paradigms prefigured in the Old Testament. As Jerome says, "Whatever was said at that time to the Israelite people now is referred to the church, so that 'holy prophets' become 'apostles and apostolic men,' and 'lying and frantic prophets' become 'all the heretics.'"[10]

The consistency of teaching between the Old and New Testaments was seen in terms of shadow and fulfillment, or else through theological themes often identified through spiritual interpretation. The most important interpretive decisions revolved around the legal material in the Pentateuch. Leviticus 11–15 says that certain animals are unclean for food. Jesus, however, indicated that all "foods" (interpreted literally) are clean, but that we should interpret the categories of clean and unclean ethically (Mark 7:14-23). In this case, at least some Christians believed that the ethical interpretation of "uncleanness" given by Jesus was the original intention of Leviticus.[11] On a different track, Jerome recognized that the Old Testament originally enjoined literal observance of the Sabbath but argued that Jesus as God had the authority to alter this command and that it was now obligatory for Christians to interpret the Sabbath figuratively.[12] As another example, at the level of the human discourse Leviticus states repeatedly that atonement and forgiveness come through animal sacrifice, but Origen follows the New Testament book of Hebrews in insisting that these sacrifices were ultimately shadows of the reality to come in the death of Jesus.[13]

Wisdom and poetic books in the Old Testament presented a particular challenge for early Christian interpreters. What was a Christian to say about Ecclesiastes 3:16-22, which says that beasts and humans go to the same place when they die and asks whether the human spirit goes up and the spirit of the beast goes down to the earth. Jerome deals with this difficult text by stating that before the coming of Jesus all human souls did indeed go down to Hades, and that "Who knows . . ." in Ecclesiastes 3:21 suggests not something impossible but something difficult.[14] What is more, Jerome points out similarities between Ecclesiastes and the Gospels, such as their teachings on the vanity of accumulating earthly wealth.[15] As for the Psalms, how were Christians, who believe in the resurrection, supposed to read a passage such as Psalm 6:5, "For in death there is no remembrance of you"? On this passage, Augustine interprets "death" as a reference to the kind of sin that makes one unmindful of God.[16] Since the New Testament gives a clearer picture of what happens to people when they die, early Christian interpreters needed to update the theology of many Old Testament wisdom texts related to death.

On the whole, the sense of theological coherence between the testaments was strongest in places where early Christian interpreters believed that they were simply following the original intentions of Old Testament writers. There is no conflict between Leviticus 11–15 and the New Testament if Moses did in fact write the food laws in the first place to teach ethics. Or again, if Moses made the bronze serpent specifically to point mysteriously to Jesus, then it was clearly in harmony with both testaments to find Jesus' crucifixion symbolized there. Still, Christians were at times willing to acknowledge differences between what they taught and what the Old Testament originally stated in its literal sense. Jerome's comments on the Sabbath are a good example. In these cases, Christians believed that the coming of Jesus brought a change to the former way of reading the Old Testament, but also that the new Christian reading was in harmony with the larger theological aim of the Old Testament passage. Augustine, who believed in spiritual fulfillments of Old Testament prophecies, nevertheless recognized that "righteous men of long ago visualized the kingdom of heaven as an earthly kingdom, and predicted it accordingly."[17] The Christian fulfillment may not perfectly match how the prediction was originally pictured, but Christians believed the fulfillment was in keeping with the spirit of the original prediction, only greater in scope.

Apparent discrepancies between passages of Scripture were considered a problem, and reconciling them was a praiseworthy activity. The ancient rabbis saw potential conflicts between the priestly regulations in the book of Ezekiel and the laws in the Torah.[18] A certain rabbi named Hananiah, son of Hezekiah, received praise for harmonizing them together. The Talmud reports, "In truth, that man, Hananiah son of Hezekiah by name, is to be remembered for blessing: but for him, the Book of Ezekiel would have been hidden [= declared non-canonical], for its words contradicted the Torah. What did he do? Three hundred barrels of oil were taken up to him and he sat in an upper chamber and reconciled them."[19]

Origen gave the following interpretation of Matthew 5:9, "Blessed are the peacemakers," as recorded by Gregory of Nazianzus and Basil the Great in the *Philocalia:*

> But there is also a third peacemaker, he who shows that what to the eyes of others seems like disagreement in the Scriptures is not really so, and who proves that harmony and concord exist, whether between the Old and the New, or the Law and the Prophets, or Gospel and Gospel, or Evangelists and Apostles, or Apostles and other Apostles. For, according to the Preacher, all the Scriptures, words of the wise, are as goads, and as nails well fastened, words which were given from collections from one Shepherd (Eccl. 12:11), and there is nothing superfluous in them. And the Word is "one Shepherd" of things relating to the Word, which do indeed sound discordant to those who have not ears to hear, but are in truth most harmonious.[20]

For Origen and other like-minded interpreters of Scripture in antiquity, finding harmony between apparently contradictory passages of Scripture was almost a spiritual exercise.

As we consider this topic today, it is clear that attempting to reconcile all biblical contradictions at the strictly literal level is too artificial to be widely convincing. Still, belief in the theological consistency of Scripture is extremely valuable in that it encourages us to seek a unified message about God in Scripture at the theological level. Many apparent discords in what biblical texts seem to say reveal points of deep importance to theology. It is beneficial for Christians to think carefully through these important points with input from each biblical testimony, and not simply to cast one biblical text aside for another.

18. Scripture Does Not Deceive

In this section I will focus primarily on an exchange that took place between Jerome and Augustine on the interpretation of Galatians. In his commentary on Galatians 2, Jerome argued that Paul did not genuinely rebuke Peter for separating himself from the Gentiles but did so only in pretense, privately knowing Peter's noble intention to win the Jews for salvation. According to Jerome, Paul's public "rebuke" of Peter was a kind of deception along the lines of acting, aimed at bringing harmony to the Jewish and Gentile believers. Augustine counters Jerome with strong affirmations that Scripture cannot deceive. The arguments of both Jerome and Augustine reflect important early Christian beliefs about the inspiration of Scripture.

The background to this story involves Plato and Origen. In the *Republic*, Plato justifies the use of deception on the part of rulers for instilling the right values in their subjects. For example, it is better for warriors to have a positive view of Hades than a negative view, because the positive view will encourage them to be brave and not fear death. Likewise, people are more likely to be good citizens if they believe that their land is their mother and that all its citizens are their brothers and sisters. These beliefs are useful, in spite of the fact that they are untrue and nothing more than myths. This kind of deception Plato refers to as a "noble falsehood." It is not proper for the general citizenry to employ falsehood, any more than it is good for patients to be less than honest with their physicians. But leaders can justifiably make use of noble falsehoods.[21]

According to Jerome, Origen quoted from this very passage in the *Republic* in his lost work, the *Miscellanies*, where Origen apparently compared some aspect of Christian teaching to Plato's concept of noble falsehood.[22] Jerome also reports that Origen, again in the *Miscellanies*, interpreted the incident between Peter and Paul in Galatians 2 as merely a pretended conflict.[23] It is not unlikely that the Platonic idea played a role in Origen's handling of Galatians 2. But more can be said about the concept of deception in Origen than simply that he was borrowing from Plato.

First, Origen developed his own theology of divine deception, offering an extended reflection on this topic in his homily on Jeremiah 20:7, "O Lord, you have deceived me, and I was deceived." Origen is unwilling to say that Jeremiah, God's prophet, is wrong, even when Jeremiah accuses God of deception. As a result, Origen must concede that God indeed deceived Jeremiah, but since it is God doing the deceiving, it must be for Jeremiah's good. Just as God's "relenting" (1 Sam. 15:11) is not like the "relenting" of people, so also God's deception is categorically unlike the deception wrought by people. Origen likens God's practice of misleading people for their own good to the practice of doctors placing honey on the rim of a cup that is filled with bitter medicine. The sweetness of the cup misleads the patient into drinking the bitter medicine, which is meant for the healing of the patient.[24] Origen also likens God's deception to a father who conceals his affection from his son and outwardly shows only displeasure, so that the son might benefit from the discipline. As a biblical precedent, Jonah's statement that Nineveh would soon be destroyed (Jon. 3:4) turned out to be a beneficial falsehood, as it led to the Ninevites' repentance. Moreover, Origen reports a tradition learned from a Jewish scholar that Jeremiah only agreed to be a prophet on the basis that he would not have to proclaim judgment against Israel; only after Jeremiah agreed to prophesy did God reveal that Israel, too, would receive the cup of God's wrath. In the end, Origen declares that he is glad to be deceived by God, provided that he knows it is truly God speaking. Even if the serpent were to speak the truth to Origen, Origen would prefer the falsehoods of God, because he knows that God acts for good.[25]

Second, Origen may have been trying to defend the reputation of the mainstream church in the third century when he applied the concept of falsehood to Galatians 2. As early as the second century certain groups within the church, such as the followers of Marcion and the so-called "Gnostics," posited that the true spiritual Christianity of Paul was incompatible with the Old Testament and with Judaic Christianity, which might be symbolized by Peter. Perhaps Origen, desiring to disprove the charge of inconsistency between the testaments, argued that the conflict reported in Galatians 2 between Peter and Paul was staged, and that in reality these two pillars of the truth taught the same Gospel.

In any case, Jerome claims to follow Origen in interpreting Paul's rebuke of Peter in Galatians 2 as mere pretense.[26] As Jerome sees it, Peter decided to withdraw from table fellowship with Gentiles not out of conviction or because he caved in to pressure, but simply as a tactic to bring the Jewish party in Galatia to the truth of the gospel. Peter, who had seen the vision of clean and unclean animals and met with the Gentile Cornelius in Acts 10, certainly knew what the gospel teaches about Jew-Gentile relations within the church. If any Gentile Christians were led astray by Peter's actions, it was only because they misunderstood his intentions. As for Paul, he certainly agreed with the idea of becoming as a Jew in order to win the Jews (1 Cor. 9:20). Paul did this sort of thing himself, and would never genuinely rebuke Peter for doing it. That would be hypocrisy. Rather, Paul outwardly acted as if he were rebuking Peter, in order to make it clear to the Gentile Christians that they should not start observing Jewish customs.

Jerome (perhaps following Origen) cites as examples of godly deception the story of David pretending to be insane when fleeing from Saul (1 Sam. 21:13-15) and the story of Jehu pretending to be a Baal worshipper in order to wipe out the Baal worshippers (2 Kings 10:18-19). Both in his *Commentary on Galatians* and in his lengthy reply to Augustine's criticism (*Epistle* 112), Jerome drives home several points in defense of his interpretation: first, the Greek commentaries that Jerome consulted, including those of Origen and John Chrysostom, support his interpretation; second, Porphyry used Galatians 2 in order to criticize Christianity, and Jerome's interpretation provides the best defense; third, we cannot charge Peter with being inconsistent with his views as presented in Acts, nor can we charge Paul with being inconsistent with his views found in 1 Corinthians and Acts, and so the incident described in Galatians 2 can only have been playacting; and fourth, not only are Jewish practices inappropriate for Gentile believers, they are also inappropriate for Jews who have accepted Christianity, a fact that Peter must have understood.[27] For these reasons and a few others, Jerome vociferously defends his position.

Augustine answers Jerome with several points. In terms of sources, Augustine points out that some of the Greek commentators used by Jerome, including Apollinaris of Laodicea and Theodore of Heraclea, were of doubtful orthodoxy. Moreover, Latin commentators such as Ambrose and Cyprian agreed with Augustine that the conflict between Peter and Paul was real.[28] Above all, Scripture is the highest authority, and what Scripture teaches should be followed above all other authorities: "Still, as I said a while ago, it is only to the canonical Scriptures that I owe such a willing submission that I follow them alone, and believe of them that their authors were not in error anywhere at all in them, nor did they set down anything so as to deceive."[29]

Augustine also argues that it is more important to defend the veracity of Scripture than to defend the veracity of characters within Scripture. Thus, it is better to allow that David sinned when he committed adultery with Uriah's wife (2 Sam. 11) than to say that Scripture lied in reporting the event. "I will read the Holy Scripture," says Augustine,

> with complete certainty and confidence in its truth, founded as it is on the highest summit of divine authority; and I would rather learn from it that men were truly approved or corrected or condemned than allow my trust in the Divine Word to be everywhere undermined because I fear to believe that the human conduct of certain excellent and praiseworthy persons is sometimes worthy of blame.[30]

Most important, Augustine believes it is totally unacceptable to suggest that Scripture could ever deceive. If one were to even allow this as a possibility, how could one trust anything that Scripture says? Augustine asserts:

> If so-called white lies are permitted in the Holy Scriptures, what authority can these writings then have? What statement, I ask you, could be quoted from these Scriptures which would have the authority to crush a wicked or a controversial error? For as soon as you have quoted it, if your opponent is of a different opinion, he will say that the text you cite is an example of the writer lying for an honorable motive.[31]

Augustine further states, "So he [Peter] was rightly rebuked, and Paul spoke the truth; otherwise, once lying is justified, Holy Scripture which has been given to promote the faith among future generations would lose its firm foundation and become completely unreliable."[32] And later on, Augustine rebukes Jerome for refusing to see "the adverse effects which would result once it was believed that a writer of the holy books could with propriety and with due reverence lie in any part of his work."[33]

From Augustine's viewpoint, no supposed benefits of Jerome's interpretation outweigh the devastatingly negative effect that Jerome's theory has on the authority of Scripture. If Scripture can lie in one passage, perhaps it is lying elsewhere. If this be allowed, then whenever someone reads something they do not like in Scripture, they will simply claim that the point in question was really just a pretense and so does not need to be heeded. Augustine's primary concern is that Jerome's interpretation undermines the authority of Scripture.

The basic principle that the divinely inspired Scriptures will not deceive people was obvious enough to most early Christians that they did not need to devote special attention to it. It was something of an innovation for Origen to suggest that Scripture might deceive us for our good,[34] and by and large this innovation did not catch on with many Christians after Origen. Its significance for our discussion lies in the conversation that it generated between Jerome and Augustine. Both were concerned about the divine nature of Scripture. Jerome, probably following Origen, wanted to protect the Scriptures from potential contradiction. Moreover, it was in keeping with traditional views of inspiration to defend the reputations of biblical "heroes" such as Peter and Paul (see section 4 above). Augustine, on the other hand, believed that the presence of deception in Scripture would detract not only from its truthfulness but also from its capacity to function as an authority. He expressed more clearly than anyone else the worry that if there is one deceptive element in Scripture, the whole of scriptural authority collapses.

Christians today do not generally imagine that biblical writers were trying to deceive their readers. On that point modern Christians share Augustine's basic concern. The concept of "deception" often implies malicious intent, and so it is natural not to associate it with Scripture. Moreover, modern commentators agree with Augustine that Jerome's reading of Galatians 2 is implausible. Some modern scholars see deceptive elements in certain biblical texts; for example, it has been argued that the author of the Pastoral Epistles (1 and 2 Timothy and Titus) was not Paul but someone pretending to be Paul and that the writer's intention was to deceive the recipients. But most Christians who have considered the matter, even those who do not believe Paul to be the author of these letters, deny that the writer's purpose was to deceive.[35] In reality, it is impossible for us to know the precise intentions of the authors of biblical books. But it does make sense for Christians to expect that the human writers of Scripture did not intend to mislead those for whom they wrote. In terms of divine inspiration, we may affirm theologically that the divine intention in Scripture is to make God known and to teach us how we are to relate to God and one another, and not to deceive or mislead us.

19. Scripture's Teaching Agrees
with a Recognized External Authority

The idea that one's interpretation of Scripture must agree with an external authority was introduced in section 5 above in the discussion of Scripture's authority. There I noted the views of Tertullian, who claimed that only those who possess the church's rule of faith can correctly interpret Scripture.[36] Now I will return to the topic of the rule of faith and try to describe how it functioned in early biblical interpretation.

Several early Christian writers make reference to a "rule of faith," which was a summary of core Christian beliefs. According to our witnesses, this rule was handed down from the apostles and could be used to distinguish between true and false teaching. Anything that disagrees with the rule of faith, even if it is supported by scriptural prooftexts, is not true Christianity. References to the rule of faith in the early church can be found in Irenaeus, Tertullian, Hippolytus, Origen, the *Didascalia apostolorum*, Cyprian, and Novatian.[37] One of the fullest accounts of the rule is provided by Irenaeus, who reports as follows:

> [The church believes] in one God, the Father Almighty, who made the heaven, and the earth, and the seas, and all that is in them, and in one Christ Jesus, the Son of God, who was made flesh for our salvation, and in the Holy Spirit, who through the prophets proclaimed the dispensations of God — the comings, the birth of a virgin, the suffering, the resurrection from the dead, and the bodily reception into the heavens of the beloved, Christ Jesus our Lord, and his coming from the heavens in the glory of the Father "to sum up all things" [cf. Eph. 1:10], and to raise up all flesh, that is, the whole human race, so that every knee may bow, of things in heaven and on earth and under the earth, to Christ Jesus our Lord and God and Savior and King, according to the pleasure of the invisible Father, and every tongue may confess him [cf. Phil. 2:10-11], and that he may execute righteous judgment on all. The spiritual powers of wickedness [cf. Eph. 6:12], and the angels who transgressed and fell into apostasy, and the godless and wicked and lawless and blasphemers among men he will send into the eternal fire. But to the righteous and holy, and those who have kept his commandments and remained in his love, some from the beginning [of life] and some since their repentance, he will by his grace give life incorrupt, and will clothe them with eternal glory.[38]

Irenaeus's version of the rule of faith is similar to what others give, although he is the only one who says that Christ "sums up all things," which fits nicely his theological understanding of "recapitulation."[39] In fact, other early Fathers also incorporate short phrases into their statements of the rule, in each case construing it in accordance with their own distinctive theological beliefs. Thus, Tertullian alone states that Christ "preached a new law." Hippolytus uniquely describes Christ as partaking of a "heavenly part" and an "earthly part." Origen is the only one to say that the rule includes belief in free will and that Scripture has two meanings, the second of which can only be understood through the aid of the Holy Spirit. Since these early Christian figures represent considerable geographical diversity, it is very likely that the basic elements of the rule of faith that they all hold in common do indeed go back to the earliest apostolic summary of Christian teaching, perhaps used in connection with baptism.

Irenaeus makes the point that even "barbarians" who do not have written Scripture believed the gospel on the basis of apostolic tradition as summarized in the rule of faith. Furthermore, Irenaeus claims that these "barbarians" are able to recognize true Christianity over against the heresies of Marcion and Valentinus (a "Gnostic") on the basis of this apostolic tradition alone, even apart from Scripture.[40] For Irenaeus, tradition plays a role alongside Scripture in the discernment of Christian truth. In order to understand this role, two important observations must be made about Scripture and the rule of faith in Irenaeus.

First, Irenaeus firmly believes that the Scriptures in their natural sense support his position. While he does concede that the Old Testament contains some parables and allegories that can be twisted into heretical meanings,[41] he nevertheless insists that the Scriptures read in their natural order confirm Christian truth. Irenaeus does not argue that Scripture could theoretically be read in different ways and that only tradition can settle which is correct. Rather, the heretics twist the Scriptures by taking passages out of context and weaving new discourses out of the words of the text.[42]

Irenaeus likens the heretics' use of Scripture to the poetic form known as the *cento*. When writing a *cento*, the poet took various lines out of a famous poem and pieced them together in a new order so that a whole new story was created out of the bits and pieces of the original poem. Irenaeus gives an example of a *cento* with a new storyline constructed out of fragments from the *Iliad* and the *Odyssey*.[43] As he emphasizes, no one who knows the actual text of Homer would be fooled into thinking that the *cento* is really saying the same thing as the original poem. It might mislead one who does not know the poems in their original form, but if one were simply to put the verses back into their context in Homer and read the poems of Homer on their own, the truth would come easily to light.

This is Irenaeus's view of how the heretics read Scripture. They have taken phrases out of the Gospels and used them to construct a detailed mythology with multiple levels of divine beings, with names such as "Wisdom" and "Logos."[44] This might sound scriptural to someone who does not know the story, but if we simply read through the Gospel texts in the right order, or even just recite the rule of faith, the actual Gospel becomes clear. In sum, the rule is an important touchstone for the church's teaching, but Irenaeus does not think the Gospel texts are unclear or that the rule is needed as a guide for interpretation. As Irenaeus sees it, the Gospel texts are sufficiently clear provided they are read in their natural order.

Second, the content of the rule of faith is quite simple, especially in comparison with later creedal formulations. The beginning statement has a "Trinitarian" framework ("God, the Father . . . Christ Jesus . . . Holy Spirit"), but it does not address in any detail the particularities of how the three relate to one another. The focus of the rule is the birth, death, resurrection, and return of Jesus and the final judgment. Nothing in the rule of faith as handed down by the apostles addressed the major doctrinal controversies of the fourth and fifth centuries. While it is certainly believable that the rule of faith helped Christians avoid the false teachings of Marcionites and Valentinians, the content of the rule would not provide much guidance in sorting out the interpretation of most passages in Scripture, except that it probably helped confirm some kind of Christological reading of the Old Testament. The rule was primarily an ecumenical statement of basic Christianity.

For Irenaeus, true Christian tradition was made public around the world in all the churches that could trace their episcopal lines back to the apostles. The apostles did not give secret teachings to a select few. Rather, they bequeathed to the churches their writings and also the tradition of their teachings, that is, the rule of faith.[45] It was a particular point of emphasis for Irenaeus that both the written testimonies of the Gospels and the rule of faith agreed with each other in support of true Christian doctrine. He did not believe that Scripture, when read in its natural order and context, might be so unclear as to require tradition to serve as an arbiter between conflicting interpretations.

In Augustine, on the other hand, we find explicit statements to the effect that tradition should serve as arbiter between competing interpretations. According to Augustine, the interpretation of Scripture should be guided by rules both positively and negatively. The positive guidance tells us what we should look for in Scripture, and the negative guidance tells us what we must not find there. Broad theological ideas and the rule of faith play a role in Augustine's "ruled" exegesis. Augustine clearly believes that apart from these guidelines it would be easy to draw wrong conclusions from Scripture.

In terms of broad theological ideas, Augustine sets forth the general rule that anything in Scripture that does not relate to good morals or true faith should be interpreted figuratively so that it does teach these things.[46] In an early work on Genesis written against the Manichees, Augustine says the following to justify his figurative reading of Genesis 2–3: "If anyone wanted to take everything that was said according to the letter, that is, to understand it exactly as the letter sounds, and could avoid blasphemies and explain everything in harmony with the Catholic faith, we should not only bear him no hostility, but regard him as a leading and highly praiseworthy interpreter."[47] In later works Augustine changes his mind about the early chapters of Genesis, deciding that they can in fact be interpreted safely at the literal level. But his general principle of interpretation did not change.[48] All Scripture must teach right morals and faith.

Augustine also states that any correct interpretation of Scripture will necessarily build up love for God and one's neighbor. If readers of Scripture miss the point of the human writer but their interpretation promotes love of God and neighbor, they are misled but not lying.[49] Augustine appears unsure how serious an error it is to miss the human writer's intention. In one passage, Augustine likens this to someone who leaves a path by mistake but still manages to reach the proper destination. This does no immediate harm, but Augustine advises that it is better to stay on the path. If interpreters make a habit of missing the human writer's point, they run the risk of ultimately going astray.[50] Elsewhere, however, Augustine suggests that even if an interpreter carves out a meaning different from what the writer meant, as long as this meaning is derived from other passages of Scripture and does not run counter to the faith, it is acceptable. Perhaps the human writer intended this meaning, too; but in any case, the Spirit of God certainly planned that this newly carved meaning would present itself to the reader.[51] In the earlier statement Augustine offers a warning to interpreters who make a habit of missing the human writer's intention. But in the later statement the writer's point is potentially meaningful, but ultimately not necessary.

A clear example of how the rule of faith functions in Augustine's scriptural interpretation is his treatment in *On Christian Teaching* of expressions that are ambiguous in their literal sense. In the ancient world, the reading aloud of a text constituted an act of interpretation. The reader had to identify which word was intended in the case of words that looked alike but were pronounced differently (an example in English: "lead" the verb versus "lead" the element). Also, readers indicated the proper punctuation of the text through pauses and emphasis, and they indicated through tone whether a sentence was a statement, a question, or an exclamation of surprise or fear.[52] When dealing with passages that are ambiguous in these ways, Augustine advises, "We must first of all make sure that we have not punctuated or articulated the passage incorrectly. Once close consideration has revealed that it is uncertain how a passage should be punctuated and articulated, we must consult the rule of faith, as it is perceived through the plainer passages of the scriptures and the authority of the church."[53] If it is determined that more than one possible sense agrees with the rule of faith, "then it remains to consult the context — the preceding and following passages, which surround the ambiguity — in order to determine which of the several meanings that suggest themselves is supported by it, and which one lends itself to acceptable combinations with it."[54] To be sure, Augustine encourages scholarly procedures in literal biblical interpretation; for example, he shows how going back to the original Greek can clear up linguistic ambiguities in the New Testament.[55] But for Augustine, the rule of faith is the final arbiter of what Scripture may be taken to mean.[56] As he states in his exposition of Psalm 75:7-8: "Some other person may produce a better interpretation, for the obscurity of the scriptures is such that a passage scarcely ever yields a single meaning only. But whatever interpretation emerges, it must conform to the rule of faith."[57]

Augustine believed that the teachings of Scripture must agree with a recognized authority. As noted above, this authority is found in "the plainer passages of the scriptures" and in "the authority of the church." Augustine referred to the church's teaching as the "rule of faith" or the "Catholic faith." The term "Catholic faith" had particular relevance for Augustine after his dispute with the Donatists, a schismatic Christian group in Augustine's North Africa that broke away from fellowship with the church worldwide (the Latin *catholicus* means "universal, relating to all"). In light of how important this concept was for Augustine's interpretation of Scripture, we must ask: What did Augustine mean by the "rule of faith" or the "Catholic faith"?

The concept of the rule of faith receives broader application in Augustine than it did in Irenaeus. Whereas Irenaeus could recount the essentially fixed content of the rule as handed down from the apostles, Augustine seems to apply the phrase "rule of faith" to his own sense of what Scripture teaches and his church affirms. Thus, he applies the term to his own explanation of the Trinity as expounded through Matthew 28:19; Deuteronomy 6:4; Galatians 4:4; and John 15:26.[58] Augustine also argues for his own particular view of original sin by saying that to deny his view is to deny the rule of faith.[59] In the controversy between the Donatists and Augustine, the Donatists cited Cyprian in support of their position. Augustine counters by stating that the authority of Peter and Paul in Galatians is greater than that of Cyprian, and that Cyprian's view does not agree with the rule of faith that the church later adopted.[60] This shows that Augustine was himself aware that the rule of faith, as he used the term, could develop over time.[61] At the beginning of an early, unfinished literal commentary on Genesis, Augustine sets forth the content of the Catholic faith as a guide for what may and may not be said about Genesis. The content that Augustine gives for the Catholic faith is his own exposition of a version of the Apostles' Creed known from Milan, where he was baptized.[62] Augustine claims this to be the universal teaching of the church. For Augustine, the authority of the church was not found in a primitive statement of belief handed down from the apostles but in the core teachings of the church in Augustine's day, as he knew and interpreted these teachings.

The idea that Scripture's message must agree with a recognized external authority has been extremely important but also problematic in the history of the church. In the earliest centuries, the rule of faith helped Christians identify the basic message of the churches founded by the apostles. As a principle of interpretation, it probably encouraged the belief that Christians should see Christ proclaimed in all the Scriptures, including the Old Testament. But as time went on and the teachings of the churches developed, appealing to a particular "rule of faith" to solve interpretive difficulties became more complicated. Thus, the teaching of the Latin-speaking churches in Augustine's day went beyond what was taught in the second century. What is more, the "Catholic faith" known to Augustine was not precisely the same as what was taught at that time in Greek, Coptic, Syriac, or Ethiopic churches. By the fifth century, there was no single rule that represented what all Christians everywhere believed. To make the rule of faith the standard for biblical interpretation could therefore have the effect of simply reinforcing the particular beliefs of the interpreter's own church context.

The potential role of creedal statements in biblical interpretation continues to be an important topic in Christian theology. On the positive side, "ruled" reading encourages Christians to interpret Scripture theologically in a distinctively Christian way. But on the negative side, such reading can also promote provincial narrowness and dogmatism. Christians in the modern world have a wide variety of perspectives on these issues. In my view, church traditions construed broadly are essential conversation partners and guides for understanding Scripture, but the evolving and diverse nature of church traditions makes it undesirable to use the teaching of any given church as the final arbiter in scriptural interpretation.

20. Scripture's Teaching Must Be Worthy of God

As early as the sixth century BCE, Greek philosophers criticized the picture of the gods presented in traditional myths. Xenophanes explained the problem clearly: "Homer and Hesiod have attributed to the gods all sorts of things which are matters of reproach and censure among men: theft, adultery, and mutual deceit."[63] One possible response would have been to reject traditional myths altogether on the grounds that they describe divine beings in a manner unworthy of the gods. But another approach was to read these myths allegorically, in order to discover what philosophical truths they might contain.[64] Theagenes of Rhegium in the sixth century BCE used allegory to explain the battle between the gods in *Iliad* 20, which otherwise presented an "unsuitable" view of the gods.[65] In the early second century CE, a philosopher named Heraclitus wrote a treatise called *Homeric Problems,* in which he gave philosophical explanations for various passages in Homer. Heraclitus justified his procedure in the opening lines of the treatise: "It is a weighty and damaging charge that heaven brings against Homer for his disrespect for the divine. If he meant nothing allegorically, he was impious through and through, and sacrilegious fables, loaded with blasphemous folly, run riot through both epics."[66] In defense of these ancient allegorists, it can hardly be doubted that Greek myths convey symbolic meanings. The ancients who read these myths symbolically were certainly justified in their expectations. At the same time, the allegorical approach had two potential pitfalls: first, it could allow philosophers to read doctrines into the early myths that did not fit well with the original symbolism; and second, it could obscure the fact that development had taken place in how people conceptualized the gods.

The portrayal of God in the Bible is less "human" than the depictions of figures such as Zeus and Poseidon in the *Iliad*. The extent and type of material that might be deemed unworthy of the deity is not the same. Nevertheless, the God of the Old Testament does express a wide array of human emotions, such as anger, regret, and compassion. He is also described as having human body parts, such as eyes, hands, and even a back (see Exod. 33:23). When ancient Jews and Christians read their Scriptures, they sometimes felt the need to explain how the human characteristics of God as described in the text fit with the true nature of the divinity. A key principle that guided their thinking on this topic was that anything genuinely taught about God in Scripture must be worthy of God.

Philo of Alexandria shows how a philosophically minded reader of the Bible might deal with depictions of God that seem less than divine. When Philo reads in Genesis 2:8 that God planted a garden in Eden, he interprets this to mean that God "plants" earthly excellence for the sake of mortals, since God fills all things and does not need a place to live; indeed, "Far be it from man's reasoning to be the victim of so great impiety as to suppose that God tills the soil and plants pleasances."[67] To interpret God's activity in this text literally would be "impiety."[68] In Genesis 8:21 it says that God "smelled the pleasing aroma," which Philo says means simply that God "accepted" the offering, since God does not possess human form (Greek *anthrōpomorphos*) and therefore has no nostrils and does not literally "smell" anything.[69] The statement in Genesis 6:7 that God is "sorry" (or "regrets") prompts Philo to remind his readers that there is no greater impiety than to suggest that the unchangeable God ever changes his mind.[70] In order to explain such phenomena in Scripture, Philo juxtaposes the phrase "God is not a man" from Numbers 23:19 with the phrase "as a man disciples his son" from Deuteronomy 8:5. Philo concludes that, while in reality God's nature is not like that of a human being, he can nevertheless be described in human terms in order to instruct humans.[71] These comments of Philo embody three important principles also found in the Church Fathers: (1) descriptions of God that are too human-like are impious if taken literally, (2) Scripture often describes God figuratively as if in human form ("anthropomorphically"), and (3) God possesses attributes that cannot be reconciled with the literal sense of certain texts.[72]

Christians began dealing with these issues in response to criticisms leveled by "heretics" against the God of the Old Testament. Such criticisms seem to underlie the argument presented in the *Pseudo-Clementine Romance* that the only true statements about God in Scripture are those that present God as good.[73] In response to "heretics" who misrepresent Scripture, Clement of Alexandria urged that we compare Scripture with Scripture and consider "what is perfectly fitting and appropriate to the Lord and Almighty God."[74] Moreover, he described those who reject the Lord as people "who do not quote or deliver the Scriptures in a manner worthy of God and of the Lord."[75] These general ideas about interpreting Scripture in a manner worthy of God were taken up by Origen and turned into a full hermeneutical principle.

Origen was the first early Christian to deal systematically with the whole Old Testament, and he found numerous occasions on which to invoke the principle that Scripture must be worthy of God. According to Origen, God inspired Scripture so that secret truths might be revealed through stories about wars and various laws. In some cases, even the simple, bodily meaning of Scripture is beneficial for common readers. But in other cases, the usefulness of Scripture is not immediately evident. In such situations, we must recognize that "the Word of God has arranged for certain stumbling blocks, as it were, and hindrances and impossibilities to be inserted in the midst of the law and the history." These stumbling blocks were recorded so that inquiring readers might examine Scripture more carefully and find "a meaning worthy of God."[76] As the first Christian to preach through Old Testament books such as Leviticus, Numbers, Joshua, and Judges, Origen had no Christian predecessors with whom he could interact. As a result, he was forced to rely on other texts of Scripture, his own Christian life experience, and reasoned judgment in deciding what the Spirit intended to teach Christians through these texts.

The wars reported in Joshua forced Origen on several occasions to search for a meaning worthy of God. For example, according to Joshua 8 Israel killed everyone in the city of Ai, "until there was left none that survived or escaped" (v. 22). The text makes clear that every human was killed, including women (vv. 23-29). Origen states near the beginning of his homily, "You ought to know that those things that are read are indeed worthy of the Holy Spirit, but in order to explain them we need the grace of the Holy Spirit."[77] Origen interprets "Ai" as "chaos,"[78] which was defeated by Jesus (= Joshua), who triumphed over the devil on the cross, as symbolized by the hanging of the king of Ai from a tree (v. 29). Only such a reading of this action is worthy of the pen of the Holy Spirit.[79] As for the Israelites killing everyone and leaving no survivors, Origen criticizes those who believe that holy persons would do such a thing. The literal sense, according to Origen, would make people cruel and thirst for human blood. The mystical meaning of this text is that we must all destroy the demons within us, allowing none to remain.[80] All holy persons must kill the inhabitants of Ai. Likewise, all Christians must strive to defeat "Hebron" (Josh. 10:23), which means "union,"[81] by destroying the union between our soul and the devil.[82] Origen gives the following general advice:

> You will read in the Holy Scriptures about the battles of the just ones, about the slaughter and carnage of murderers, and the saints spare none of their deeply rooted enemies. If they do spare them, they are even charged with sin, just as Saul was charged because he had preserved the life of Agag king of Amalek.[83] You should understand the wars of the just by the method I set forth above, that these wars are waged by them against sin.[84]

As far as Origen is concerned, God's intention in inspiring these accounts is to encourage his followers to fight against the sin within us.[85]

Origen also made important observations about the nature of scriptural language about God. In his *Homilies on Jeremiah,* Origen addresses a number of difficult expressions in Scripture, such as God's "relenting" of doing something (Jer. 18:10), God's hope that "perhaps" something will happen (36:3), and God's deceiving Jeremiah (20:7). In each case, Origen's goal is to find an interpretation that is "worthy of God."[86] Origen appeals to the idea of "anthropomorphism," and he speaks of God "condescending" to us. Just like Philo, Origen plays on the tension between Numbers 23:19 ("God is not a man") and Deuteronomy 8:5 ("as a man disciples his son").[87] But his most interesting comment comes when he compares scriptural language about God to homonyms in human speech. Homonyms are words that share the same spelling and sound but have different meanings (in English, the "bank" of a river over against a financial "bank"). Although these words look and sound alike, they have different meanings. As Origen explains, the same is true for words such as "regret" or "wrath" with reference to God. Even if we use the same words to describe human "wrath" or "regret," these words mean something different when applied to God.[88] Origen believes that scriptural words that describe God take on unique, divinely appropriate significations.

God's moral superiority over humans was a foundational principle for Origen. In his view, people who interpret all biblical texts literally end up making impious assertions about God. Origen offers the following criticism of scriptural literalists: "Moreover, even the simpler of those who claim to belong to the Church, while believing indeed that there is none greater than the Creator, in which they are right, yet believe such things about him as would not be believed of the most savage and unjust men."[89] If killing every person in a city is morally reprehensible when a human does it, then such an action cannot be ascribed to God.[90] For Origen, God is not only different from humanity but also morally perfect in a way recognizable to human sensibilities.

Origen's commentaries were widely read and appreciated by later Christian commentators. Even those who criticized his speculative theology adopted many of his principles for interpreting the Old Testament. The impact of Philo and other Hellenistic Jewish writers was also significant in dealing with "human" depictions of God in Scripture.

On the question of whether or not God has a "hand" (see Exod. 13:9: "with a strong hand the Lord has brought you out of Egypt"), Eusebius of Caesarea quotes the early Jewish philosopher Aristobulus, who says that readers must "hold fast the fitting conception of God" and be careful not to "fall off into the idea of a fabulous anthropomorphic conception." They must not take the "hand of the Lord" literally but recognize that it represents God's power.[91] On Genesis 1:4, Didymus the Blind tells his readers that they should understand "God saw the light" in a manner worthy of God.[92] Gregory of Nyssa interprets the death of Egypt's firstborn in Exodus 12:29 allegorically, stating, "How could a concept worthy of God be preserved in the description of what happened if one looked only at the history? The Egyptian acts unjustly, and in his place is punished his newborn child, who in his infancy cannot discern what is good and what is not."[93] Basil the Great and Gregory of Nazianzus quote several passages from Origen in their *Philocalia* where Origen reconciles the concept of free will with the hardening of Pharaoh's heart in Exodus.[94] The underlying concern of these passages is that "it is unworthy of God to bring about the hardening of any man's heart."[95] Numerous examples of this kind can be given, especially from writers known to have read Origen or Philo.

Concern to interpret Scripture in a manner worthy of God is also evident in Antiochene commentators. John Chrysostom often describes God's strategy of depicting the divine in a human-like way as "condescension" *(synkatabasis)*.[96] Chrysostom says the following about Genesis 2:21, "God . . . took one of his ribs":

Notice the condescension of Sacred Scripture in the words employed with our limitations in mind: "God took one of his ribs," the text says. Don't take the words in human fashion; rather, interpret the concreteness of the expressions from the viewpoint of human limitations.[97] You see, if he had not used these words, how would we have been able to gain knowledge of these mysteries which defy description? Let us therefore not remain at the level of the words alone, but let us understand everything in a manner proper to God because applied to God. That phrase, "He took," after all, and other such are spoken with our limitations in mind.[98]

If the account of God making the woman out of the man's rib seems too commonplace for the deity, we must keep in mind that God communicates with us in this way for our benefit. Our part is to recognize God's gracious condescension to our human limitations, and to interpret the text in a manner proper to God, seeking to know what mystery it teaches.

Theodoret of Cyrus is another Antiochene who shows particular care not to take human-like language about God in Scripture too literally. Regarding the phrase in Jeremiah 4:28, "I shall not relent," Theodoret warns that we should not take this to suggest that God could ever "relent," since "The phrase 'I shall not relent' is anthropomorphic, the divinity being immune to passion, and it has the meaning, I thought fit to exact retribution."[99] Again, Jeremiah 9:9 says, "And shall not my soul take vengeance on a nation such as this?" Theodoret comments, "He used the phrase 'my soul' in human fashion: the divine is not composed of body and soul, being simple, lacking composition and form. His words are adjusted to our capacity to receive."[100] In addition to Theodoret's use of the term "anthropomorphism" and his explanation that God adjusts his communication to us to match our capacity to receive, it is notable that Theodoret warns the reader not to interpret the text in such a way that it threatens the immutability or simple nature of God. For Theodoret, these are attributes that necessarily belong to God.

Examples similar to these could be offered from the writings of Latin Church Fathers. I will wrap up this discussion with a comment from Augustine. Like many others, Augustine insists that we must understand God's body parts as his various capacities, and he often points out the inappropriateness of taking scriptural language about God too literally.[101] As for moral behavior, Augustine says, "Any harsh or even cruel word or deed attributed to God or his saints that is found in the holy scriptures applies to the destruction of the realm of lust."[102] In a manner similar to Origen, Augustine asserts that nothing morally unworthy of God should be taken literally in Scripture.

The basic concern for the Christian interpreters discussed in this section was that human-like qualities ascribed to God in Scripture should not be interpreted as teaching anything contrary to the loftiest conceptions of God. We may ask: Where did these lofty conceptions come from? To some degree, these conceptions came to Christian readers through the teachings of the New Testament and through the Greek philosophical tradition. This is part of the truth, and to recognize it is to acknowledge the progressive nature of scriptural revelation and also the efficacy of moral and theological reasoning. But there is more to be said. Another part of the truth is that Christian theological conceptions developed substantially out of Old Testament texts, and values found in the Old Testament strongly shaped later Christian ideas. So it is not accurate to say that Christians simply imposed these later categories on the Old Testament. Besides, it is simplistic and uncharitable to assume that scriptural writers intended all their accounts to be taken literally in the first place. Did Old Testament writers really believe that God had a physical arm and back, when even the highest heavens cannot contain God (1 Kgs. 8:27)? It is better to assume that Old Testament writers already connected abstract ideas with the concrete images they used. Christian readers who inherited the biblical tradition relied on certain parts of Scripture to guide them in interpreting other parts. These interpreters sought to evaluate and organize the ideas presented to them in Scripture, with the goal of more precisely defining the nature of the deity. Some anachronism naturally came into play, but the theological process dealt substantially with Scripture's imagery and was guided by recognizable principles.

Modern Christians with strong historical sensibilities are quick to caution against ascribing later Christian theological ideas to the human writers of the Old Testament. Understanding the human author's discourse is valuable, and to appreciate the Old Testament at this level we must avoid anachronism. Yet, when we come to decide what these texts teach us about God, it is right to look at the whole of Scripture and to assess the biblical witness through prayer and reason and with the instruction of our traditions and communities. This may point us toward theological conclusions that stay close to the historical sense but are not identical with it. For example, many Christians today are troubled by the divine commands in the Old Testament to destroy whole populations of people through warfare. The question is not simply one of practical ethics, since Christians can always say that the Sermon on the Mount overrides the Old Testament as a contemporary ethical guide. The question has to do with the doctrine of

God: Did the same God who condemned the shedding of innocent blood (e.g., Jer. 7:1-11), required compassion for the vulnerable (e.g., Exod. 22:21-27), and revealed himself supremely in Jesus also command the Israelites to kill whole groups of people, including women and children? It is theologically appropriate for Christians not to believe that God gave such commands. Some Christians argue that God did not command such actions and that the Israelites did not do them, but that the language in Scripture that suggests otherwise is simply exaggeration and rhetoric common to the ancient Near East.[103] Another approach is to suggest that, even if Israel performed such actions, God did not command them, and the scriptural texts in question reveal that biblical writers folded their own military practices into the divine teaching that instructed Israel to remain absolutely separate from wicked Canaanite moral and religious customs. If this explanation were correct, these texts within the context of all Scripture truthfully point to God's fierce opposition to human evil. In any case, the question has to do with the doctrine of God, and therefore ultimately must be settled at the theological level. The complexities of this kind of theological reasoning are such that no individual's perception of what Scripture teaches on a given topic can serve as the final authority for what every Christian should believe on that topic. Still, Christians must work through biblical texts in this way in order to grasp God's teaching in Scripture.

The Church Fathers believed that God inspired Scripture for the purpose of instruction, and they naturally expected everything taught by the Spirit of God in Scripture to be true. The inner coherence of Scripture's message was a logical entailment of this way of thinking. Moreover, it made sense to assume that what Scripture teaches will agree with other reliable sources of truth. These other sources included non-scriptural traditions handed down from the apostles, the perceived consensus of the church in one's own time, and the highest ideals of our religious sensibilities. None of the Church Fathers seriously questioned the truthfulness of Scripture. But as we have seen throughout this study, the question of how to interpret Scripture so as to arrive at the truth was a complex matter.

CHAPTER SEVEN

Conclusions

Variety and Difference

Based on the above survey of early Christian beliefs about biblical inspiration, two important observations can be made: first, a variety of ideas existed in antiquity regarding what the divine inspiration of Scripture entailed and how to understand those entailments; and second, some notions associated with inspiration in antiquity are no longer fully plausible from a modern standpoint. The significance of these two observations must be spelled out before moving on to discuss the relevance of ancient Christian thinking about inspiration for today.

First, the fact that so many different ideas came to be associated with the concept of inspiration shows that belief in the inspiration of Scripture is not simply an "up" or "down" issue. All the early Christians discussed in this book could justly be described as having a "high" view of biblical inspiration, but their beliefs varied as to the precise impact of inspiration on Scripture. In some instances, apparently significant beliefs stood in conflict with one another; for example, Augustine was concerned that Jerome's interpretation of the confrontation between Paul and Peter in Galatians violated the principle that Scripture does not deceive, whereas Jerome thought that Augustine's interpretation left Scripture open to the charge of internal contradiction. This illustrates how challenging it can be to determine what conceptions of inspiration best capture Christian beliefs about Scripture. The church today can learn an important lesson from this. The greatest benefit for the church in its understanding of Scripture will be gained by open discussion of inspiration grounded in faith and learning, which seeks to describe with ever greater clarity the nature of inspired Scripture. Such discussion does more good for the church than simply affirming the truthfulness of Scripture in abstract. Just as many in the church today are, within certain limits, comfortable disagreeing with fellow Christians on such an important topic as the Lord's Supper, so also Christians today can agree to disagree on the precise implications of biblical inspiration. Charitable disagreement and discussion can significantly increase the understanding that most Christians in the pews have of this important doctrine.

Second, the diversity of early Christian thinking about inspiration and the gap between ancient and modern perspectives make it impossible for anyone today to claim absolute continuity with the early church. As noted in the Introduction, early Christian conceptions of inspiration took shape within the context of early Jewish and Greco-Roman ideas about sacred texts. In view of the contextual nature of early Christian ideas about Scripture, it is perfectly understandable that Christians in the contemporary world have felt free and even obligated to recast the essential elements of inspiration into modern (or post-modern) garb. But once we have done this recasting, it is important for the sake of charity that we acknowledge how we differ from the great authorities of the past. For example, some contemporary Christians may share Origen's belief in the theological unity of Scripture, but if they do not endorse Origen's approach to allegorical interpretation, then they are in continuity with his belief in unity but in discontinuity with his belief in allegory. As another example, some today may share Augustine's belief that all Scripture points to Christ, but if they do not share his belief in the hidden significance of scriptural details (such as numerals), then their relationship to Augustine's thought is one of both continuity and discontinuity. It is highly problematic to claim to adhere to the "traditional" view on inspiration, when in fact one is only adhering to a select portion of some ancient viewpoint. In particular, it is not valid to lay claim to an ancient belief (such as Scripture's theological unity), while at the same time rejecting the hermeneutical basis of that belief (namely, that Scripture has a spiritual sense). No point of doctrine related to inspiration can be regarded as settled by tradition when only part of the traditional perspective is in view. Of course, I do not see any other way to proceed except to say that some traditional ideas are still enduring and others should be left in the past; but if this is so, then theological reflection on inspiration cannot simply be an affirmation of the "traditional" view but must consist of cogent arguments for how the church can best explain biblical inspiration today.[1]

There is a long tradition in the church of people appealing to traditional sources for their own purposes while concealing the points where they are not in harmony with those sources. In this regard I hope that this book is not traditional. I believe that acknowledging both our similarities *and* our differences from the past gives us the greatest opportunity to learn the right lessons from our traditions. This kind of honesty promotes charity, since we are recognizing that no one has a monopoly on the Christian tradition. It also promotes critical reflection on the past and the present, which helps us to see truth more clearly.

Continuity and Meaningfulness

In order to be faithful to Scripture and mindful of Christian tradition, it is important to identify some of the essential beliefs about inspiration from the early church that continue to impress themselves upon modern believers. Of course, certain aspects of ancient thinking about scriptural inspiration are best left in the past. For example, the search for mystical meanings in virtually all proper names in Scripture, the exposition of trivial details, and the practice among some interpreters of ignoring the context of the human writer are all dimensions of ancient interpretation that do not work.[2] Yet, the Church Fathers have much to teach us about how Scripture can and should be meaningful for Christians. Above all, ancient Christian thinking about inspiration shows us that we must interpret Scripture in light of its divine purpose: to guide people in knowing and following God.

The continuing relevance of ancient biblical interpretation is most obvious where Church Fathers made significant use of the *ad litteram/iuxta historiam* sense, as is commonly found among Antiochenes such as Theodoret and John Chrysostom, but also among many others. Qualities found in these readers that connect with modern emphases include concern for what the words of Scripture would have meant in their original contexts, attention to the logical flow and main themes of literary compositions, and interest in what we call literary genre. At its best, modern biblical studies attempts to understand biblical literature along these lines.[3] Focus on the *ad litteram* sense is what most distinctively characterizes modern biblical studies, both in the academy and in the church. I think the attention that has been paid to the contextual and literary meaning of Scripture has been beneficial for modern Christians. What is in view is not taking everything "literally" in the Bible, but rather paying attention to the text's own discourse at the human level. Each biblical text has something to contribute to the theological message of Scripture, and attention to the *ad litteram* sense allows for the voice of each biblical text to be heard. Respect for the "surface meaning" of biblical texts keeps us from simply reading any content we like onto the texts. In order to be challenged by Scripture, we must be in genuine contact with what biblical texts actually said. This is best accomplished when *ad litteram* interpretation is alive and well. It is a positive state of affairs, therefore, that the modern church has picked up and developed the ancient Christian interest in the *ad litteram/iuxta historiam* sense of Scripture.

Nevertheless, the almost exclusive focus on the *ad litteram* sense of Scripture in much modern Christianity is problematic. Research into the *ad litteram* sense alone cannot uncover the contemporary significance of Scripture. The results of "literal" biblical exegesis can only be past-tense claims, such as, "This is what Jeremiah said to the Judeans," or "This is what Peter said to the first-century church." But how is the historical intention of Jeremiah's injunction to keep the Sabbath (Jer. 17:19-27) to be applied today? How are we to apply Peter's instructions (e.g., 1 Pet. 2:13–3:7) today if we live in a culture without an emperor and with different conceptions and laws regarding slavery? Furthermore, for many scriptural texts — for example, narratives such as Judges or Acts — it is unclear whether *ad litteram* exegesis can recover even the writer's intended "message" for the original audience. The New Testament renders problematic the idea that Old Testament laws can apply to Christians today in their historical sense, and it is doubtful that New Testament perspectives on topics such as spiritual gifts (e.g., 1 Cor. 12:31; 14:1), jewelry (e.g., 1 Pet. 3:3; 1 Tim. 2:9), and hairstyles (e.g., 1 Cor. 11:14-15) can be appropriated today without some theological translation. Finally, it is impossible based on strictly "literal" exegesis of the Old Testament to explain from the Old Testament that Jesus was the Christ and that he rose from the dead on the third day (see Acts 18:28; 1 Cor. 15:4). Deeper reflection is obviously needed on how we can best move beyond the *ad litteram* sense to a legitimate modern Christian reading of all Scripture.

In my view, the church today suffers from two major problems that flow from the overriding emphasis in modern times on "literal" exegesis: first, some interpreters focus so much on exegesis that they neglect the contemporary meaningfulness of Scripture, leaving Christian readers and hearers unclear as to why they should be concerned about Scripture at all; and second, many modern teachers of Scripture arbitrarily devise their own (sometimes idiosyncratic) applications of biblical texts and impose them on others as if with divine authority, supported by historical exegesis but no clear explanation as to how the contemporary significance was determined.[4] If Scripture is to speak credibly to contemporary Christians, the exposition of Scripture must move beyond simply recounting the *ad litteram* sense toward reasoned theological interpretation set forth with charity. Good biblical interpretation for the church is closely connected to the human discourse of biblical texts, but the message of Scripture is not always equivalent to the intention of its human writer. Insights from the early church can be particularly helpful in our search to discover Scripture's theological message.

Therefore, although it is often not obvious to modern Christians, we have much to learn from the Church Fathers about how to interpret Scripture beyond the "literal" level. As stated above, commitment to biblical inspiration is not an "up" or "down" affair, and no one today believes everything that early Christians believed about Scripture. The challenge is to identify the most insightful dimensions of early Christian thought and to explain how these dimensions continue to be significant. Christians will naturally differ to some degree in identifying these key insights. Without trying to be exhaustive, I will offer a few suggestions as to how early Christian notions of divine inspiration can help Christians today perceive the meaningfulness of Scripture.

To begin, the ancient belief that God intended Scripture for religious instruction, training in righteousness, and preparation for good works is fundamental to our understanding of what we should look for in Scripture (see, e.g., 2 Tim. 3:16-17; 1 Cor. 10:11; Rom. 15:4). Believing that what we learn as true from Scripture will not contradict any genuine truth derived from secular learning can encourage healthy theological dialogue between scriptural theology and the natural and social sciences. The idea that Scripture solves every problem that we put to it, which can lead to absurd interpretations if taken to an extreme, can also be construed more moderately as an encouragement for Christians to read Scripture and look for values, stories, and images that they can use to help them in any situation in life. Even granting the diversity of perspectives found in the Bible, a nuanced conception of the unity and internal harmony of Scripture can keep Christians from discarding certain biblical texts in favor of others, challenging them to wrestle with every text to see what lesson it has to teach. In addition, the belief that Scripture has multiple senses, although not necessarily viable in the thoroughly supernatural way imagined by some early Christians, is a helpful reminder that even while a scriptural text is literally talking about one thing, it can also be talking about something else (*allēgoreō*, "speak about something other"). Thus, Genesis 22 is a story about God, Abraham, and Isaac but can also be described as a story about trust. The capacity of stories and poems to be about something beyond the "literal" sense is basic to their enduring significance. When construed with proper nuance, many ancient perspectives on inspiration turn out to be quite insightful.

Four ideas in particular derived from ancient thinking about inspiration deserve special mention because of their importance for Christian biblical interpretation. The first idea draws from a number of general categories to focus on the figure of Jesus. Whether Scripture was regarded as predicting Jesus in the future, or talking about Jesus through a "higher" sense, or even speaking in the voice of Jesus, early Christians used many ancient notions about sacred texts to envision Jesus as the center of scriptural interpretation. Of course, particularly at the level of the human discourse of Old Testament texts, much of what the early church thought about Jesus as the subject of Scripture cannot be argued in precisely the same way today. But it remains a key Christian belief that Old Testament stories, imagery, and aspirations are summed up in Jesus, and that the example and teachings of Jesus serve as a lens through which all interpretations of Scripture must pass; in this regard, the injunctions to love God and one's neighbor come prominently to mind. Thus, the early church can challenge the modern church to see connections between the subject matter of all scriptural texts and Jesus, and also to interpret the meaningfulness of all scriptural texts through the lens of Jesus' mission and teachings.

Second, the idea that proper interpretation of Scripture takes place within the church points to the necessity of community and traditions in discovering the meaningfulness of Scripture. Authoritative texts survive and maintain their vitality through communities that recognize their authority and continue to reinterpret their significance. As with both the Bible and the U.S. Constitution, interpretive communities develop traditions and precedents that guide later interpreters who will have to reapply the authoritative texts in new situations. Unlike the U.S. Constitution, however, Christian Scripture is preserved in more than one community, and the nature of leadership and authority in these communities varies. Yet it is surely wise to say that Christian interpreters should pay respectful attention to traditions of scriptural interpretation and also to the voices of those within their Christian communities who offer counsel based on Scripture.

The third idea that bears special importance for biblical interpretation is that Scripture's teaching must be worthy of God. The biblical text that comes first to my mind is Abraham's statement, followed by God's replies, in Genesis 18:25: "Shall not the Judge of all the earth do what is just?" Abraham knows something true about God's character and posits that God will act according to this truth, and God concurs. Similarly, Jesus argues on the basis of Scripture and moral reasoning that it is obviously acceptable to do a person good on the Sabbath (Matt. 12:9-14). Human reason apart from God does not generate its own independent truths, but moral reasoning that draws on tradition, community, and spiritual insight is an essential part of organizing and prioritizing the ideas of Scripture into a coherent theological picture that is worthy of God.

The fourth idea from antiquity that I wish to highlight for its importance for understanding Scripture is the belief that divine illumination is required for biblical interpretation. It is not plausible to argue that divine illumination will bestow upon the reader special knowledge of the historical sense of Scripture beyond what can be known through scholarly investigations. It might be argued that virtues such as patience, charity, and humility can be beneficial for any intellectual exercise and that if divine aid promotes these virtues then illumination might be beneficial even for the academic study of Scripture. Yet the most important role that divine illumination plays in biblical interpretation has to do with the perception on the part of its readers and hearers of what God is teaching them through the text. Responsible Christian interpretation of Scripture involves genuine contact with the *ad litteram* sense of the text, focus on Jesus as guide and ultimate subject matter, a teachable spirit with respect to Christian traditions and communities, and careful theological and moral reasoning. But in the end, this process will not lead Christians to hear God's applied message in Scripture without what John Goldingay calls "inspired intuition."[5] Although much work can be done to guide the Christian reader in the right direction, the application of Scripture requires something beyond research and reasoning. As modeled by Origen, the mysterious insight that allows us to perceive the meaning of the gospel for us in Scripture comes through prayer and receptivity to divine illumination.

Obviously, these ancient ideas as applied to biblical interpretation raise important questions about the nature and function of Scripture's authority. I will now offer a few brief comments on how this might be viewed along the lines sketched out above.

Hermeneutics and Authority

The most significant ideas associated with the doctrine of inspiration in the early church had to do with scriptural interpretation. This necessarily raises questions about the authority of Scripture. It is certainly possible for people to agree that Scripture is authoritative while disagreeing on how to interpret it. But from a practical standpoint one cannot detach Scripture's authority from the questions "What does Scripture mean?" and "How do we know what Scripture means?" To speak of Scripture's "authority" is to affirm something about the present-day meaning of Scripture. As the testimony of the early church suggests, a number of complex hermeneutical values must be at work in order for the ever-present Christian message of Scripture to be heard. This complexity has important implications for our understanding of scriptural authority.

To state the matter directly: the interpretative practices that foster the continued meaningfulness of Scripture involve elements of subjectivity. There are a variety of ways that one might see Jesus as central to Christian biblical interpretation. A variety of traditions and communities exist that lay claim to authentic Christianity. Concepts such as moral reasoning or the application of biblical "principles" involve enough of the interpreter's perceptions to leave room for subjectivity.[6] Private experiences of divine illumination when reading Scripture are obviously subjective. But the fact that a perception is subjective does not mean that it is not real: what we experience subjectively can be true. But when it comes to making authoritative appeals within a community, the issue of subjectivity must be carefully considered.

One way to address the issue of subjectivity is to appeal to an authoritative interpreter. For example: even with the U.S. Constitution, which reflects a literary genre directly tied to its purpose and was composed within a relatively short time frame and with specific aims in view, judges are still necessary to serve as the final arbiters of its present-day significance.[7] It might seem, then, all the more necessary for an authoritative interpreter to preside over Scripture, which represents a wide range of literary genres, covers the eras of both ancient Israel and the early church, and speaks of spiritual realities.

The presumed need for authoritative scriptural interpretation is sometimes used as an argument in favor of a particular Christian group serving as the authoritative interpreter. Yet, the desire among some for an authoritative interpreter cannot serve as evidence that there is such an interpreter. This is simply wish fulfillment. In order for a group to make a just claim to be the divinely authorized interpreter of Scripture, that group would need to offer a historical explanation for the existence of such an office, show itself to be in sufficient continuity with the early church to make credible its claims to that office, and demonstrate that it alone among all worldwide Christian groups holds the office. I do not believe that any Christian group today is capable of making these claims credibly. Moreover, although it is certainly true that the Christian canons of Scripture (for example, the Syrian Orthodox, Coptic Orthodox, Armenian Apostolic, Roman Catholic, and Protestant canons) are the products of historical processes within the churches of the first several centuries of Christianity,[8] it does not follow from this that every organization in later times that claims to be "the church" has the divine authority to dictate to the rest of humanity what biblical texts mean. Therefore, while Christian communities are essential for hearing the message of Scripture, I do not believe that appealing to authoritative interpreters within specific communities can address the issue of subjectivity in biblical interpretation.

Another approach to dealing with the subjective element in scriptural interpretation is to ground the authority of Scripture in the *ad litteram* sense together with principles to guide Christians as they move from the biblical text to the modern world. The element of subjectivity is reduced by the *ad litteram* exegesis on the one hand and by the guiding principles on the other. I think there is much good in this approach. The attention given to the "literal" sense (the discourse of the human writer) puts the reader in contact with the distinctive content of each passage, and the guiding principles can help readers apply the text's message to their lives. Still, I have two concerns regarding this approach: first, although it is possible to identify general guidelines that can help Christian readers connect the Old Testament to Christ,[9] no set of rules can capture the full range of possible connections between the themes and images of the Old Testament and our experience of God in Christ, and we should be cautious about limiting such connections to what may be discerned strictly through rules; and second, even when readers of Scripture genuinely engage the content of the text and thoughtfully look for Scripture's present message, in the end this still does not eliminate the subjective dimension of biblical interpretation. One need only consider the diversity of beliefs and practices in the church associated with baptism or Christian involvement in war to see that "literal" exegesis combined with interpretive principles is not entirely sufficient to resolve the issue of subjectivity.

In the end, however, a measure of subjectivity in interpretation is only a major problem if the goal of biblical hermeneutics is to eliminate all subjectivity. But if some subjectivity is embraced, then readings in contact with the *ad litteram* sense that take full advantage of the theological resources seen in the early church can be fully appropriate for Christians today, despite their subjectivity. Still, the implications of such thinking for biblical authority must be recognized.

Many Christians have believed that they are able to "prove" all their views from Scripture, just as Paul in Acts 9:22 is said to have confounded the Jews who lived in Damascus "by proving that Jesus was the Christ." The book of Acts reports Paul spending an entire day demonstrating the truth about Jesus from the Law of Moses and the Prophets (Acts 28:23; see also 13:23; 17:11; 26:23). Although Paul's unique mission was based on a direct call from God, he is described in disputation as proving his case from Scripture. The scriptural text was the ultimate authority, and in his cultural setting Paul was seen as primarily an expounder of Scripture.

But the nature of Paul's arguments would work differently for us today. As an example, Hosea 1:10 and 2:23 originally spoke about the restoration of Israel to its former status as the "people of God." But Paul quotes these verses to explain how God made "people of God" out of some Gentiles (Rom. 9:25-26). In defense of the essential truthfulness of Paul's argument, there is a theological connection between God's desire to remake Israel as a people after they have been alienated from God and God's desire to make a people out of Gentiles who were alienated from God. Paul's argument can be read today as showing Christians how to relate their story to the story of Israel in the Old Testament. But Paul's argument presumes more than simply a recitation of the *ad litteram* sense of Hosea. In an ancient context it would have served as proof for at least some listeners. But in view of the original meaning of Hosea, Paul's quotation would not function in the same way today for informed readers outside the church. From our perspective today, Paul's use of Hosea is grounded in Paul's (the interpreter's) direct experience with God. In other words, the authority of the interpreter (Paul) is bound up with the authority of the text that he is interpreting. We can accept what he has to say about God's work in Christ as capturing the essence of what Hosea says about God, but our different perspective on the locus of interpretive authority is theologically significant for us. Specifically, we who do not share in Paul's context and divinely assigned mission must construe the authority of our own interpretations of Scripture differently than how Paul's interpretations are presented in the book of Acts.

I suggest that Christians can and should continue to read Scripture with Christ as the focus, in thoughtful conversation with their Christian community, informed by Christian tradition and scholarship, and guided by moral reason and prayer, seeking to meet God and develop spiritually by reading and hearing the sacred text. As many Christians past and present testify, an approach to Scripture such as this is the best way to receive what God has to teach us through Scripture. But as we see today more clearly than ever, the results of such distinctively Christian reading will often be too subjective and personal to function as an absolute "authority" in an interpersonal sense. Modern Christians do not need to give up the spiritual dimension of their reading of Scripture. They simply need to be more humble about what they discover about God in Scripture, in recognition of the subjective nature of Christian biblical interpretation.

It is not that the category of "authority" does not properly belong to Scripture. God speaks to Christians through Scripture, and Christians believe themselves to be under the authority of God. When Christians read Scripture, they do so with the belief that they will hear God's message and should follow God's authority.[10] But the complex nature of biblical hermeneutics means that the authority of Scripture functions to mediate God's authority to me as an individual Christian, and does not give me divine authority to exercise over others. I may testify to what I take Scripture to be saying, and I may even try to persuade fellow Christians to adopt my position, but for God to exercise authority through Scripture to these other persons through my doing so, they would need to come to the same perception as I have in their own reading of Scripture. This way of thinking about Scripture and divine authority seems to me to be the most ethical way to address the issue of subjectivity in biblical hermeneutics. Divine authority resides in Scripture, not in my interpretation of Scripture.

Liberty in Faith and Responsibility

It remains central to Christianity that Scripture is profitable for instruction in the Christian faith. The concept of Scripture as the supreme authority in Christian belief and practice was already qualified or nuanced in antiquity (section 5 above). As we consider reading Scripture in a full Christian sense today, I believe we should nuance our conception of Scripture's authority by affirming that the final locus of interpretive authority rests in the relationship between God and the individual Christian. It is not that Christians should try to interpret and live out Scripture individualistically. The meaning of Scripture is discerned in community and lived out in community. Nevertheless, in terms of Scripture's authority, the final point of discernment as to the significance of Scripture for today must lie with the individual Christian. Seeking to be receptive to God, the individual Christian must be at liberty to make the ultimate decisions as to how Scripture relates to her or him.

In my view, respect for individual Christian liberty in biblical interpretation fits well with the core values of the church. First, if such a view of biblical authority is adopted, then Christians who wish to teach, encourage, or correct one another from Scripture will need to take the posture of trying to persuade their fellow Christians rather than commanding them. "The kings of the Gentiles exercise lordship over them, and those in authority over them are called benefactors. But not so with you. Rather, let the greatest among you become as the youngest, and the leader as one who serves" (Luke 22:25-26). When we try to persuade others, we are not presuming to be in charge over them but are granting that they may or may not agree with us, and all we can do is offer counsel and try to point them toward God. By imagining biblical instruction as persuasion, we are better able to serve others and genuinely show love through our appeals to Scripture. Second, belief that our primary task with Scripture is to testify and convince makes perfect sense together with the idea that God desires genuine and sincere faith rather than feigned obedience. Christianity is a matter of the heart and of inward persuasion of the mind. As such, true Christian faith cannot be coerced. Our goal with Scripture should not be to win arguments but to convince the heart. This dovetails nicely with the idea of individual liberty in scriptural interpretation. Third, recognizing the necessary role of the individual interpreter's conscience affords greater opportunity for Christian ministry to involve the whole body of Christ. Every Christian can and should take responsibility to understand their own Christian faith to whatever degree possible, and this should promote active participation by more members of the church.

Christian liberty in scriptural interpretation obviously implies a measure of responsibility. If what matters most is not what is written in church record books but what Christians actually believe and do, then it is essential for every Christian to understand the message of Scripture as clearly as possible. Our role within the church includes building each other up in this regard and helping one another to take this responsibility seriously. Whereas someone else may file our income taxes for us and free us from a degree of responsibility for whatever payment we make, there is no one who can free us from our responsibility before God. Even if some people do not want this responsibility, I believe that it is ours as moral beings made uniquely in God's image. God is merciful and certainly recognizes that we are all far from reaching perfect understanding. But it is within our power and responsibility to understand and practice the teachings of Scripture as well as opportunity allows and to remember that we will be judged according to the measure that we judge others (Matt. 7:1-5).

Recognizing the role of individual Christians in perceiving the authority of God in Scripture does not detract from fellowship among Christians; it merely presumes that churches are voluntary organizations within society and that diverse church communities must live together side by side. Christians can join together in churches whose understanding of Christian life is sufficiently similar to their own to allow them to experience Christian life together as an immediate community, and these individual Christian communities can relate to each other as parts of the larger body of Christ. This is a common way for churches to be organized in the modern world, and in general I regard this as positive, although I think more should be done to encourage all Christians to cooperate with each other. One obvious result of embracing a spiritual hermeneutic that places such emphasis on individual believers is that diverse interpretations of Scripture will coexist within the church. In my view, when handled with charity this diversity is good for the church.

The Benefits to the Church of Diverse Interpretations of Scripture

For certain kinds of scriptural interpretation, multiple readings of the same biblical text can comfortably exist side by side. One Christian might read the David and Goliath story and see David as a symbol of divine mission, confidence in God, and deliverance for the people that within the framework of the Christian Bible points to Christ. Another Christian might read the David and Goliath story within the context of the David narratives from 1 Samuel to 1 Kings and see themes that illuminate the nature of the spiritual progress (or regress) that can take place in the life of faith. Especially when spiritual or devotional readings are grounded in broader theological truths and relate directly to the religious life of the individual, these readings can be legitimately convincing and meaningful for the reader or hearer without having to rule out different spiritual readings of the same passage. It is not that anything can legitimately be found in any passage, but more than one insight relevant to a person's spiritual life can exist for any given passage of Scripture. In this sense, multiple valid readings can coexist without being in competition with each other. Because different people may benefit most at any given time from different insights found in Scripture, in these cases diversity in biblical interpretation is obviously helpful for the church.

For other kinds of scripture interpretation, however, it is not possible for multiple views to coexist without being in competition with each other. This is particularly the case when it comes to establishing practical guidelines for behavior. For example, in the nineteenth century many Christians in the United States argued that Noah's curse in Genesis 9:24-27, viewed in light of Scripture as a whole (e.g., Eph. 6:5; Col. 3:22; 1 Tim. 6:1; Tit. 2:9; 1 Pet. 2:18), offered a divine mandate for slavery.[11] Many other Christians disagreed, and in this century virtually all Christians have come to believe that the best overall reading of Scripture's values leads us to reject the institution of slavery as unethical. This serves as an example of interpretive differences that cannot simply coexist in harmony. In terms of applying the message of Scripture to the real world, one interpretation must be better than the other. In these cases, all Christians would desire that the better interpretation be embraced rather than the worse, even as they disagree over what constitutes the better interpretation.

Many matters of biblical interpretation fall somewhere between the Christological reading of David on the one hand and the issue of slavery on the other. Christians read Scripture differently on a host of theological topics, including divine sovereignty and human free will, the theological meaning of the Eucharist, and the nature of the final consummation of the world. Topics such as these have sometimes been at the center of great conflicts within the church, and Christians continue to disagree about them. Many Christians today are willing to recognize the genuine faith of those who differ with them on these topics, but this does not suggest that the best answers to these questions are unimportant. Diverse interpretations of texts such as Romans 9, 1 Corinthians 11, and the book of Revelation create meaningful differences within and between churches, but today they are not usually divisive to the highest degree.

Valuing diversity in scriptural interpretation does not imply that one does not believe in absolute truths. Rather, vibrant and charitable discussions based on Scripture among diverse voices in the church contribute to helping people find what is true. Within individual churches, in Bible study groups, in denominational assemblies, in Christian education, and in any organization where Christians come together and live out their faith, it is profitable for different ways of reading Scripture to be set forth. It is especially important for different ecclesiastical communions to listen to each other, and also churches in different cultures. Some of the practical benefits of diversity in scriptural interpretation are as follows:

1. Since no person is infallible, it is always possible that any given Christian is misguided in his or her interpretation of Scripture. By listening to readings of Scripture proposed by others, we might be corrected toward a better interpretation. To have diverse readings of Scripture within the church increases the chances that the best reading is to be found somewhere in the body of Christ. Diversity is no cause for worry, but I think it is very worrisome when some authority within a church has the power to suppress the views of other Christians. Unless this authority is infallible, we cannot assume that it will always have the best interpretation. In at least some cases, therefore, such an authority will use its power to suppress the best interpretation and enforce a worse one. Therefore, since no Christian individual or institution is infallible, the church benefits most by listening to diverse interpretations of Scripture.

2. One's views may be only partly correct, reflecting only half of the truth; the other half of the truth may be found in a different reading of Scripture suggested by someone else. The idea that different readings contain partial truths is an attractive way to understand many longstanding issues of disagreement among Christians, such as the debate surrounding divine sovereignty and human free will. Especially when our attempts to interpret Scripture lead us to reflect on the most profound truths about God, we often need insights from other Christians in order to grasp the full measure of what Scripture has to say. If we were somehow to eliminate diversity in biblical interpretation, we would certainly lose out on important insights into Scripture that fill up what is lacking in our own grasp of the truth.

3. Even if the reading suggested by someone else is not the best idea at present, in a later time or in a different circumstance it might become instructive, in which case other Christians will be glad to have heard it.[12] For example, some Christians have appealed to the Old Testament to suggest that Christians can properly engage in war, where the goals are defense and justice, and the motivation is self-sacrifice.[13] Even if the original circumstance that gave rise to such a suggestion did not constitute a credible case of "just war," the scriptural reasoning that went into the suggestion has

value for Christians later on who wish to pursue the same question in a different setting. One can also imagine that biblical texts could be employed within a particular culture against polygamous marriages in a way that is unhelpful, but that the same or similar arguments against polygamy make good sense in other cultures. In cases such as these, the fact that diverse readings of Scripture are available to be consulted does not hinder truth but helps discerning Christians to find truth.

4. The toleration and even appreciation of diverse readings of Scripture provide ample opportunity for Christians to show each other love and humility. To tolerate other interpretations does not mean to agree with them, and toleration does not imply that there is no correct answer. Seeking to understand how others read Scripture demonstrates humility because we recognize that we are not infallible. Since our own knowledge is imperfect, we must be teachable in order to reach the truth. Furthermore, genuinely listening to the opinions of others shows that we love them. If we want others to listen to us, then we should listen to others.

5. Christians can grasp the truth better if they are put in positions where they must explain and defend their beliefs to others with different views. Engaging in the kind of dialogue that involves laying out the scriptural warrants and reasons behind one's own interpretations promotes internalization of the truth. We all come to Scripture with a set of beliefs about how we should understand and apply it. Through contact with diverse approaches to Scripture we are forced to return to the text in fresh ways and sharpen our interpretive thinking, with the result that we will either modify our views if they are found lacking, or else we will understand our views at a deeper level and make them truly our own. The process of working out a defense for our position helps us to take it truly to heart.

6. The most effective way for Christians to gain confidence that they have arrived at the best interpretation is to know that all possible interpretations have been considered and the most convincing one selected. No person who is truly aware of the world around them wants to hold a certain view simply because it is the only one they have heard. If Christians know that they have been exposed to the best possible arguments in favor of competing positions, they can justifiably be confident in the position that they select.

7. Diversity of views and the free flow of ideas promote vibrant Christianity, as seen in the eras of the Church Fathers and the Reformation. The period of late antiquity (200-600 CE) saw intense interactions between various groups of Christians, Jews, and "pagans" in the Greco-Roman

world, giving rise to the intellectual and spiritual achievements of the "golden age" of the Church Fathers. Likewise, the rise of diverse ideas in the period of the Renaissance fueled creative religious awakenings in the west through the Protestant and Roman Catholic Reformations.[14]

Diversity in scriptural interpretation offers many benefits for the church. It is therefore helpful for Christians to know others who hold differing views, so that each Christian can hear opposing viewpoints precisely as their adherents would explain them. This provides the best opportunity for finding the soundest readings of Scripture. Obviously, the existence of diverse interpretations means that some error coexists with truth. Although obviously not ideal, this is unavoidable in our present state. The benefits that come when diversity is embraced far outweigh any benefits that might come from ignoring or suppressing it. It should not be regarded as a problem that there is interpretive pluralism in the church's reading of Scripture. In fact, this is a fruitful product of the democratization of Christian life embodied in the principle of *sola scriptura*.

The early church believed that God inspired the Scriptures in order to instruct humanity. Despite some variety of views on the precise implications of inspiration, all Christians regarded Scripture as authoritative and true in its message. Most believed that Scripture communicated in special ways as a result of being inspired and that some kind of spiritual perception was necessary in order to understand it properly. Above all, ancient Christians believed that Scripture had a spiritual sense that focused somehow on Christ. As the early church recognized, Scripture continues to instruct because of its divine subject matter, because of the events it describes, and because its symbols and metaphors continue to point people to God. Although many early Christian beliefs about inspiration cannot be brought into the modern world without at least some qualifications, certain key ideas related to spiritual perception, moral reasoning, profitability for the soul, and unity of purpose are essential for a fully Christian appreciation of Scripture today. This rich and complex manner of reading Scripture underscores the element of subjectivity involved in interpretation. In my view, this subjectivity means that scriptural authority should be construed as functioning ultimately between God and the individual Christian. This dovetails well with the reality of pluralism in the interpretation of Scripture, which is not a problem but a blessing for the church.

Notes

Chapter One. Introduction

1. The historical process by which the Bible was created, which I have explained generally and briefly here, was complex and led to some variations in the books that were included within different communities; see p. 180, n. 8; Lee M. McDonald, *The Biblical Canon* (Peabody: Hendrickson, 2007).

2. Jerome, *Commentary on Micah* 7:5-7 (*Corpus Christianorum, Series Latina* 76, p. 513).

3. For a reliable and concise historical overview of biblical interpretation during this period, see Manlio Simonetti, *Biblical Interpretation in the Early Church*, trans. John A. Hughes (Edinburgh: Clark, 1994). For more in-depth discussions of specific topics and figures, see Charles Kannengiesser, ed., *Handbook of Patristic Exegesis: The Bible in Ancient Christianity*, 2 vols. (Leiden: Brill, 2004). A book that helpfully addresses many issues related to the inspiration of Scripture is Robert M. Grant, *The Letter and the Spirit* (London: SPCK, 1957).

4. Jerome, *Epistle* 127.7.

5. I have written an article on Marcella: Michael Graves, "The Biblical Scholarship of a Fourth-Century Woman: Marcella of Rome," *Ephemerides Theologicae Lovanienses* 87 (2011): 375-91.

6. On the *Code of Hammurabi*, see Victor H. Matthews and Don C. Benjamin, *Old Testament Parallels: Laws and Stories from the Ancient Near East*, 3rd ed. (New York: Paulist, 2006), p. 109. The prologue to the *Code of Hammurabi* calls the king a "Good Shepherd" whose responsibilities include establishing justice and equitably allotting pasture and water rights (Matthews and Benjamin, *Old Testament Parallels*, p. 106). In Exodus 21:2-11, male slaves go free in the seventh year, but female slaves designated as wives do not go free. In Deuteronomy 15:12-18, provision is made for both male and female slaves to go free in the seventh year.

7. For example, see Isocrates, *Nicocles* 61; *To Nicocles* 24; *To Demonicus* 14; and *Panegyricus* 81; *Letter of Aristeas* 207; Tobit 4:15; Philo (quoted in Eusebius, *Preparation for the Gospel* 8.7.6). See also the Rabbinic sage Hillel: "What is hateful to you, do not do to your neighbor: that is the whole Torah, while the rest is the commentary thereof; go and learn it"

(Babylonian Talmud, *Shabbat* 31a; see *The Babylonian Talmud*, "Shabbath I," trans. H. Freedman, ed. I. Epstein [London: Soncino, 1938]), p. 140). This basic idea is also found in Zoroastrian, Confucian, Buddhist, and ancient Indian literatures; see John Nolland, *The Gospel of Matthew*, NIGTC (Grand Rapids: Eerdmans, 2005), p. 329.

8. See Matthews and Benjamin, *Old Testament Parallels*, pp. 167-69, Judges 2:11-15, and in general Judges 3–16.

9. For example, see Joshua 8:31-32; 23:6; 1 Kings 2:3; 2 Kings 14:6; Ezra 3:2; 7:6; Nehemiah 8:1; and Daniel 9:11-13. The legal material in the Pentateuch is presented literarily as direct revelation from God, but the discovery of Near Eastern law codes similar to the legal material in the Pentateuch confirms the idea that "a substantial part of biblical law was based upon pre-existing Near Eastern laws"; see Samuel Greengus, *Laws in the Bible and in Early Rabbinic Collections* (Eugene: Cascade, 2011), p. 1. This suggests that the revelation of this legal material was not purely "direct" divine discourse; rather, the ultimate presentation of these laws involved divinely prompted human composition that made use of previous sources. This may be likened to the inspiration that Christians believe took place in the composition of the Gospel of Luke (see Luke 1:1-4).

10. For example, Irenaeus describes the law as punishment for the sin of the golden calf (*Against Heresies* 4.15.1-2; 4.16.5). Theodoret says that God permitted animal sacrifices in the law as a concession to the Israelites, who had become accustomed to animal sacrifices in Egypt (*Commentary on Jeremiah* 7:21-23).

11. 2 Peter 3:15-16 offers an example of a New Testament book reflecting on another New Testament book as Scripture.

12. See I. Howard Marshall, *Biblical Inspiration* (Grand Rapids: Eerdmans, 1982), pp. 22-30.

13. Some commentators argue that Paul intended to say that Deuteronomy 25:4 relates *not only* to oxen *but also* to people. They see Paul as deriving a principle from this law about oxen and reapplying it to people. It is certainly fair to say that Paul's point does make sense along these lines, but it is not what Paul actually says. The idea that God originally intended such Old Testament laws in a non-literal sense as applying primarily to people was not by any means an absurd belief in Paul's context (for example, see *Letter of Aristeas* 144; Philo, *Noah's Work as a Planter* 113; *Allegories of the Laws* 3.147; and other passages from Philo cited below; *Epistle of Barnabas* 10:9). It is important to appreciate this if one is to understand how the Church Fathers appropriated Paul. On 1 Corinthians 9:9-10, see Hans Conzelmann, *1 Corinthians*, Hermeneia (Philadelphia: Fortress, 1975), pp. 154-55; Richard B. Hays, *First Corinthians*, Interpretation (Louisville: John Knox, 1997), p. 151; and F. F. Bruce, *1 and 2 Corinthians*, NCBC (Grand Rapids: Eerdmans, 1971), pp. 84-85. As Bruce states, "His [Paul's] argument may clash with modern exegetical method and western sentiment, but he must be allowed to mean what he says."

14. See Daniel I. Block, *Judges, Ruth,* New American Commentary (Nashville: Broadman & Holman, 1999), pp. 57-70; and Trent C. Butler, *Judges,* Word Biblical Commentary (Nashville: Nelson, 2009), pp. li-lxiv, lxxv-lxxxiv. On the tendency among Greco-Roman readers of Scripture to idealize biblical characters, see for example Josephus, *Jewish Antiquities* 5.230 and 5.317 and section 4 below.

15. See the reasonable comments of Richard N. Longenecker, *Biblical Exegesis in the Apostolic Period*, 2nd ed. (Grand Rapids: Eerdmans, 1999), p. 197. See also Moisés Silva, "The

New Testament Use of the Old Testament: Text Form and Authority," in *Scripture and Truth*, ed. D. A. Carson and John D. Woodbridge (Grand Rapids: Baker, 1992), pp. 163-64.

16. For an excellent description of the importance of the literal sense in modern biblical studies, see John Barton, *The Nature of Biblical Criticism* (Louisville: Westminster John Knox, 2007).

17. Porphyry, *On the Cave of the Nymphs* 78.

18. Philo, *On Mating with Preliminary Studies* 11-19. See also Plutarch, *The Education of Children* 7D, who says that those who wear themselves out on preliminary education and do not attain to philosophy are like the suitors in the *Odyssey* who could not approach Penelope and therefore consorted with her maidservants.

19. Babylonian Talmud, *Sanhedrin* 67b; Midrash *Genesis Rabbah* 47.9.

20. Cornutus, *Traditions of Greek Theology* 2-3.

21. This *Commentary on Habakkuk* is often known as the *Habakkuk Pesher*. "*Pesher*" is an Aramaic word meaning "interpretation." In the commentary "*pesher*" is often used to introduce an interpretation. For an English translation of this commentary, see Geza Vermes, *The Complete Dead Sea Scrolls in English* (New York: Penguin, 1997), pp. 478-85.

22. Many scholars have identified the "Wicked Priest" as Jonathan (d. 143 BCE) or Simon (d. 134 BCE), who were brothers of Judas Maccabaeus. Yet there is also evidence to suggest that several historical persons known to the Qumran community were referred to as the "Wicked Priest." See Maurya P. Horgan, *Pesharim: Qumran Interpretations of Biblical Books* (Washington: Catholic Biblical Association of America, 1979), pp. 6-8; Timothy H. Lim, *Pesharim* (London: Sheffield Academic, 2002), pp. 65-78. The *Habakkuk Pesher* uses the word "Kittim" to refer to the Romans.

23. It is impossible to know whether Trypho was a real individual. The dialogue itself appears to be a literary creation of Justin.

Chapter Two. Usefulness

1. Strabo, *Geography* 1.2.3-9. See also Horace, *Art of Poetry* 333 and 344: "Poets aim either to benefit, or to amuse, or to utter words at once both pleasing and helpful to life." "He has won every vote who has blended profit and pleasure, at once delighting and instructing the reader" (Loeb Classical Library).

2. *Saint Basil: Exegetic Homilies*, trans. A. C. Way, Fathers of the Church (Washington: Catholic University of America Press, 1963), p. 151. See also Athanasius, *Letter to Marcellinus*, on the idea that the Psalms contain all that is in the Old Testament in concentrated form.

3. Gregory of Nyssa, *Life of Moses*, prologue 8-10.

4. Gregory of Nyssa, *Life of Moses*, prologue 15; see *Gregory of Nyssa: The Life of Moses*, trans. A. J. Malherbe and E. Ferguson, Classics of Western Spirituality (New York: Paulist, 1978), p. 33.

5. Gregory of Nyssa, *Life of Moses* 1.77.

6. Gregory of Nyssa, *Life of Moses* 2.49; see *Gregory of Nyssa: The Life of Moses*, Malherbe and Ferguson, p. 65.

7. *Gregory of Nyssa: The Life of Moses*, Malherbe and Ferguson, p. 65.

8. See also Maximus the Confessor: "For though Holy Scripture, being restricted chronologically to the times of the events which it records, is limited where the letter is con-

cerned, yet in spirit it always remains unlimited as regards the contemplation of intelligible realities"; *The Philokalia. The Complete Text, compiled by St. Nikodimos of the Holy Mountain and St. Makarios of Corinth,* vol. 2, trans. G. E. H. Palmer, P. Sherrard, and K. Ware (London: Faber and Faber, 1981), p. 207.

9. *Philocalia* 12.2; see *The Philocalia of Origen,* trans. G. Lewis (Edinburgh: Clark, 1911), p. 56.

10. *Philocalia* 12.1; see *The Philocalia of Origen,* Lewis, p. 55.

11. Augustine, *On Christian Teaching* 3.10.14; see *Saint Augustine: On Christian Teaching,* trans. R. P. H. Green, Oxford World's Classics (Oxford: Oxford University Press, 1999), p. 75.

12. Philo, *Allegories of the Laws* 3.147 (Loeb Classical Library).

13. The Hebrew text has *qereb,* which means "inward parts." The ancient Greek translation of the Old Testament (called the "Septuagint"; see section 16 below) used the Greek word *koilia,* which means "belly." Philo is basing his comments on the Greek translation.

14. See also Philo, *Allegorical Interpretations* 3.239; *On Dreams* 300-302.

15. This is the first of the so-called "Thirty-Two 'Rules' *(Middot)* of R. Eliezer." See H. L. Strack and G. Stemberger, *Introduction to the Talmud and Midrash,* trans. and ed. M. Bockmuehl (Minneapolis: Fortress, 1996), p. 23.

16. Midrash *Genesis Rabbah* 1.14.

17. *Saint Ambrose: Hexaemeron, Paradise, and Cain and Abel,* trans. John J. Savage, Fathers of the Church (New York: Fathers of the Church, 1961), p. 369.

18. See *Cyril of Alexandria: Commentary on Isaiah. Vol. 1: Chapters 1–14,* trans. Robert C. Hill (Brookline: Holy Cross Orthodox, 2008), p. 84. For the word "strength," Cyril's Greek text has *ischys* ("strength"), whereas the Hebrew text has *mish'an* ("support").

19. For Didymus, see *Didyme L'aveugle. Sur la Genèse,* vol. 2, ed. and trans. Pierre Nautin, Sources chrétiennes (Paris: Cerf, 1978), p. 113. For Ephrem, see *Hymns on Paradise: St. Ephrem,* trans. Sebastian Brock (Crestwood: St. Vladimir's Seminary Press, 1990), p. 89.

20. Ambrose, *Cain and Abel* 8.29.

21. Didymus, *Commentary on Zechariah* 1:7.

22. Augustine, *Tractates on the Gospel John* 9.6.

23. Augustine, *Tractates on the Gospel John* 10.12.

24. Augustine, *Tractates on the Gospel John* 122.8.

25. Augustine, *Harmony of the Gospels* 2.4.13.

26. Augustine, *Expositions of the Psalms* 1.1.

27. *Jean Chrysostome. Homélies sur Ozias,* ed. and trans. Jean Dumortier, Sources chrétiennes (Paris: Cerf, 1981), p. 92.

28. *Saint John Chrysostom. Homilies on Genesis 1–17,* trans. Robert C. Hill, Fathers of the Church (Washington: Catholic University of America Press, 1986), p. 195.

29. Origen, *Philocalia* 2.4. See also Hippolytus, *Commentary on Daniel* 1.7: "The sacred scriptures proclaim to us nothing idle"; see *Hippolyte: Commentaire sur Daniel,* ed. and trans. Maurice Lefèvre, Sources chrétiennes (Paris: Cerf, 1947), p. 80.

30. An important book in modern studies of the Bible as "literature" is Robert Alter, *The Art of Biblical Literature* (New York: Basic, 1981). For a Christian approach to reading the Bible as "literature" which sees divine intention behind the literary crafting of the human authors of the Bible, see Leland Ryken, *How to Read the Bible as Literature* (Grand Rapids: Zondervan, 1985).

31. Mishnah, *Avot* 5.22; see *The Mishnah,* trans. H. Danby (Oxford: Oxford University Press, 1933), p. 458 (translation updated). On Ben Bag-Bag, see also Babylonian Talmud, *Eruvin* 27b. Ben Bag-Bag is referring to the "Torah," which for him probably meant the first five books of the Hebrew Bible ("Old Testament"). But "Torah" might also refer to the Hebrew Bible as a whole, or perhaps even to the Hebrew Bible as explained by Jewish sages (including what became known later as "oral Torah").

32. Babylonian Talmud, *Menahoth* 99b; see *The Babylonian Talmud,* "Menahoth," trans. Eli Cashdan, ed. I. Epstein (London: Soncino, 1948), pp. 609-10.

33. In some cases, the Jewish sage whose opinion is reported in the Midrash or Talmud seems to think that the scripture text that he quotes really does "prove" his point. But in other cases, the prooftext is seen merely as a "support" *(asmakhta)* for a view that has been derived through other means; for example, Babylonian Talmud, *Chullin* 17b.

34. *Letter of Aristeas* 144; see Moses Hadas, ed. and trans., *Aristeas to Philocrates (Letter of Aristeas)* (New York: Harper, 1951), p. 159.

35. *Letter of Aristeas* 146-51.

36. *Epistle of Barnabas* 10. Irenaeus continues this symbolic reading of the dietary laws, but he adds an "anti-heresy" dimension to the symbolism *(Against Heresies* 5.8.3).

37. Gregory of Nyssa, *Life of Moses* 2.105-8; see *Gregory of Nyssa: The Life of Moses,* trans. Malherbe and Ferguson, pp. 78-79.

38. Jerome, *Homilies on the Psalms* 17; see *The Homilies of Saint Jerome,* vol. 1, trans. M. L. Ewald, Fathers of the Church (Washington: Catholic University of America Press, 1964), p. 131.

39. Tertullian, *On Baptism* 6-7.

40. Cyprian, *Epistle* 63.

41. On this topic, see J. N. D. Kelly, *Early Christian Doctrines,* rev. ed. (New York: HarperCollins, 1978), pp. 301-43.

42. For example, see Justin Martyr, *Dialogue with Trypho* 129.4; Tertullian, *Against Praxeas* 11.3; Athenagoras, *Plea for the Christians* 10.2; Theophilus of Antioch, *To Autolycus* 2.10; Origen, *On First Principles* 4.4.1; Hiliary of Poitiers, *On the Trinity* 12.35-37; and Athanasius, *Against the Arians* 2.16.18–2.22.82; *On the Opinion of Dionysius* 10-11. On the use of Proverbs 8 in early discussions of Christology, see Jaroslav Pelikan, *The Christian Tradition: A History of the Development of Doctrine,* vol. 1: *The Emergence of the Catholic Tradition (100-600)* (Chicago: University of Chicago Press, 1971), pp. 186-97.

43. As stated by Pelikan, *Christian Tradition,* p. 193: "Although the transmission of the documents of Arianism is even more confused than that of other heretical literature, it does seem clear that the Arian controversy broke out over the exegesis of Proverbs 8:22-31." ⁻

44. For an example of this discussion, see Gary T. Meadors, ed., *Four Views on Moving beyond the Bible to Theology* (Grand Rapids: Zondervan, 2009).

45. Eusebius, *Preparation for the Gospel* 7.5; see *Eusebius: Preparation for the Gospel,* vol. 1, trans. E. H. Gifford (Oxford: Clarendon, 1903), pp. 326-27.

46. Ambrose, *On Isaac* 8.79.

47. Ambrose, *On Joseph* 1.1; see *Saint Ambrose: Seven Exegetical Works,* trans. Michael P. McHugh, Fathers of the Church (Washington: Catholic University of America Press, 1972), p. 189.

48. Ancient Jewish authors who wrote in Greek also showed a tendency to extol the virtues of biblical characters, as is illustrated by the idealized pictures that Josephus paints of

Gideon ("a man of moderation and a model of every virtue") and Samson (apart from his weakness for women, which is merely "human nature," "testimony is due to him for his surpassing excellence in all the rest"); see *Jewish Antiquities* 5.230, 317 (Loeb Classical Library).

49. See also *1 Clement* 17: "Let us be imitators also of those who in goat-skins and sheep-skins went about proclaiming the coming of Christ; I mean Elijah, Elisha, and Ezekiel among the prophets, with those others to whom a like testimony is borne [in Scripture]. Abraham . . . Job. . . ."

50. John Chrysostom, *Homilies on Genesis* 47.2; see *Saint John Chrysostom: Homilies on Genesis 46–67*, trans. Robert C. Hill, Fathers of the Church (Washington: Catholic University of America Press, 1992), pp. 14-24.

51. John Chrysostom, *Homilies on Genesis* 47.5.

52. John Chrysostom, *Homilies on Genesis* 47.6.

53. John Chrysostom, *Homilies on Genesis* 47.8.

54. John Chrysostom, *Homilies on Genesis* 47.9.

55. John Chrysostom, *Homilies on Genesis* 47.11.

56. John Chrysostom, *Homilies on Genesis* 47.12.

57. John Chrysostom, *Homilies on Genesis* 47.14.

58. *Saint Ambrose: Seven Exegetical Works,* trans. McHugh, 119-84.

59. Ambrose, *Jacob and the Happy Life* 2.2.6-9.

60. Ambrose, *Jacob and the Happy Life* 2.2.9.

61. Ambrose, *Jacob and the Happy Life* 2.1.1.

62. Ambrose, *Jacob and the Happy Life* 2.4.16.

63. Ambrose, *Jacob and the Happy Life* 2.4.17.

64. Ambrose, *Jacob and the Happy Life* 2.5.20.

65. Ambrose, *Jacob and the Happy Life* 2.5.25.

66. Ambrose, *Jacob and the Happy Life* 2.5.20.

67. Ambrose, *Jacob and the Happy Life* 2.5.21-22.

68. Ambrose, *Jacob and the Happy Life* 2.5.23.

69. Ambrose, *Jacob and the Happy Life* 2.6.26.

70. Ambrose, *Jacob and the Happy Life* 2.6.28.

71. Ambrose, *Jacob and the Happy Life* 2.7.30.

72. Ambrose, *Jacob and the Happy Life* 2.7.30.

73. Ambrose, *Jacob and the Happy Life* 2.9.37-40.

74. In particular, Ambrose drew heavily from Philo and Origen.

75. For example, see Philo, *Every Good Man Is Free;* Cicero, *Tusculan Disputations* 5; Epictetus, *Discourses* 4.1; Seneca, *Epistle* 92; Plutarch, *Stoic Self-Contradictions* 1046.

76. Augustine, *On Christian Teaching* 3.12.18-20; 3.18.26.

77. Augustine, *On Christian Teaching* 3.22.32.

78. Augustine, *On Christian Teaching* 3.14.22–3.15.23.

79. Thus Theodoret of Cyrus, *The Questions on the Octateuch,* defends Abraham from the charges of lacking faith (Gen. Qu. 66), lust (Gen. Qu. 68), and harshness (Gen. Qu. 73). He even defends Jacob from lying in Gen. 27:27-29 (Gen. Qu. 82) and Gideon from introducing idol worship (Judg. Qu. 17) and explains that Samson failed to keep Nazarite dietary rules because they had become obsolete (Judg. Qu. 22).

80. For example, see *The Homilies of Saint Jerome,* vol. 2, trans. M. L. Ewald, Fathers of the Church (Washington: Catholic University of America Press, 1965), pp. 165, 239; *Philocalia*

1.29 compiled by Gregory of Nazianzus and Basil the Great; and Augustine, *On Christian Teaching* 3.11.17: "Any harsh or even cruel word or deed attributed to God or his saints that is found in the holy scriptures applies to the destruction of the realm of lust" (*On Christian Teaching*, Green, p. 77).

81. For example, see Cyril of Alexandria's admission of Hezekiah's sin of pride in his *Commentary on Isaiah* 39.

82. See Shimon Bar-Efrat, *Narrative Art in the Bible* (Sheffield: Sheffield Academic, 1992), pp. 47-92.

83. For a defense of the authoritative nature of church practices not supported by Scripture (but not contradicted by it), see Basil the Great, *On the Holy Spirit* 27.66-67.

84. Cyril of Jerusalem, *Catechetical Lectures* 4.17; see *Cyril of Jerusalem and Nemesius of Emesa*, trans. William Telfer, Library of Christian Classics (Philadelphia: Westminster, 1955), pp. 108-9.

85. Gregory of Nyssa, *On the Soul and the Resurrection*; see *St. Gregory of Nyssa: The Soul and the Resurrection*, trans. Catharine P. Roth (Crestwood: St. Vladimir's Seminary Press, 1993), p. 50.

86. Basil, *Letter* 189.3; see *Saint Basil: Letters*, vol. 2 (186-368), trans. A. C. Way, Fathers of the Church (New York: Fathers of the Church, 1955), p. 27.

87. See, for example, Clement of Alexandria, *Miscellanies* 4.1 (Ante-Nicene Fathers 2, 409); Hippolytus, *Against Noetus* 9; Athanasius, *Against the Heathen* 1.1.3; *Life of Antony* 16; *On the Councils of Ariminum and Seleucia* 1.6; Ambrose, *Exposition of the Christian Faith* 4.1.1; John Chrysostom, *Homilies on Genesis* 13.8, 13.

88. See John Calvin, *Institutes of the Christian Religion* (1559) 1.6-7; 4.8.

89. See Charles Hodge, *Systematic Theology*, vol. 1 (New York: Scribner, 1873), pp. 182-88; see also the *Westminster Confession of Faith* 1.4-7.

90. Tertullian, *Prescription against Heretics* 19; see *Tertullian: On the Testimony of the Soul, and "Prescription" of Heretics*, trans. T. Herbert Bindley (London: SPCK, 1914), pp. 59-60. See also *Early Latin Theology*, trans. S. L. Greenslade, Library of Christian Classics (Philadelphia: Westminster, 1956), pp. 42-43.

91. Tertullian remained comfortable with this rule even after he became associated with a group called the "Montanists" and separated from the mainstream church.

92. For example, see Tertullian, *Against Hermogenes* 22; *Against Praxeas* 11.

Chapter Three. The Spiritual and Supernatural Dimension

1. Justin Martyr, *Dialogue with Trypho* 7; see *St. Justin Martyr*, trans. Thomas B. Falls and rev. by Thomas P. Halton (Washington: Catholic University of America Press, 2003), p. 14.

2. Justin Martyr, *Dialogue with Trypho* 92; see *St. Justin Martyr*, Falls and Halton, p. 142.

3. Justin Martyr, *Dialogue with Trypho* 119; see *St. Justin Martyr*, Falls and Halton, p. 178.

4. Origen, *Homilies on Ezekiel* 2.2; see *Origen: Homilies 1-14 on Ezekiel*, trans. Thomas P. Scheck, Ancient Christian Writers (New York: Paulist, 2010), p. 47.

5. Origen, *Homilies on Exodus* 1.1; see *Origen: Homilies on Genesis and Exodus*, trans. Ronald E. Heine, Fathers of the Church (Washington: Catholic University of America Press, 1982), p. 227.

6. *Origen: Homilies on Genesis and Exodus,* Heine, p. 227.

7. The Hebrew word *nephesh* (Greek: *psychē*) in v. 5 can mean "soul" or "person."

8. Origen, *Homilies on Exodus* 1.2.

9. Origen, *Homilies on Exodus* 1.2. See also Origen's *Homily on Leviticus* 5.2: "But where shall I find an approach to the divine Scripture that teaches me what 'an oven' is? I must call upon Jesus my Lord that he may make me as the seeker find and may open to the one knocking, that I may find in Scriptures 'the oven' where I can bake my sacrifice that God may accept. Indeed, I think I have found it in Hosea the prophet where he says . . ." (quoting Hos. 7:4); see *Origen: Homilies on Leviticus 1–16,* trans. Gary Wayne Barkley, Fathers of the Church (Washington: Catholic University of America Press, 1990), p. 99.

10. Origen, *Homilies on Exodus* 1.4.

11. See, for example, *Homilies on Exodus* 2.4; *Homilies on Joshua* 8.1; *Commentary on the Song of Songs,* prologue (near the end); and Origen, *Homilies on Jeremiah, Homily on 1 Kings 28,* trans. John Clark Smith, Fathers of the Church (Washington: Catholic University of America Press, 1998), pp. 94, 207, 209, and 216.

12. The significance of this passage for Origen can be seen in *On First Principles* 4.2.6.

13. For example, see Philo, *Allegorical Interpretation* 2.5, 10; *On the Contemplative Life* 29; *On the Cherubim* 25.

14. For example, see Porphyry, *On the Cave of the Nymphs* 1; *Life of Pythagoras* 12. For an earlier use, see Strabo, *Geography* 1.2.7.

15. For example, Clement of Alexandria, *Miscellanies* 6.15; 6.124.5 (Ante-Nicene Fathers 2, p. 509; Griechischen Christlichen Schriftsteller 15, p. 494); and Methodius of Olympus, *Banquet of the Ten Virgins* 3.1.

16. Didymus the Blind explicitly draws the connection between Philo and Paul in the allegorical interpretation of Sarah and Hagar; see *Didyme L'aveugle. Sur la Genèse,* vol. 2, ed. and trans. Pierre Nautin, Sources chrétiennes (Paris: Cerf, 1978), p. 202.

17. Philo, *On Mating with Preliminary Studies* 23.

18. See *Gregory of Nyssa: The Life of Moses,* trans. A. J. Malherbe and E. Ferguson, Classics of Western Spirituality (New York: Paulist, 1978), p. 30.

19. *Gregory of Nyssa: Homilies on the Song of Songs,* trans. Richard A. Norris, Jr., Writings from the Greco-Roman World (Atlanta: Society of Biblical Literature, 2009), p. 293.

20. *Theodoret of Cyrus: Commentaries on the Prophets,* vol. 1, trans. Robert C. Hill (Brookline: Holy Cross Orthodox, 2006), p. 21.

21. John Cassian, *Conferences* 14.2.1; see *John Cassian: The Conferences,* trans. Boniface Ramsey, Ancient Christian Writers (New York: Newman, 1997), p. 505.

22. John Cassian, *Conferences* 14.3.1.

23. John Cassian, *Conferences* 14.8.1.

24. Athanasius, *On the Incarnation* 57; see *Athanasius:* Contra Gentes *and* De Incarnatione, ed. and trans. Robert W. Thomson (Oxford: Clarendon, 1971), p. 275.

25. For example, see Donald Bloesch, *Holy Scripture: Revelation, Inspiration and Interpretation* (Downers Grove: InterVarsity, 1994), pp. 127, 159-60, 202; Stanley J. Grenz, *Theology of the Community of God* (Nashville: Broadman & Holman, 1994), pp. 499-500; Peter C. Hodgson, *Christian Faith: A Brief Introduction* (Louisville: Westminster John Knox, 2001), p. 33; and Kevin J. Vanhoozer, *The Drama of Doctrine: A Canonical Linguistic Approach to Christian Theology* (Louisville: Westminster John Knox, 2005), p. 230.

26. Origen, *On First Principles,* preface, 8; see *Origen: On First Principles,* trans. G. W. Butterworth (New York: Harper & Row, 1966), p. 5.

27. Augustine, *On Christian Teaching* 3.5.9; see *Saint Augustine: On Christian Teaching,* trans. R. P. H. Green, Oxford World's Classics (Oxford: Oxford University Press, 1999), p. 72.

28. Augustine, *Literal Commentary on Genesis* 1.1.1; see *St. Augustine: The Literal Meaning of Genesis,* vol. 1, trans. John Hammond Taylor, S.J., Ancient Christian Writers (New York: Paulist, 1982), p. 19.

29. The Greek word *anagōgē* ("anagogy") means "elevation," and was a common term in the early church for the higher or spiritual sense of Scripture.

30. Diodore of Tarsus, *Commentary on the Psalms,* prologue; see Karlfried Froehlich, ed. and trans., *Biblical Interpretation in the Early Church* (Philadelphia: Fortress, 1984), p. 86.

31. Gregory of Nazianzus, *Orations* 45.12.

32. Philo, *On the Life of Abraham* 89-93.

33. An analogy might be helpful here. In 1946 George Orwell wrote a political allegory called *Animal Farm.* It would be missing the point of the book to try to operate an actual farm based on principles learned from *Animal Farm.* The point of the book is not to teach farming techniques but to make a statement about human politics. This is similar to the view of the *Epistle of Barnabas* regarding the allegorical intention of Moses in writing Old Testament laws.

34. Origen, *Homilies on Leviticus* 1.2; see *Origen: Homilies on Leviticus 1–16,* Barkley, pp. 29-30.

35. Jerome, *Commentary on Jeremiah* 17:21-27.

36. Origen, *On First Principles* 4.2.9; see *Origen: On First Principles,* Butterworth, p. 285.

37. Origen, *On First Principles* 4.3.1. Jerome similarly insisted that Psalm 98:8, "Let the rivers clap their hands," should not be taken literally (*Homilies on the Psalms* 25; see *The Homilies of Saint Jerome,* vol. 1, trans. M. L. Ewald, Fathers of the Church [Washington: Catholic University of America Press, 1964], p. 201). Modern readers would agree, seeing this simply as a figure of speech.

38. Origen, *On First Principles* 4.3.2.

39. For example, see Irenaeus, *Against Heresies* 5.33.3. See also sections 13, 14, and 17 below.

40. Augustine, *Confessions* 5.14.24; 6.4.6.

41. Clement of Alexandria, *Miscellanies* 5.6.32.1–40.4 (Ante-Nicene Fathers 2, pp. 452-54); see also Philo, *On the Special Laws* 1.66-75; *Life of Moses* 88-93.

42. Justin Martyr, *Dialogue with Trypho* 111. On Rahab's scarlet cord as a symbol of Jesus' death, see also Origen, *Homilies on Joshua* 6.4.

43. Cyril of Alexandria, *Sermons on Luke* 127.

44. See Origen, *Homilies on Exodus* 1.4. On this topic, see Elizabeth Ann Dively Lauro, *The Soul and Spirit of Scripture within Origen's Exegesis* (Leiden: Brill, 2004).

45. John Cassian, *Conferences* 14.8.

46. See Henri de Lubac, *Medieval Exegesis: The Four Senses of Scripture,* vol. 1, trans. Mark Sebanc (Grand Rapids: Eerdmans, 1998), p. 1. The Latin goes like this: "*Littera gesta docet, quid credas allegoria, moralis quid agas, quo tendas anagogia.*"

47. This point is made by Robert Alter, *The Art of Biblical Poetry* (New York: Basic, 1985), pp. 148-49.

48. Tertullian, *Apology* 20.

49. Origen, *On First Principles* 4.1.6.

50. Eusebius, *Proof of the Gospel* 1.1, etc.

51. Theophilus, *To Autolycus* 1.14; see *Theophilus of Antioch: Ad Autolycum*, trans. Robert M. Grant (Oxford: Clarendon, 1970), p. 19.

52. Prooftexts for this section include Isaiah 7:9; John 8:24; Habakkuk 2:4; Genesis 15:6; and Galatians 3:6-9. For Cyprian's *Testimonies to Quirinus*, see Ante-Nicene Fathers 5, pp. 507-57.

53. See Roger Nicole, "New Testament Use of the Old Testament," in *Revelation and the Bible*, ed. Carl F. H. Henry (Grand Rapids: Baker, 1958), p. 137.

54. Matthew 1:22; 2:15, 17, 23; 4:14; 8:17; 12:17; 13:14, 35; 21:4; 26:54, 56; 27:9.

55. On the theory that Mark was the first Gospel written, see David A. deSilva, *An Introduction to the New Testament* (Downers Grove: InterVarsity, 2004), pp. 158-71; and Raymond E. Brown, *An Introduction to the New Testament* (New York: Doubleday, 1997), pp. 111-16.

56. A note in the ESV Bible suggests "even" as an alternative rendering. This captures the poetic sense of the original Hebrew better, but the ESV rightly keeps "and" in the text because it shows Matthew's interpretive use of the quotation.

57. Midrash *Genesis Rabbah* 75.6.

58. R. Judah said, "From one ox many oxen came forth, and from one donkey many donkeys came forth." Directly after R. Judah's comment, R. Nehemiah points out that the words are singular simply because this is the normal idiom, that is, these are collective nouns. But R. Judah knows this, too; it would be impossible to read Hebrew and not understand this point of grammar. The difference of opinion between R. Judah and R. Nehemiah has to do simply with the insightfulness of this particular homiletical interpretation.

59. The two animals in Matthew 21:1-7 were often interpreted allegorically by the Church Fathers. Justin Martyr took the donkey to stand for the Jewish Christians and the colt to stand for Gentile Christians (*Dialogue with Trypho* 53), whereas Hilary of Poitiers interpreted the two animals as Christians from among Samaritans and Gentiles (*Commentary on Matthew* 21.1; see Sources chrétiennes 258, pp. 120-22). See also Origen, *Commentary on John* 10.18.

60. Hilary of Poitiers, *Treatise on Mysteries* 1.1; see *Hilary de Poitiers: Traité de mystères*, ed. and trans. Jean-Paul Brisson, Sources chrétiennes (Paris: Cerf, 2005), p. 72.

61. Irenaeus, *Against Heresies* 4.26.1; Origen, *On First Principles* 4.1.6. See also Irenaeus, *Against Heresies* 4.9.3; 4.14.3; 4.25-28; Hippolytus, "Fragments on Daniel" 2.5 (Ante-Nicene Fathers 5, p. 179); Theodoret, *Commentary on Daniel* 7:23; and Gregory the Great, "Fragment II on Gen. 24" in *The Homilies of Saint Gregory the Great on the Book of the Prophet Ezekiel*, trans. Theodosia Gray, ed. P. J. Cownie (Etna: Center for Traditionalist Orthodox Studies, 1990), p. 292.

62. Eusebius, *Commentary on Isaiah* 1. For an example of prophecy that is said to point directly to Christ in the literal sense, see Eusebius's comments on Isaiah 11:1-13. See also Tertullian, *On the Resurrection of the Flesh* 20.

63. Origen, *Against Celsus* 1.50; see *Origen: Contra Celsum*, trans. Henry Chadwick (Cambridge: Cambridge University Press, 1965), p. 47.

Chapter Four. Mode of Expression

1. See Sophocles, *Oedipus the King* 1524-27; Euripides, *Phoenician Women* 1688; Plutarch, *On the Oracles of Pythia* 24-25, 30.

2. Cornutus, *Traditions of Greek Theology* 35.3; see *Lucius Annaeus Cornutus' Epidrome (Introduction to the Traditions of Greek Theology)*, trans. Robert Stephen Hays (Ph.D. dissertation, University of Texas at Austin, 1983), p. 121. See also 17.3: "One must not conflate the myths or transfer the names from one to another. There are situations where fictional accretions have been added to the genealogies which were passed on according to these myths by people who do not understand the message they cryptically contain, but use them as they do mere fictions. In these situations, one ought not to give them a place contrary to reason" (pp. 78-79).

3. Heraclitus, *Homeric Problems* 24.1-3; see *Heraclitus: Homeric Problems*, ed. and trans. D. A. Russell and David Konstan, Writings from the Greco-Roman World (Atlanta: Society of Biblical Literature, 2005), p. 47.

4. The second-century Greek philosopher and critic of Christianity Celsus, against whom Origen wrote his defense of Christianity, *Against Celsus*, also interpreted Greek myths allegorically by pointing to enigmas (see *Against Celsus* 6.42). The rhetorician Quintilian, however, used the word "enigma" to describe an allegorical statement that was too obscure for its own good (*Institutes of Oratory* 8.6.52).

5. Philo, *On the Special Laws* 1.200; see also *Allegories of the Laws* 3.226.

6. Clement of Alexandria, *Miscellanies* 5.4.21.4–23.2 (Ante-Nicene Fathers 2, p. 449, translation updated).

7. Justin Martyr, *Dialogue with Trypho* 76. Justin uses the verb *ainissetai*, which is related to the noun "enigma."

8. Justin Martyr, *Dialogue with Trypho* 86. On Moses' or Aaron's staff and the stick from Exodus 15:25 as the cross, see also Ephrem, *Commentary on Exodus* 7.4; 14.3; 16.1; 17.2.

9. Justin Martyr, *Dialogue with Trypho* 90; Augustine, *On Christian Teaching* 2.6.7.

10. Clement of Alexandria, *Miscellanies* 1.12.55.1–56.3 (*Clement of Alexandria: Stromateis, Books One to Three*, trans. John Ferguson, Fathers of the Church [Washington: Catholic University of America Press, 1991], pp. 63-64); *Miscellanies* 6.15.126.1–131.5 (Ante-Nicene Fathers 2, pp. 509-10); *Who Is the Rich Man?* 5.2; see Matthew 7:6.

11. Origen, *On First Principles* 4.1.6-7; 4.2.7-8.

12. Origen, *Philocalia* 2.2; *Against Celsus* 7.10. See also Hippolytus, *Fragment on Proverbs*: "'To understand the difficulties of words'; for things spoken in strange language by the Holy Spirit become intelligible to those who have their hearts right with God" (Ante-Nicene Fathers 5, p. 172).

13. Philo, *On the Life of Abraham* 147.

14. Didymus the Blind, *On Genesis* 168; see *Didyme L'aveugle. Sur la Genèse*, vol. 2, ed. and trans. Pierre Nautin, Sources chrétiennes (Paris: Cerf, 1978), pp. 62-64.

15. Clement of Alexandria, *Miscellanies* 6.15.126.1-2, 127.3-4 (Ante-Nicene Fathers 2, pp. 509-10); Origen, *On First Principles* 4.2.8.

16. Clement of Alexandria, *Miscellanies* 6.15.127.5–128.1 (Ante-Nicene Fathers 2, p. 510); John Chrysostom, *On the Obscurity of the Old Testament* 1; see *St. John Chrysostom: Old Testament Homilies*, vol. 3, trans. Robert C. Hill (Brookline: Holy Cross Orthodox, 2003), pp. 8-25.

17. Jerome, *Commentary on Jeremiah* 25:26c.

18. Augustine, *On Christian Teaching* 2.6.7-8; see also 4.7.15.

19. Ephrem, *Hymns on Paradise* 1.2; see *Hymns on Paradise: St. Ephrem,* trans. Sebastian Brock (Crestwood: St. Vladimir's Seminary Press, 1990), p. 78.

20. Clement of Alexandria, *Miscellanies* 6.15.126.1 (Ante-Nicene Fathers 2, p. 509).

21. Gregory the Great, *Homilies on Ezekiel* 10.31.

22. Cyril of Alexandria, *Commentary on Isaiah*, preface.

23. Augustine, *On Christian Teaching* 3.11.17.

24. See Origen's treatment of Genesis 18, according to which Abraham serves his three guests "hidden and mysterious loaves of bread," and "Everything he [Abraham] does is mystical, everything is filled with mystery." Secret and hidden meanings stand behind every peculiar element in the story (*Homilies on Genesis* 4.1-2).

25. For example, see Tertullian, *On Modesty* 17.18; *Against Marcion* 1.9; *On the Resurrection* 19, 21; *Against Praxeas* 20 (the many statements interpret the few); Irenaeus, *Against Heresies* 2.27.1; Augustine, *On Christian Teaching* 2.9.14. See also Quintilian, *Institutes of Oratory* 5.10.8.

26. See Augustine's comments in *On Christian Teaching* 2.12.17-18; 2.13.19-20.

27. Modern scholars have identified significant parallels between the description of the Tabernacle in Exodus and the account of creation in Genesis 1–2. Perhaps, as many ancient interpreters believed, the Tabernacle was in some way meant to be a depiction of the universe. On this topic, see James K. Bruckner, *Exodus,* NIBC (Peabody: Hendrickson, 2008), pp. 231-32.

28. See Hesiod, *Theogony* 133, 226.

29. The whole work is devoted to the subject of names and things, but see especially *Cratylus* 383a-384d; 424b-c; 428d-431e.

30. Plato, *Cratylus* 425d-426b.

31. See Cicero, *The Nature of the Gods* 3.24; Origen, *Against Celsus* 1.24. According to Diogenes Laertius, *Lives of the Philosophers* 7.200, the Stoic Chrysippus wrote two substantial works on etymologies.

32. Cornutus, *Traditions of Greek Theology* 4.

33. *Iamblichus: On the Mysteries of the Egyptians, Chaldeans, and Assyrians,* trans. Thomas Taylor, 2nd ed. (London: Bertram Dobell & Reeves and Turner, 1895), pp. 293, 297-98 (translation updated).

34. See Yair Zakovitch, "Inner-biblical Interpretation," in *A Companion to Biblical Interpretation in Early Judaism,* ed. Matthias Henze (Grand Rapids: Eerdmans, 2012), pp. 49-50.

35. *Mekhilta de-Rabbi-Ishmael,* tractate *Amalek* 1.

36. Philo, *On the Cherubim* 56 (Loeb Classical Library). For other passages where Philo discusses his theory of etymologies, see *Allegories of the Laws* 3.95; *On Agriculture* 1-2; and *Questions and Answers on Genesis* 2.77.

37. Philo, *On Planting* 134-35. On "Judah" as "praise" elsewhere in Philo, see *Allegories of the Laws* 1.80; 3.146; *On Dreams* 2.34.

38. In the prologue to his *Book of Hebrew Names* Jerome says that, according to Origen, Philo had compiled the prototype Greek-Hebrew word list. Eusebius of Caesarea says the same thing (*Ecclesiastical History* 2.18.7), probably in dependence on Origen. It is debatable

whether Philo knew enough Hebrew to have compiled such a list. But if Philo is not the author of the list known to Origen, he must have made use of this list or one like it.

39. For "Israel" to mean "the man who sees God," one must expand the Hebrew consonants to *'ysh r'h 'l*, literally "man seeing God." See Philo, *On Dreams* 2.173; *On Mating with Preliminary Studies* 51; *On Flight and Finding* 208; *Questions and Answers on Genesis* 3.49; Origen, *Homilies on Numbers* 11.4; Didymus, *Commentary on Zechariah* 6:12-15.

40. For example, see Justin, *Dialogue with Trypho* 125; Clement of Alexandria, *The Instructor* 1.6.

41. Origen, *Homilies on Joshua* 23.4; see *Origen: Homilies on Joshua*, trans. Barbara J. Bruce, ed. Cynthia White, Fathers of the Church (Washington: Catholic University of America Press, 2010), pp. 200-201.

42. Origen, *Homilies on Numbers* 25.3; see *Origen: Homilies on Numbers*, trans. Thomas P. Scheck, ed. C. A. Hall, Ancient Christian Texts (Downers Grove: InterVarsity, 2009), pp. 155-56. This etymology ultimately goes back to the Aramaic word *ryq'*, which also underlies the statement of Jesus in Matthew 5:22 that one should not say *"raka"* to one's brother.

43. For examples in Gregory of Nyssa, see *Gregory of Nyssa: Homilies on the Song of Songs*, trans. Richard A. Norris, Jr., Writings from the Greco-Roman World (Atlanta: Society of Biblical Literature, 2009), pp. 17, 153, 225, 229.

44. *Saint Cyril of Alexandria: Commentary on the Book of Exodus, First Discourse*, trans. Evie Zachariades-Holmberg (Rollinsford: Orthodox Research Institute, 2010), pp. 68-70. "Jethro" is being associated with the Hebrew word *yeter*, "what is left remaining," and "Reuel" is interpreted as "shepherd" *(ro'eh)* of "God" *('el)*. See also *Cyril of Alexandria: Commentary on Isaiah. Vol. 1: Chapters 1–14*, trans. Robert C. Hill (Brookline: Holy Cross Orthodox, 2008), p. 187.

45. Didymus the Blind, *Commentary on Zechariah* 14:10. On "Rimmon" as "lofty," see Hebrew *rwm*, "to be high," and *ramah*, "high place."

46. See *Didyme L'aveugle. Sur la Genèse*, vol. 2, Nautin, pp. 10-12.

47. "Hezekiah" is "strength" *(hzq)* of "YHWH" *(yh)*. "Isaiah," which would be better interpreted as "deliverance" *(yesha')* of "YHWH" *(yh)* (as in *Onomastica Sacra* 165.97; 173.69; 191.65), was also interpreted in some Greek sources as "elevation of God" (see *Onomastica Sacra* 202.79). Interestingly, Maximus interprets "Saul" as "Hades requested" (related to *Sheol*) or "borrowed" (passive participle of *sh'l*, "to ask for"). See *St. Maximus the Confessor's Questions and Doubts*, trans. Despina D. Prassas (Dekalb: Northern Illinois University Press, 2010), pp. 137-39; Maximus the Confessor, *Questions to Thalassius I* (*Corpus Christianorum, Series Graeca* 7, pp. 379-83); and Maximus the Confessor, *Questions to Thalassius II* (*Corpus Christianorum, Series Graeca* 22, pp. 251-55).

48. See *The Philokalia: The Complete Text, compiled by St. Nikodimos of the Holy Mountain and St. Makarios of Corinth*, vol. 2, trans. G. E. H. Palmer, P. Sherrard, and K. Ware (London: Faber and Faber, 1981), p. 207. The interpretation of proper name etymologies generally plays a smaller role among the Antiochene interpreters; but for an example, see Theodoret of Cyrus, *Questions on First Kingdoms* (= 1 Samuel) 59, where Theodoret makes use of the etymological meaning "fool" for Nabal in 1 Samuel 25.

49. Ambrose, *Cain and Abel* 1.6.24. For a theoretical statement on the interpretive significance of etymologies, see the prologue to Ambrose's *Commentary on Psalm 118*.

50. Hilary, *Tractates on the Psalms* 51:3; 67:14.

51. Augustine, *On Christian Teaching* 2.16.23; see *Saint Augustine: On Christian Teaching,* trans. R. P. H. Green, Oxford World's Classics (Oxford: Oxford University Press, 1999), p. 43.

52. Augustine, *Expositions of the Psalms* 59.9.

53. For examples, see Jerome's treatment of "Sheshach" in his *Commentary on Jeremiah* 25:26c, and his comments on "Abraham" in his *Hebrew Questions on Genesis* 17:4-5.

54. Jerome, *Commentary on Jeremiah* 32:42-44.

55. Jerome, *Homilies on the Psalms* 15 (on Psalm 83:6-11). As Jerome explains, "Unless we interpret this passage as we have done, what benefit is it to the churches of Christ to read of the tents of Edom, and the Ishmaelites, and so on, with all the other names" (*The Homilies of Saint Jerome,* vol. 1, trans. M. L. Ewald, Fathers of the Church [Washington: Catholic University of America Press, 1964], p. 114). In his *Commentary on Galatians* 1:11-12, Jerome says that the Greek translators of the Old Testament had to coin new words to express the new things that had been expressed uniquely in Hebrew.

56. Isidore of Seville, *Etymologies* 7.6-10; 9.1. On Hebrew as the original language of creation, see also Jerome, *Commentary on Isaiah* 13:10; *Commentary on Amos* 5:8-9.

57. This quotation comes from a third-century source cited by Eusebius of Caesarea, *Ecclesiastical History* 5.28.18.

58. Philo, *On the Special Laws* 4.49 (Loeb Classical Library).

59. Athenagoras, *A Plea for the Christians,* 7, 9; see *Early Christian Fathers,* trans. Cyril C. Richardson, Library of Christian Classics (Philadelphia: Westminster, 1953), pp. 307-8.

60. See also Basil the Great, *Homilies on the Psalms* 17.3; Justin Martyr, *Apology* 1.36; *Dialogue with Trypho* 115.

61. For example, regarding sūra 2:216-17, which deals with the possibility of fighting in the prohibited month in response to an attack, the thirteenth-century Persian Qur'anic commentator al-Baiḍāwī gave an account of a conflict between followers of Muhammad and a caravan of the hostile tribe Quraish as the situation directly addressed by this revelation; see Helmut Gätje, *The Qur'ān and Its Exegesis* (Oxford: Oneworld, 1996), pp. 212-14. A famous work titled *Occasions of Revelation (asbāb al-nuzūl)* was composed by the eleventh-century Islamic scholar al-Wāhidī. On the essentially interpretive (rather than historical) nature of this "occasion of revelation" material, see Andrew Rippin, "The Function of *asbāb al-nuzūl* in Qur'ānic Exegesis," in *The Qur'an and Its Interpretive Tradition* (Aldershot: Ashgate, 2001), section XIX (originally published in the *Bulletin of the School of Oriental and African Studies* 51 [1988]: 1-20).

62. For example, see Babylonian Talmud, *Pesahim* 6b; *Mekhilta de-Rabbi Ishmael,* tractate *Shirata* 7. Thus, Abraham could be said to have kept the whole Torah of Moses, even though this is impossible according to human chronology (Mishnah, *Qiddushin* 4:14; Tosefta, *Qiddushin* 5:21; Babylonian Talmud, *Yoma* 28b).

63. *Song of Songs Rabbah* 1.10.2.

64. Again, a rabbinic saying captures this idea: "Words of Torah may be poor in their own context, but rich in another context" (Talmud Yerushalmi, *Rosh Hashanah* 3:5, 58d).

65. Origen, *Homilies on Jeremiah* 8.3-5; Jerome, *The Homilies of Saint Jerome,* vol. 1, Ewald, p. 195; *The Homilies of Saint Jerome,* vol. 2, Ewald, p. 112.

66. *Didymus the Blind: Commentary on Zechariah,* trans. Robert C. Hill (Washington: Catholic University of America Press, 2006), pp. 115-21.

67. Didymus refers to Jesus as "the human being assumed by God the Word," and he

says that those who imitate Christ are "also called Christs on account of being sharers in him of whom it is said, 'Christ the power and wisdom of God' (1 Cor. 1:24)."

68. Relevant to this discussion is Augustine's belief that Christ is directly the speaker in all of the Psalms. According to Augustine, the fact that certain verses say things that Christ might not be expected to say simply shows that Christ speaks in the Psalms both through his own *persona* (the "head" of Christ) and also through the *persona* of the church (the "body" of Christ). Thus, in his exposition of Psalm 31, Augustine sees Christ the head speaking in v. 5 ("Into your hands I commit my spirit"; see Luke 23:46), and his body the church speaking in v. 10, "My life is spent in sorrow . . . my strength is weakened in iniquity"; see *Saint Augustine: Expositions of the Psalms 1–32*, trans. Maria Boulding, Works of Saint Augustine (Hyde Park: New City, 2000), pp. 321-58. Augustine never interprets a Psalm as if David or any other Old Testament character were speaking out of his own context, even when the Psalm itself suggests an "occasion of revelation." For example, at Psalm 18, which begins, "A Psalm of David, . . . who addressed the words of this song to the Lord on the day when the Lord rescued him from the hand of all his enemies, and from the hand of Saul," Augustine says, "Accordingly Christ and the Church, the whole Christ, Head and body, are speaking here when the Psalm begins"; see *Saint Augustine: Expositions of the Psalms 1–32*, Boulding, p. 189.

69. *Philocalia* 2.3; see *The Philocalia of Origen*, trans. G. Lewis (Edinburgh: Clark, 1911), p. 32.

70. As both Origen and Augustine point out, this approach to biblical interpretation requires exhaustive knowledge of Scripture and a sharp memory; see Origen, *Commentary on Matthew* 10.15; and Augustine, *On Christian Teaching* 2.9.14.

71. See Michael Graves, "The 'Pagan' Background of Patristic Exegetical Methods," in *Ancient Faith for the Church's Future*, ed. M. Husbands and J. P. Greenman (Downers Grove: InterVarsity, 2008), pp. 105-7.

72. See *Theodore of Mopsuestia: Commentary on the Twelve Prophets*, trans. Robert C. Hill, Fathers of the Church (Washington: Catholic University of America Press, 2004), pp. 116-20. See also Theodore's observation that Psalm 68:18 was not originally a prophecy about Christ but was simply quoted by Paul in Ephesians 4:7-11 as an idea applicable to Christ (*Theodore of Mopsuestia: Commentary on Psalms 1–81*, trans. Robert C. Hill, Writings from the Greco-Roman World [Atlanta: Society of Biblical Literature, 2006], pp. 876-78).

73. See also Athanasius, *Oration against the Arians* 1.54, "Now it is right and necessary, as in all divine Scripture, so here, faithfully to expound the time of which the apostle wrote, and the person, and the point; lest the reader, from ignorance missing either these or any similar particular, may be wide of the true sense."

74. Cyril introduced his *Commentary on Isaiah* with a general description of the historical setting: "Blessed Isaiah, then, prophesied in the time of the reign of Uzziah, Jotham, Ahaz, and Hezekiah. Come now, let us recall the times of each one, and mention in passing how he lived; from this we shall learn that the word of prophecy was appropriate and relevant to what was done in each period" (Cyril of Alexandria, *Commentary on Isaiah*, preface); see also Cyril's comments at Isaiah 13:2 and 14:1-3.

75. For example, see Jerome, *Commentary on Jeremiah* 2:36b-37; 5b-6a; 7:12; 12:5; 22:13-17; 22:18-19; 24:1-10; 25:32-33; 26:17-19; 29:21-23.

76. For example, see *Sifre to Numbers* 112; Babylonian Talmud, *Berakhot* 31b; *Yebamot* 71a; *Sanhedrin* 64b; 90b.

77. *Diodore of Tarsus: Commentary on Psalms 1–51,* trans. Robert C. Hill, Writings from the Greco-Roman World (Atlanta: Society of Biblical Literature, 2005), p. 143.

78. Qur'an 11:13. See *The Qur'an,* trans. Muhammad A. S. Abdel Haleem, Oxford World's Classics (Oxford: Oxford University Press, 2004), p. 137. See also Qur'an 10:38; 17:88.

79. For an introduction to this dimension of the Qur'an, with an accompanying CD, see Michael Sells, *Approaching the Qur'an: The Early Revelations,* 2nd ed. (Ashland: White Cloud, 2007).

80. See Al-Sayyid Abu al-Qasim al-Musawi al-Khui, *The Prolegomena to the Qur'an* (New York: Oxford University Press, 1998), pp. 42-44. See also Abdullah Saeed, "The Self Perception and the Originality of the Qur'an," in *Communicating the Word: Revelation, Translation, and Interpretation in Christianity and Islam,* ed. David Marshall (Washington: Georgetown University Press, 2011), pp. 102-3.

81. On this topic in general, see Michael Graves, "The Literary Quality of Scripture as Seen by the Early Church," *Tyndale Bulletin* 61 (2010): 161-82.

82. Arnobius, *Against the Pagans* 1.58-59; see Arnobius of Sicca, *The Case against the Pagans,* vol. 1, trans. George E. McCracken (New York: Newman, 1949), p. 104. See also the criticisms of Celsus in Origen, *Against Celsus* 6.1-2, and Lactantius, *Divine Institutes* 6.21.

83. Tatian, *Address to the Greeks* 29; see *Tatian: Oratio Ad Graecos and Fragments,* trans. Molly Whittaker (Oxford: Clarendon, 1982), p. 55. See also Clement of Alexandria, *Protrepticus* 8.

84. Origen, *Philocalia* 4.2; see *The Philocalia of Origen,* Lewis, p. 36.

85. John Chrysostom, *Commentary on Saint John the Apostle and Evangelist,* trans. T. A. Goggin (New York: Catholic University of America Press, 1957), p. 18.

86. Origen, *Against Celsus* 6.1-5.

87. Lactantius, *Divine Institutes* 5.1.15-16.

88. As an example, see Basil the Great, *Address to Young Men on Greek Literature;* Gregory of Nazianzus, *Orations* 4.5.

89. Socrates Scholasticus, *Ecclesiastical History* 3.16; Sozomen, *Ecclesiastical History* 5.18; Jerome, *Chronicon* CE 329; *On Illustrious Men* 84.

90. Origen, *Against Celsus* 7.59; Eusebius, *Preparation for the Gospel* 11.5.2.

91. Jerome, *Epistles* 22.30; 125.12.

92. This quotation comes from Jerome's preface to his Latin translation of Eusebius's *Chronicon* (see Griechischen Christlichen Schriftsteller 47, pp. 3-4).

93. Jerome, *Commentary on Isaiah* 5:7c; see Roger Gryson, *Commentaire de Jérôme sur le Prophète Isaïe. Livres I-IV* (Freiburg: Herder, 1993), pp. 275-76.

94. See Michael Graves, *Jerome's Hebrew Philology* (Leiden: Brill, 2007).

95. But see also the brief comment of Ambrose, *Epistle* 21: "Many persons say that our sacred writers did not write in accordance with the rules of rhetoric. We do not take issue with them: the sacred writers wrote not in accord with rules, but in accord with grace, which is above all rules of rhetoric. They wrote what the Holy Spirit gave them to speak. Yet, writers on rhetoric have found rhetoric in their writings and have made use of their writings to compose commentaries and rules"; see *Saint Ambrose: Letters,* trans. Mary M. Beyenka (New York: Catholic University of America Press, 1954), p. 115.

96. Augustine, *Confessions* 3.5.9; 5.14.24; *The First Catechetical Instruction* 9.13.

97. Augustine, *On Christian Teaching* 2.6.7-8 (written c. 396), on the "great pleasure" to

be had in finding the allegorical sense of the Song of Songs, and *The First Catechetical Instruction* 8.12, on the "marvelous sublimity" under the simple language of Scripture.

98. See *On Christian Teaching* 4.6.9–4.7.21, which Augustine wrote in the late 420s.

99. In addition to the passage cited in the previous note, see *On Christian Teaching* 2.19.29. According to Augustine, there are two kinds of learning: that which was instituted by humans and that which already existed (or was instituted by God) and has merely been observed by humans.

100. For example, see Harold Bloom, *The Shadow of a Great Rock: A Literary Appreciation of the King James Bible* (New Haven: Yale University Press, 2011); and Robert Alter, *Pen of Iron: American Prose and the King James Bible* (Princeton: Princeton University Press, 2010).

Chapter Five. Historicity and Factuality

1. There is some difficulty related to the chronology of these two figures. Herod the Great died in 4 BCE, but the only governorship easily identifiable by our sources (primarily Josephus) did not begin until 6 CE. On this topic, see I. Howard Marshall, *The Gospel of Luke: A Commentary on the Greek Text* (Grand Rapids: Eerdmans, 1978), pp. 102-4.

2. Paul's number in Galatians is apparently based on the ancient Greek translation of Exodus 12:40, which says, "The time that the people of Israel lived in Egypt *and Canaan* was 430 years." In other words, Paul's figure includes the period in Canaan covering Abraham's later life and the lives of Isaac and Jacob, together with Israel's time in Egypt. On this reckoning, Israel's time in Egypt would be just over 200 years. According to the Hebrew text of Exodus 12:40, "The time that the people of Israel lived in Egypt was 430 years." This figure of 430 years in Egypt is closer to the 400 years of affliction mentioned in Genesis 15:13-14. It is a matter of debate which text represents the original reading.

3. Josephus likewise approaches biblical narratives as essentially historical. Furthermore, Josephus praises the consistency of Israel's Scriptures in contrast to the contradictory histories written by the Greeks, whose authors are said to have lacked reliable records and to have written more to impress their readers than for the sake of accuracy (Josephus, *Against Apion* 1.3-5, 8).

4. See Markus Barth and Helmut Blanke, *The Letter to Philemon: A New Translation with Notes and Commentary* (Grand Rapids: Eerdmans, 2000), pp. 278-80.

5. See *Jerome's Commentaries on Galatians, Titus, and Philemon*, trans. Thomas P. Scheck (Notre Dame: University of Notre Dame Press, 2010), pp. 365-66.

6. *Theodore of Mopsuestia: Commentary on the Twelve Prophets*, trans. Robert C. Hill, Fathers of the Church (Washington: Catholic University of America Press, 2004), p. 200.

7. See Cyril of Alexandria, *Commentary on Jonah* 1:17; Jerome, *Commentary on Jonah* 2:2. Cyril mentions a story in which Hercules was swallowed by a sea monster. Jerome lists several stories from Ovid's *Metamorphoses*.

8. *On Unbelievable Tales* 15; see Jacob Stern, *Palaephatus, On Unbelievable Tales: Translation, Introduction, and Commentary* (Wauconda: Bolchazy-Carducci, 1996), p. 46.

9. See Luc Brisson, *How Philosophers Saved Myths,* trans. Catherine Tihanyi (Chicago: University of Chicago Press, 2004); T. James Luce, *The Greek Historians* (New York: Routledge, 1997).

10. See Louis H. Feldman, *Josephus's Interpretation of the Bible* (Berkeley: University of California Press, 1998), pp. 427-33.

11. Philo, *On Mating with Preliminary Studies* 180 (Loeb Classical Library).

12. Philo, *On Drunkenness* 144 (Loeb Classical Library).

13. *Leviticus Rabbah* 1; Babylonian Talmud, *Megillah* 13a.

14. *Philocalia* 15.15; see *The Philocalia of Origen,* trans. G. Lewis (Edinburgh: Clark, 1911), pp. 73-74 (translation updated). See also *Against Celsus* 1.42.

15. *Commentary on John* 10.143-49; see *Origen, Commentary on the Gospel According to John Books 1-10,* trans. Ronald E. Heine, Fathers of the Church (Washington: Catholic University of America Press, 1989), pp. 288-90.

16. See also *Philocalia* 1.16: "And this we ought to know, that the chief purpose was to show the spiritual connections both in past occurrences and in things to be done. Wherever the Word found historical events capable of adaptation to these mystic truths, He made use of them, but concealed the deeper sense from the many; but where in setting forth the sequence of things spiritual there was no actual event recounted for the sake of the more mystic meaning, Scripture interweaves the imaginative with the historical, sometimes introducing what is utterly impossible, sometimes what is possible but never occurred. Sometimes it is only a few words, not literally true, which have been inserted; sometimes the insertions are of greater length"; see *The Philocalia of Origen,* Lewis, p. 17 (translation updated).

17. *Philocalia* 15.17. It should also be noted that Origen defended the historicity of many passages of Scripture, including the story of Noah's ark, against pagan criticism (*Homilies on Genesis* 2.2).

18. But see Joshua 5:4-6.

19. Jerome, *Against Jovinianus* 1.21 (Nicene and Post-Nicene Fathers, series 2, vol. 6, pp. 361-62). Jerome interprets "Gilgal" as "revelation" and takes the overthrow of Jericho as the overthrow of the world by the preaching of the Gospel (following Origen). Jerome also argues that when Joshua enters the land, the waters of marriage dry up. This is part of Jerome's argument in favor of chastity.

20. *Homilies on Ezekiel* 2.1.3; see *The Homilies of Saint Gregory the Great on the Book of the Prophet Ezekiel,* trans. Theodosia Gray, ed. P. J. Cownie (Etna: Center for Traditionalist Orthodox Studies, 1990), pp. 158-59.

21. See Origen, *Against Celsus* 4.39-40; *On First Principles* 3.2.1; 4.3.1.

22. See Didymus, *Commentary on Genesis* 3; Ambrose, *Paradise.*

23. Ambrose, *Paradise* 11-18; see *Saint Ambrose: Hexameron, Paradise, and Cain and Abel,* trans. John J. Savage, Fathers of the Church (New York: Fathers of the Church, 1961), pp. 293-99. On the cardinal virtues, see Plato, *Protagoras* 330b; 349b; 359a (five virtues: the four plus "piety"); *Republic* 4.427e, 433a-c; *Laws* 1.631c-d; 12.965d (four virtues); Wisdom of Solomon 8:7; Cicero, *On Ends* 5.23.67; *On Duties* 1.2.5; Ambrose, *Exposition of the Gospel of Luke* 5.62-68.

24. Diodore of Tarsus, *Commentary on Psalm 118,* preface; see Karlfried Froehlich, ed. and trans., *Biblical Interpretation in the Early Church* (Philadelphia: Fortress, 1984), p. 90.

25. Theodoret, *Questions on the Octateuch,* Qu 25 and Qu 29 on Genesis.

26. Theodore of Mopsuestia, *Commentary on Galatians* 4:22-31; see Froehlich, *Biblical Interpretation in the Early Church,* p. 97.

27. Diodore of Tarsus, *Commentary on the Psalms,* prologue; see Froehlich, *Biblical Interpretation in the Early Church,* p. 85.

28. See Dimitri Z. Zaharopoulos, *Theodore of Mopsuestia on the Bible: A Study of His Old Testament Exegesis* (New York: Paulist, 1989), pp. 46-47. The source for this quotation is the ninth-century writer Isho'dad of Merv.

29. Zaharopoulos, *Theodore of Mopsuestia on the Bible,* pp. 46-47. For charges made against Theodore based on his views of Job, see John Behr, *The Case against Diodore and Theodore: Texts and Their Contexts* (Oxford: Oxford University Press, 2011), pp. 411-13.

30. Diodore of Tarsus, *Commentary on Psalm 118,* preface; see Froehlich, *Biblical Interpretation in the Early Church,* p. 91.

31. Philo, *On Rewards and Punishments* 55 (Loeb Classical LIbrary).

32. Augustine, *Letter* 143.7.

33. Cyril of Alexandria, *Commentary on Isaiah* 1:2-3; see *Cyril of Alexandria: Commentary on Isaiah.* Vol. 1: *Chapters 1–14,* trans. Robert C. Hill (Brookline: Holy Cross Orthodox, 2008), p. 21.

34. Aristotle, *Poetics* 25 (Loeb Classical Library): *Peri problēmatōn kai lyseōn* ("Concerning problems and their solutions").

35. An example of an allegedly impossible narrative is the story of Achilles chasing Hector around the city of Troy in *Iliad* 22. An example of an alleged contradiction is the description of Aeneas's spear failing to penetrate Achilles' shield in *Iliad* 20.258-72; the spear is stopped by the gold (outer?) layer, but is also said to have penetrated two bronze (inner?) layers.

36. Philo, *Noah's Work as a Planter* 113 (Loeb Classical Library). Readers today may find Philo's comments fascinating as a window into how people prepared food in the ancient world.

37. Matthew 4:11-13.

38. See Mark 11:15-19; Matt. 21:12-17; Luke 19:45-48.

39. John 2:1; 2:12, 14-22; 3:22-24.

40. Origen, *Commentary on John* 10.14; see *Origen, Commentary on the Gospel According to John Books 1-10,* trans. Ronald E. Heine, Fathers of the Church (Washington: Catholic University of America Press, 1989), p. 257.

41. Origen, *Commentary on John* 10.19; see *Origen, Commentary on the Gospel According to John Books 1-10,* Heine, p. 259. See also *Commentary on John* 10.10, 18-22, 27, 129-30, 143-49, 197-200.

42. Augustine, *City of God* 18.44; see *St. Augustine Concerning The City of God against the Pagans,* trans. Henry Bettenson (London: Penguin, 1984), pp. 822-23.

43. See Matthew 26:6-13 and John 12:1-8 on the many parallels and differences between these accounts.

44. Jerome, *Commentary on Matthew* 26.7-8; see *St. Jerome: Commentary on Matthew,* trans. Thomas P. Scheck, Fathers of the Church (Washington: Catholic University of America Press, 2008), p. 293. On the figure of speech *syllēpsis,* see H. Lausberg, D. E. Orton, and R. D. Anderson, eds., *Handbook of Literary Rhetoric* (Leiden: Brill, 1998), paragraphs 702, 703, and 706. Jerome refers to *synecdochē* ("the whole stands for part, or the part for the whole") in his *Commentary on Jonah* 2:1 to explain why Jesus likens his time in the grave to Jonah's "three days and three nights" (Matt. 12:40), when Jesus was not in the grave for three full days and nights (see also Quintilian 8.6.19; Cicero, *On the Orator* 3.168).

45. Jerome, *Homily* 75; see *The Homilies of Saint Jerome,* vol. 2, trans. M. L. Ewald, Fa-

thers of the Church (Washington: Catholic University of America Press, 1965), pp. 121-23. This problem had been raised by Porphyry in his work *Against the Christians*.

46. Jerome, *Homilies on the Psalms* 11; see *The Homilies of Saint Jerome*, vol. 1, trans. M. L. Ewald, Fathers of the Church (Washington: Catholic University of America Press, 1964), pp. 81-83. Jerome addresses several other textual difficulties in this passage. On Jerome's attempts to resolve the apparent quotation from Zechariah ascribed to Jeremiah in Matthew 27:9-10, see Jerome's *Homilies on the Psalms* 11; *Epistle* 57.7; and *Commentary on Matthew* 27:9-10. Jerome suggests scribal error, the loose citation practices of the apostles, and even the possibility that the text was in an apocryphal work on Jeremiah. But in the end, he concedes that the passage is from Zechariah: "Yet, it still seems more likely to me that the testimony was taken from Zechariah by a common practice of the evangelists and apostles. In citation they bring out only the sense of the Old Testament. They tend to neglect the order of the words" (see *St. Jerome: Commentary on Matthew*, Scheck, p. 310).

47. Theodoret, *Questions on the Octateuch*, Qu 2 on Judges; see *Theodoret of Cyrus: The Questions on the Octateuch*, vol. 2, Hill, p. 311.

48. See *Jerome's Commentaries on Galatians, Titus, and Philemon*, trans. Thomas P. Scheck (Notre Dame: University of Notre Dame Press, 2010), p. 101; Jerome, *Against Helvidius* 4. On the custom of historians describing things not as they were but as they were widely thought to be, see also Jerome, *Commentary on Jeremiah* 28:10-17, on the false prophet Hananiah being called a "prophet." This topic is addressed in Aristotle's *Poetics* 25.

49. It is interesting that neither Theodore nor Jerome explicitly comments on what kind ("genre") of literature Jonah is. Still, they both make observations that run parallel to some modern readings of the book. For example, Theodore doubts that the sailors in Jonah 1 actually made sacrifices while still on the boat and insists that Jonah must have preached more than what is reported in Jonah 3 since the Ninevites would never have repented based on the short remark in v. 4 spoken by an unknown foreigner (see Theodore, *Commentary on Jonah* 1:16; 3:5), and Jerome says that the description of the animals wearing sackcloth in 3:8 should be interpreted allegorically (see Jerome, *Commentary on Jonah* 3:6-9).

50. Tertullian, *Against Marcion* 4.2; see *Tertullian: Adversus Marcionem, Books 4 and 5*, trans. Ernest Evans (Oxford: Clarendon, 1972), p. 263.

51. John Chrysostom, *Homilies on Matthew* 1.6 (Nicene and Post-Nicene Fathers 10, p. 3).

52. Tertullian, *Prescription against the Heretics* 7 (Ante-Nicene Fathers 3, p. 246). See also *Tertullian: On the Testimony of the Soul, and "Prescription" of Heretics*, trans. T. Herbert Bindley (London: SPCK, 1914), p. 45; and *Early Latin Theology*, trans. S. L. Greens5lade, Library of Christian Classics (Philadelphia: Westminster, 1956), p. 36.

53. For example, see Lactantius, *Divine Institutes* 3.26-30.

54. For example, see Origen, *Against Celsus* 6.2-10; 8.2-4. Whereas Scripture's simple style benefits many, Origen says, Plato's refined style benefits few, if anyone at all (6.2). But later on Origen says that Plato did help humankind (6.2) and said something well (6.3), yet what Plato said well did little good (6.4-5), even though he did teach profound philosophy about the highest good (6.5). The passage about the devil inspiring a saying of Plato is found in *Against Celsus* 8.4 (see Plato, *Phaedrus* 246e-247a). Origen appears to have been somewhat conflicted about Platonic thinking; see Joseph W. Trigg, *Origen: The Bible and Philosophy in the Third-Century Church* (Atlanta: John Knox, 1983); Mark J. Edwards, *Origen against Plato* (Aldershot: Ashgate, 2002).

55. Gregory the Great was another early Christian figure who often exhibited a negative attitude toward non-Christian learning; for example, on the sentence "There was no blacksmith to be found in Israel" (1 Sam. 13:19), Gregory says, "What therefore does this mean, except that we do not equip ourselves for spiritual wars through secular literature but through divine literature?" See Gregory the Great, *Commentary on 1 Kingdoms* (= 1 Samuel) 5.84 (*Corpus Christianorum, Series Latina* 144, p. 471).

56. Eusebius of Caesarea, *Preparation for the Gospel* 2.1; 9.27; 13.12.

57. See Clement of Alexandria, *Miscellanies* 1.15.66.1–73.6; 1.21.101.1–22.150.5; 1.25.165.1– 166.5 (see *Clement of Alexandria: Stromateis, Books One to Three*, trans. John Ferguson, Fathers of the Church [Washington: Catholic University of America Press, 1991], pp. 72-78, 99- 135, 144-46). The quotation from Numenius is in *Miscellanies* 1.22.150.4 (*Clement of Alexandria,* Ferguson, p. 135). On the partial benefits to be found in Greek philosophy, see *Miscellanies* 6.10.80.1–83.3 (Ante-Nicene Fathers 2, pp. 498-99).

58. Tatian, *Address to the Greeks* 31, 36-41; Justin, *1 Apology* 59; Theophilus, *To Autolycus* 3.23; Augustine, *City of God* 18.37. Augustine suggests that it was Jeremiah who introduced Plato to the writings of Moses while they were both in Egypt, and "it was this that enabled him [Plato] to learn and write the things for which he is justly praised" (Augustine, *On Christian Teaching* 2.28.43; see *Saint Augustine: On Christian Teaching*, trans. R. P. H. Green, Oxford World's Classics [Oxford: Oxford University Press, 1999], p. 55).

59. Justin, *2 Apology* 10; see *Saint Justin Martyr*, trans. Thomas B. Falls, Fathers of the Church (New York: Christian Heritage, 1948), p. 129. See also Jerome, *Commentary on Daniel* 1:2: "By these vessels we are to understand the dogmas of truth. For if you go through all of the works of the philosophers, you will necessarily find in them some vessels of the portions of God. For example, you will find in Plato that God is the fashioner of the universe, in Zeno the chief of the Stoics, that there are inhabitants in the infernal regions and that souls are immortal, and that honor is the one (true) good. But because the philosophers combine truth with error and corrupt the good of nature with many evils, for that reason they are recorded to have captured only a portion of the vessels of God's house, and not all of them in their completeness and perfection"; see *Jerome's Commentary on Daniel*, trans. Gleason L. Archer, Jr. (Grand Rapids: Baker, 1958), p. 20.

60. Justin, *2 Apology* 13; see *Saint Justin Martyr*, Falls, pp. 133-34. See the related comments of Jerome, *Commentary on Matthew* 25:26-28: "'You reap where you have not sown, and you gather where you have not scattered,' we understand that the Lord accepts the good life even of the Gentiles and philosophers. He regards those who behave justly one way, and those who behave unjustly in another way. Those who neglect the written law will be condemned in comparison with the one who serves the natural law"; see *St. Jerome: Commentary on Matthew*, Scheck, p. 288.

61. Examples of this can be found throughout the book. To offer another clear illustration: Origen says that Solomon intended to teach the three branches of philosophy through his wisdom books: moral philosophy through Proverbs, natural philosophy through Ecclesiastes, and inspective (or "contemplative") philosophy through the Song of Songs. These three branches were already prefigured in the patriarchs Abraham, Isaac, and Jacob. According to Origen, it was from Solomon that the Greeks learned these philosophical categories (Origen, *Commentary on the Song of Songs*, prologue); see *Origen: The Song of Songs, Commentary and Homilies*, trans. R. P. Lawson, Ancient Christian Writers (New York: Newman, 1956), pp. 39-42, 44-45. Ambrose similarly finds the threefold wisdom of "pagan" philoso-

phers, that is, natural, moral, and rational philosophy, symbolized by the three wells that Isaac dug in Genesis 26:19-23 (Ambrose, *Commentary on the Gospel According to Luke,* prologue); see Boniface Ramsey, *Ambrose,* The Early Church Fathers (London: Routledge, 1997), pp. 161-62. Obviously, Origen and Ambrose did not actually learn these categories from Scripture but from their "pagan" education.

62. Basil, *Address to Young Men on Greek Literature* 4.1 (Loeb Classical Library).

63. Augustine, *On Christian Teaching* 2.40.60.

64. Gregory of Nyssa, *Life of Moses,* 2.115-16; see also 2.37-41; Augustine, *On Christian Teaching* 2.18.28; 2.40.60–2.42.63. See also Origen's comments in *Philocalia* 13.1-4. See Exodus 3:20-22; 11:2-3; 12:35-36.

65. Noteworthy in this connection was the attempt by Julian ("Julian the Apostate," emperor 361-63) to forbid Christians from teaching in the schools. Julian wanted to cut Christians off from the educational system. If Christians did not believe in the traditional Greek and Roman gods, Julian reasoned, then they should not be teaching the traditional literature. Julian said, "Let them [that is, the Christians] betake themselves to the churches of the Galilaeans to expound Matthew and Luke" (Julian, *Epistle* 36, Loeb Classical Library).

66. Origen, *On First Principles* 4.3.1; see *Origen: On First Principles,* trans. G. W. Butterworth (New York: Harper & Row, 1966), p. 288.

67. Origen, *Homilies on Genesis* 1.2, 5-7; see *Origen: Homilies on Genesis and Exodus,* trans. Ronald E. Heine, Fathers of the Church (Washington: Catholic University of America Press, 1982), pp. 48-49, 53-56.

68. Ephrem, *Commentary on Genesis* 1.1; 5.1; see *St. Ephrem the Syrian: Selected Prose Works,* Fathers of the Church (Washington: Catholic University of America Press, 1994), pp. 74, 77-78, 91. Ephrem does make a point to say that the plants and animals were created old in appearance, even though they were young in age (*Commentary on Genesis* 25.1).

69. John Chrysostom, *Homilies on Genesis* 2-10.

70. Ambrose, *The Six Days of Creation* 2.5; see *Saint Ambrose: Hexameron, Paradise, and Cain and Abel,* trans. John J. Savage, Fathers of the Church (New York: Fathers of the Church, 1961), p. 5.

71. For example, see *Saint Ambrose: Hexameron, Paradise, and Cain and Abel,* Savage, pp. 5-6 (Moses' education), p. 21 (earth upheld by God), p. 23 (disparaging philosophers), p. 24 (their opinions cannot withstand Moses' words), pp. 52-53 (heavens spherical with square-shaped roof), p. 87 (God, not sun, makes vegetation). For a defense that Hezekiah's shadow really moved back ten steps (2 Kings 20:9) and that the sun stood still for Joshua (Joshua 10:12-14), see Hippolytus, *Commentary on Daniel* 1.7-8; see *Hippolyte: Commentaire sur Daniel,* ed. and trans. Maurice Lefèvre, Sources chrétiennes (Paris: Cerf, 1947), pp. 80-84.

72. Basil, *The Six Days of Creation* 9.1; see *Saint Basil: Exegetic Homilies,* trans. A. C. Way, Fathers of the Church (Washington: Catholic University of America Press, 1963), pp. 135-36. As Basil says, "Those who interpret allegorically think that they are wiser than the revelations of the Spirit."

73. Basil, *The Six Days of Creation* 1.2.

74. Basil, *The Six Days of Creation* 7.1; see *Saint Basil: Exegetic Homilies,* Way, pp. 105-6. Basil's treatment of the animals in homilies 7 and 8 is particularly interesting.

75. See Augustine, *Literal Commentary on Genesis* 8.2.5. Augustine contrasts this "literal" treatment with his former work on Genesis directed against the Manichees, which ap-

proached the text primarily through figures and enigmas (see Augustine's *Two Books on Genesis against the Manichees* 2.2.3).

76. Augustine, *Literal Commentary on Genesis* 1.2.5; 1.4.9; 1.9.16; 1.10.20 (God's first utterance was immaterial); 1.1.2 (on the "deep"); 1.5.11 (on the "waters"). See also *Literal Commentary on Genesis* 1.6.12 on the Trinity.

77. See Augustine, *Literal Commentary on Genesis* 1.19.38; 1.21.41; 2.9.21; see *St. Augustine: The Literal Meaning of Genesis*, vol. 1, trans. John Hammond Taylor, S.J., Ancient Christian Writers (New York: Paulist, 1982), pp. 42, 45, 59.

78. Augustine, *Literal Commentary on Genesis* 1.19.39; see *St. Augustine: The Literal Meaning of Genesis*, vol. 1, Taylor, pp. 42-43. See also *Literal Commentary on Genesis* 1.10.21; 2.1.4; 2.9.20.

79. The Aramaic portions of the Old Testament are Daniel 2:4b–7:28; Ezra 4:8–6:18 and 7:12-26; Jeremiah 10:11; and the phrase "heap of witness" in Genesis 31:47. Aramaic is an ancient Semitic language closely related to Hebrew. Aramaic inscriptions have been dated to as early as the tenth century BCE. Aramaic was later used as an administrative language by the Babylonian Empire, which explains the presence of Aramaic in books related to Judah's exile in Babylon.

80. For examples of Aramaic sayings of Jesus, see Mark 5:41; 15:34. On the languages of Jesus and the Gospels, see Michael Graves, "The Languages of Palestine," in *Dictionary of Jesus and the Gospels*, 2nd ed., ed. Joel B. Green, Jeannine K. Brown, and Nicholas Perrin (Downers Grove: InterVarsity, 2013).

81. See Natalio Fernández Marcos, *The Septuagint in Context: Introduction to the Greek Versions of the Bible*, trans. W. G. E. Watson (Leiden: Brill, 2001), pp. 320-37.

82. The letters *aleph-daleth-mem* in Hebrew can be pronounced as either "Edom" or "*adam.*" The Old Testament context favors "Edom," since it is followed by the phrase "and all the nations," implying that one nation has just been mentioned. In the Hebrew manuscripts that survive to us, a vowel letter marking an "o" sound for "Edom" was added to make the meaning clear, but this vowel letter was apparently lacking in the Hebrew text used by the Septuagint translators, which only exacerbated their difficulties with this text.

83. The historical setting of the quotation in Acts 15 is also significant. The quotation of Amos 9 essentially follows the Septuagint. But would we not expect James, speaking in Jerusalem, to quote the Hebrew text? Is it possible that he did and that the writer of Acts then gave the text in the Septuagint-based form?

84. See Rudolph Pfeiffer, *History of Classical Scholarship: From the Beginning to the Hellenistic Age* (Oxford: Clarendon, 1968), pp. 171-279.

85. The statement of Aristobulus on the translation of the Law, preserved in Eusebius's *Preparation for the Gospel* 13.12, was not very influential.

86. Moses Hadas suggests a date shortly after the translation of Sirach in 132 BCE; see Moses Hadas, ed. and trans., *Aristeas to Philocrates (Letter of Aristeas)* (New York: Harper, 1951), p. 54. For another translation, see "Letter of Aristeas," in *The Old Testament Pseudepigrapha*, vol. 2, ed. James H. Charlesworth (New York: Doubleday, 1985), pp. 7-34.

87. *Letter of Aristeas* 307; see *Aristeas to Philocrates*, Hadas, p. 221.

88. Josephus, *Jewish Antiquities* 12:11-118.

89. Philo, *Life of Moses* 2.37.

90. Philo, *Life of Moses*, 2.36.

91. Justin, *1 Apology* 31.

92. Justin, *Dialogue with Trypho* 71.

93. Irenaeus, *Against Heresies* 3.21.2.

94. Irenaeus, *Against Heresies* 3.21.3-4.

95. *Exhortation to the Greeks* 13. The story of the separate cells is not mentioned in the earliest sources and is no doubt fictitious, but this apparently did not stop ancient "tour guides" from capitalizing on the story.

96. Clement of Alexandria, *Miscellanies* 1.22.148.1–149.3 (see *Clement of Alexandria*, Ferguson, p. 134-35).

97. Eusebius, *Preparation for the Gospel* 8.1–15.9.

98. For example, see Cyril of Jerusalem, *Catechetical Lectures* 4.34; John Chrysostom, *Homilies on Genesis* 4.9; *Homilies on Matthew* 5.4; Epiphanius, *On Weights and Measures* 3-11; Augustine, *On Christian Teaching* 2.15.22.

99. It should be noted that in the first three centuries Tertullian alone mentions the *Letter of Aristeas* by name. His version of the Septuagint legend follows the *Letter* more closely than those of other writers do, lacks the supernatural elements, and even gives the number of translators as seventy-two (Tertullian, *Apology* 18.5-8).

100. Philo, *Life of Moses* 2.38-40.

101. On Origen's *Hexapla*, see Marcos, *Septuagint in Context*, pp. 204-22.

102. See Origen's *Epistle to Africanus* (Ante-Nicene Fathers 4, pp. 386-92). For examples of Origen interpreting more than one text, see his *Homilies on Jeremiah* 14.3-4; 15.5. Other Church Fathers quote alternative translations and expound them; for example John Chrysostom, *Homilies on the Psalms* 8.5; 10.11; Jerome, *Commentary on Jeremiah* 2:23c-24; 15:12; 22:13-17.

103. See especially Origen, *Commentary on Matthew* 15.14 (Griechischen Christlichen Schriftsteller 40, pp. 387-89). Origen says that he intends to "heal" the disagreements in the copies of the Old Testament. He seems to think that by getting closer to the Hebrew, he is restoring the original Septuagint. It would be possible to read this passage as if Origen intends actually to correct the Septuagint based on the Hebrew, but this would not match Origen's views as stated in his *Epistle to Africanus* or his general practice of basing his interpretations on the Septuagint. See also Origen's *Homilies on Jeremiah* 15.5; 16.5,10.

104. Hilary, *Tractate on the Psalms* 2.2-3.

105. Theodore of Mopsuestia, *Commentary on Habakkuk* 2:11.

106. On Jerome's life and biblical interpretation as it relates to Hebrew, see *Jerome: Commentary on Jeremiah*, trans. Michael Graves, ed. C. A. Hall, Ancient Christian Texts (Downers Grove: InterVarsity, 2011), pp. xxiii-li.

107. For example, see Jerome, *Commentary on Jeremiah*, prologue: "The book of Baruch, which is included in the popular edition of the Seventy but is not found in the Hebrew, and the pseudepigraphic letter of Jeremiah, I have judged to be totally unworthy of treatment. But out of the Hebrew founts I have endeavored to straighten out the order of Jeremiah, which had been confused by scribes, and to complete what was lacking in the book, so that you may have the new out of the old, and the true prophet in place of the false and corrupted one" (see *Jerome: Commentary on Jeremiah*, Graves, p. 1). This quotation shows the implications of Jerome's turn to the Hebrew for the question of what books should be included in the canon. At the same time, he had a strong conservative streak and continued his whole life to quote "apocryphal" books, such as Wisdom of Solomon and Ecclesiasticus, even though they were not in the Hebrew canon; see his comments in the

preface to his translation of Samuel-Kings (Nicene and Post-Nicene Fathers, series 2, vol. 6, p. 490).

108. In addition to Jerome's prefaces, see Rufinus, *Apology against Jerome* 2.32-37.

109. On Augustine's initial reaction, see Augustine, *Epistles* 28 and 71. See also *On Christian Teaching* 2.15.22 (written in 396); *Epistle* 82. Augustine's more open attitude can be found in *City of God* 18.42-44 (written after 420) and *On Christian Teaching* 4.7.15 (written in the late 420s).

110. See H. F. D. Sparks, "Jerome as Biblical Scholar," in *The Cambridge History of the Bible*. Volume 1: *From the Beginnings to Jerome,* ed. P. R. Ackroyd and C. F. Evans (Cambridge: Cambridge University Press, 1970), p. 521.

111. Nevertheless, Jerome complains that some people grumbled against him even for correcting Latin Gospel texts according to the original Greek; see *Vulgate Gospels,* preface (Nicene and Post-Nicene Fathers, series 2, vol. 6, p. 488).

112. Jerome got his start in Hebrew studying with a Jewish convert to Christianity (Jerome, *Epistle* 125.12).

113. The following is an example of interpretation based on a textual detail in translation: In the Hebrew language, there is a way of expressing emphasis in doing an action, saying "he will *surely* do it" rather than simply "he will do it." This is done by placing the infinitive of the verb next to the indicative form of the verb. Thus, in Genesis 2:17, *mot tamut* means "You shall *surely* die" (literally, "to die, you shall die"). The translators of the Septuagint and the Old Latin version did not always translate this construction idiomatically, and it caused problems for commentators. Thus, at Exodus 22:23 (Hebrew *'anneh te'anneh,* "If you do *in fact* afflict them . . ."), the Septuagint translated in a wooden fashion: "If *with affliction* you afflict them. . . ." According to Philo, this implies that one can also afflict someone with good; otherwise, it would be superfluous to say "*with affliction* you afflict them" (*On Mating with Preliminary Studies* 178). The same phenomenon occurred in Latin. For *mot tamut* in Genesis 2:17, the Old Latin version translated "*by death* you shall die" (instead of "You shall *surely* die"). Augustine explains that the text points to two acts of dying, the first and the second (see Rev. 20:6, 14; 21:8). Augustine's comment makes better sense when we realize that two "dying" words are before him in the text. In the idiom of the Hebrew language, there are not two deaths involved. But the peculiar reading of the Old Latin, which followed the Septuagint in its wooden translation of the underlying Hebrew idiom, gave Augustine an open door to identify two deaths in the passage (Augustine, *City of God* 13.12).

Chapter Six. Agreement with Truth

1. Tertullian, *On Monogamy* 11; see *Tertullian: Treatises on Marriage and Remarriage,* trans. William P. Le Saint, Ancient Christian Writers (New York: Newman, 1951), p. 98. See also Tertullian's treatise *On the Soul* 21, where he indicates that his opponents quoted Luke 6:43, "For no good tree bears bad fruit, nor again does a bad tree bear good fruit," in order to prove that the fundamental nature of human beings cannot change. Tertullian counters by quoting other passages of Scripture, such as Matthew 3:9, "God is able from these stones to raise up children for Abraham," Ephesians 2:3, and 1 Corinthians 6:11, which show that the nature of people *can* change by God's power. Tertullian's point is that Luke 6:43 cannot teach something different from these texts: "Holy Scripture, however, is never contradictory"; see

Tertullian: Apologetical Works, and Minucius Felix: Octavius, trans. R. Arbesmann, E. J. Daly, and E. A. Quain, Fathers of the Church (Washington: Catholic University of America Press, 1950), p. 229.

2. *Exhortation to the Greeks* 8; see *Saint Justin Martyr,* trans. Thomas B. Falls, Fathers of the Church (New York: Christian Heritage, 1948), p. 384. Although not written by Justin, the *Exhortation to the Greeks* was preserved as part of the corpus of Justin Martyr's writings and is included along with Justin's works in the Fathers of the Church series.

3. Augustine, *Reply to Faustus the Manichaean* 11.5-6; see *Saint Augustine: Answer to Faustus, a Manichean,* trans. Roland Teske, S.J., Works of Saint Augustine (Hyde Park: New City, 2007), p. 119.

4. Jerome, *Commentary on Galatians* 5:2.

5. Origen, *Homilies on Jeremiah* 5.12.1.

6. Didymus the Blind, *Commentary on Ecclesiastes,* fragment from a papyrus found at Tura in Egypt. On this difficult text I have followed the edition of Michael Fiedrowicz, *Principes de l'interprétation de l'Écriture dans l'Église ancienne* (Berne: Lang, 1998), pp. 78-80. Didymus also mentions in this text a criticism made by Porphyry against Christian spiritual interpretation, and he describes an allegorical reading of Homer such that Achilles is likened to Christ and Hector to the devil.

7. Justin, *Dialogue with Trypho* 94.

8. Cyril of Jerusalem, *Catechetical Lectures* 16.4; see *Cyril of Jerusalem and Nemesius of Emesa,* trans. William Telfer, Library of Christian Classics (Philadelphia: Westminster, 1955), p. 169. See also Jerome's *Commentary on Ecclesiastes* 11:6-8; 12:12, where he argues that the Old and New Testaments are a single body and that all the various books of Scripture theologically comprise a single book.

9. Origen, *Homilies on Numbers* 9.4; see *Origen: Homilies on Numbers,* trans. Thomas P. Scheck, ed. C. A. Hall, Ancient Christian Texts (Downers Grove: InterVarsity, 2009), p. 39.

10. Jerome, *Commentary on Ezekiel* 13:1-3a (*Corpus Christianorum, Series Latina* 75, p. 137). See also Jerome, *Commentary on Jeremiah* 30:18-22: "Whatever took place 'carnally' among the former people is fulfilled spiritually in the church" (see *Jerome: Commentary on Jeremiah,* trans. Michael Graves, ed. C. A. Hall, Ancient Christian Texts [Downers Grove: InterVarsity, 2011], p. 188).

11. For example, see *Epistle of Barnabas* 10; Irenaeus, *Against Heresies* 5.8.3.

12. The Sabbath was commanded not only in the Law (e.g., Exod. 20:8-11; Num. 15:32-36; Deut. 5:12-15) but also in the Prophets (e.g., Isa. 56:6; Jer. 17:19-27). On Jesus and the Sabbath, see Matt. 12:1-14; Mark 2:23-28; Luke 6:1-5; and John 5:18. On Jerome's views, see *Homily* 72 (see *The Homilies of Saint Jerome,* vol. 2, trans. M. L. Ewald, Fathers of the Church [Washington: Catholic University of America Press, 1965], p. 139); and *Commentary on Jeremiah* 17:21-27.

13. See Leviticus 4:20, 26, 31, 35; 5:10, 13, 16, 18; 6:7; 19:22; Hebrews 10:1-4, 11; Origen, *Homilies on Leviticus* 2.2.5; 3.5.1; 8.5.3; 10.1.2; 12.1.1; 13.3.3; 15.3.2. As Hebrews 10:4 states, "It is impossible for the blood of bulls and goats to take away sins."

14. Jerome, *Commentary on Ecclesiastes* 3:18-21; see *St. Jerome: Commentary on Ecclesiastes,* trans. Richard J. Goodrich and David J. D. Miller, Ancient Christian Writers (New York: Newman, 2012), pp. 63-64. Jerome points to Genesis 37:35; Job 17:13; 21:13; 24:19; and Luke 16:19-31 to show that before Christ's death all souls went to Hades, and Luke 23:43 among other texts to show that Christ opened the way to Paradise.

15. Jerome, *Commentary on Ecclesiastes* 2:18-19. Jerome cites as parallel the parable of the rich fool in Luke 12:16-21.

16. Augustine, *Expositions of the Psalms* 6.6; see also 38.22, on Psalm 39:13, ". . . before I depart and am no more"; 87.11-12, on Psalm 88:11, "Is your steadfast love declared in the grave, or your faithfulness in ruin?"

17. Augustine, *On Christian Teaching* 3.12.20; see *Saint Augustine: On Christian Teaching*, trans. R. P. H. Green, Oxford World's Classics (Oxford: Oxford University Press, 1999), p. 78.

18. For example, compare Ezekiel 18:2-4, 19-20 ("the soul who sins shall die") with Exodus 20:5 ("visiting the iniquity of the fathers on the children to the third and the fourth generation of those who hate me"). See also the differently stated laws in Ezekiel 44:22 and Leviticus 21:14 and also in Ezekiel 44:31 and Leviticus 22:8. Moreover, Ezekiel 45:20 mentions a sacrifice that is not explicitly prescribed in the Pentateuch.

19. Babylonian Talmud, *Shabbat* 13b (see *The Babylonian Talmud*, "Shabbath I," trans. H. Freedman, ed. I. Epstein [London: Soncino, 1938], p. 55). See also Babylonian Talmud *Hagigah* 13a; *Menahoth* 45a. One of the so-called "Thirteen *Middot* ['Hermeneutical Rules'] of Rabbi Ishmael" was the principle that "two passages opposing one another and conflicting with one another stand as they are, until a third passage comes and decides between them." On the thirteen rules of Rabbi Ishmael, see H. L. Strack and G. Stemberger, *Introduction to the Talmud and Midrash*, trans. and ed. M. Bockmuehl (Minneapolis: Fortress, 1996), pp. 20-22. For an example of this principle, see *Mekhilta de-Rabbi Ishmael*, tractate *pisha* 4, where Rabbi Akiba resolves the conflict between Exodus 12:5, "you may take it [the Passover lamb] from the sheep or from the goats," and Deuteronomy 16:2, ". . . from the flock or the herd." Akiba cites Exodus 12:21 as deciding in favor of Exodus 12:5, that the Passover lamb can come only from the flock and not from the herd. This presumably leaves Deuteronomy 16:2 free to be used for some other purpose; see *Mekhilta de-Rabbi Ishmael*, ed. and trans. Jacob Z. Lauterbach, 2nd ed., vol. 1 (Philadelphia: Jewish Publication Society, 2004), pp. 22-23.

20. *Philocalia* 6.1; see *The Philocalia of Origen*, trans. G. Lewis (Edinburgh: Clark, 1911), pp. 42-43.

21. See Plato, *Republic* 3.386a-c, 414b-415e.

22. Jerome, *Against Rufinus* 1.18. Origen is said to have quoted Plato's *Republic* in book six of the *Miscellanies*.

23. Jerome, *Epistle* 112 (*Epistle* 75 in the Augustine corpus).

24. On the use of honey to cover the bitter taste of medicine, see Lucretius, *On the Nature of Things* 1.935-50; 4.10-25.

25. Origen, *Homilies on Jeremiah* 19.15.3-9; 20.1.1–20.5.5; see *Origen: Homilies on Jeremiah, Homily on 1 Kings 28*, trans. John Clark Smith, Fathers of the Church (Washington: Catholic University of America Press, 1998), pp. 217-33.

26. Jerome, *Epistle* 112.

27. Jerome, *Commentary on Galatians* 2.11-13; *Epistle* 112.

28. Augustine, *Epistle* 82.3.23; see *Saint Augustine: Letters*, vol. 1 (1-82), trans. W. Parsons, Fathers of the Church (New York: Fathers of the Church, 1951), pp. 410-11.

29. Augustine, *Epistle* 82.3.24; see *Saint Augustine: Letters*, vol. 1 (1-82), Parsons, p. 411.

30. Augustine, *Epistle* 82.2.5; see *Saint Augustine: Letters*, vol. 1 (1-82), Parsons, pp. 393-94.

31. Augustine, *Epistle* 40.3; see Carolinne White, *The Correspondence (394-419) between Jerome and Augustine of Hippo* (Lewiston: Mellen, 1990), p. 76.

32. Augustine, *Epistle* 40.5; see White, *Correspondence,* p. 78.

33. Augustine, *Epistle* 40.7; see White, *Correspondence,* p. 78. See also Augustine's *Epistle* 82.1.3: "For, I admit to your Charity [that is, Jerome] that it is from those books alone of the Scriptures, which are now called canonical, that I have learned to pay them such honor and respect as to believe most firmly that not one of their authors has erred in writing anything at all. If I do find anything in those books which seems contrary to truth, I decide that either the text is corrupt, or the translator did not follow what was really said, or that I failed to understand it"; see *Saint Augustine: Letters,* vol. 1 (1-82), Parsons, p. 392. See also Augustine's *On Lying* 8 (Nicene and Post-Nicene Fathers 3, p. 461; Fathers of the Church 16, pp. 62-63); and *To Consentius: Against Lying* 26 (Nicene and Post-Nicene Fathers 3, p. 493; Fathers of the Church 16, pp. 157-59).

34. But see Clement of Alexandria, *Miscellanies* 7.9.53, regarding the one who truly possesses Christian knowledge (the "Gnostic" in Clement's terminology): "Whatever then he has in mind, that he has also on his tongue, when addressing those worthy to hear it from their agreement with him, since both his word and his life are in harmony with his thought. For he not only thinks what is true, but he also speaks the truth, except it be medicinally, on occasion; just as a physician, with a view to the safety of his patients, will practice deception or use deceptive language to the sick, according to the sophists"; see *Alexandrian Christianity,* trans. J. E. L. Oulton and H. Chadwick, Library of Christian Classics (Philadelphia: Westminster, 1954), pp. 126-27 (see also Ante-Nicene Fathers 2, p. 538).

35. For a solidly Christian discussion that does not see Paul as the author of these letters, see I. H. Marshall, *The Pastoral Epistles,* International Critical Commentary (Edinburgh: Clark, 1999), pp. 57-92.

36. See Tertullian, *Prescription against Heretics* 19.

37. Irenaeus, *Against Heresies* 1.10.1; 3.4.2; Tertullian, *Against Praxeas* 2; *Prescription against Heretics* 13.1-6; and *Concerning the Veiling of Virgins* 1.3; Hippolytus, *Homily on the Heresy of Noetus* 17-18; Origen, *On First Principles* preface, 4-10; *Didascalia apostolorum* 15.26; Cyprian, *Epistle* 73.5.2; and Novatian, *On the Trinity* 9. On this section, see Michael Graves, "Evangelicals, the Bible, and the Early Church," in *Evangelicals and the Early Church,* ed. G. Kalantzis and A. Tooley (Eugene: Cascade, 2012), pp. 202-7.

38. Irenaeus, *Against Heresies* 1.10.1; see *Early Christian Fathers,* trans. Cyril C. Richardson, Library of Christian Classics (Philadelphia: Westminster, 1953), p. 360 (translation updated).

39. On Irenaeus's distinctive addition to the rule of faith, see *St. Irenaeus of Lyons: Against Heresies,* trans. and annotated by Dominic J. Unger, with further revisions by John J. Dillon, Ancient Christian Writers (New York: Paulist, 1992), pp. 183 n. 1, 185 n. 11.

40. Irenaeus, *Against Heresies* 3.4.2.

41. Irenaeus, *Against Heresies* 1.3.6.

42. Irenaeus, *Against Heresies* 1.8.1.

43. Irenaeus, *Against Heresies* 1.9.4.

44. See also the description by Clement of Alexandria, *Miscellanies* 7.16.96, who says that heretics quote Scripture only piecemeal and without regard for the context, and that they tend to focus on names alone (*Alexandrian Christianity,* Oulton and Chadwick, pp. 155-56; Ante-Nicene Fathers 2, pp. 551-52).

45. Irenaeus, *Against Heresies* 3.2.1-2; 3.3.1–4.3.

46. Augustine, *On Christian Teaching* 3.10.14.

47. Augustine, *Two Books on Genesis Against the Manichees* 2.2.3; see *Saint Augustine, On Genesis: Two Books on Genesis against the Manichees and On the Literal Interpretation of Genesis: An Unfinished Book*, trans. Roland J. Teske, S.J., Fathers of the Church (Washington: Catholic University of America Press, 1991), p. 95.

48. On the change in Augustine's view of the value of the literal sense of Genesis, see Augustine, *Literal Commentary on Genesis* 8.2.5. See also 1.14.28: "Now, it is obvious that everything subject to change is fashioned out of something formless; and furthermore, our Catholic faith declares, and right reason teaches, that there could not have existed any matter of anything whatsoever unless it came from God"; see *St. Augustine: The Literal Meaning of Genesis*, vol. 1, trans. John Hammond Taylor, S.J., Ancient Christian Writers (New York: Paulist, 1982), p. 35.

49. Augustine, *On Christian Teaching* 1.36.40.

50. Augustine, *On Christian Teaching* 1.36.41.

51. Augustine, *On Christian Teaching* 3.27.38.

52. On this aspect of ancient interpretation, see Michael Graves, *Jerome's Hebrew Philology* (Leiden: Brill, 2007), pp. 26-35.

53. Augustine, *On Christian Teaching* 3.2.2; see *On Christian Teaching*, Green, p. 68.

54. *On Christian Teaching*, Green, p. 68.

55. Augustine, *On Christian Teaching* 3.4.8.

56. See also Augustine, *On Christian Teaching* 3.3.6: "The points that I have just made about the problems of punctuation also apply to the problems of reading aloud. These too, unless they are simply mistakes due to a reader's gross carelessness, are resolved by considering either the rules of faith or the surrounding context" (*On Christian Teaching*, Green, p. 70). Augustine's perspective is different from that of Irenaeus. In *Against Heresies* 3.7.2, Irenaeus also says that one must observe proper reading aloud in Paul's letters in order to avoid blasphemies. But Irenaeus does not suggest that one needs the rule of faith in order to ascertain the correct sense of the text.

57. Augustine, *Expositions of Psalms* 74.12; see *Saint Augustine: Expositions of the Psalms*, vol. 4, trans. Maria Boulding, Works of Saint Augustine (Hyde Park: New City, 2002), p. 50.

58. Augustine, *On the Trinity* 15.28.51. See also Augustine's appeal to the rule of faith in his predestinarian explanation of John 17:5 (*Tractates on the Gospel of John* 105.8).

59. Augustine, *On Original Sin* 2.34.29.

60. Augustine, *On Baptism against the Donatists* 2.1.2.

61. For a related idea on development, see Augustine, *Expositions of the Psalms* 67.39, where he explains that certain meanings in Scripture lie hidden and are not made known in a form useful to everyone until they are needed to give answer to heretics.

62. See *Two Books on Genesis Against the Manichees* 2.2.3; see *Saint Augustine, On Genesis: Two Books on Genesis against the Manichees and On the Literal Interpretation of Genesis: An Unfinished Book*, Teske, pp. 145-47.

63. J. H. Lesher, *Xenophanes of Colophon, Fragments: A Text and Translation with a Commentary* (Toronto: University of Toronto Press, 1992), fragment 11.

64. For an outright rejection of Homeric poetry, see Plato, *Republic* 10.

65. On Theagenes, see Hermann Diels and Walther Kranz, *Die Fragmente der Vorsokratiker*, vol. 1, 6th ed. (Berlin: Weidmann, 1952), pp. 51-52. Pherecydes of Syros was an-

other sixth-century BCE philosopher who applied allegory to ancient myths (see Origen, *Against Celsus* 6.42).

66. *Homeric Problems* 1.1-2; see *Heraclitus: Homeric Problems,* trans. D. A. Russell and D. Konstan, Writings from the Greco-Roman World (Atlanta: Society of Biblical Literature, 2005), p. 3. Heraclitus probably lived in the late first or early second century CE.

67. Philo, *Allegorical Interpretation* 1.43-45 (Loeb Classical Library). Origen agrees with Philo's interpretation of Genesis 2:8, saying, "And who is so silly as to believe that God, after the manner of a farmer, 'planted a paradise eastward in Eden,' and set in it a visible and palpable 'tree of life,' of such a sort that anyone who tasted its fruit with his bodily teeth would gain life" (*On First Principles* 4.3.1; see *Origen: On First Principles,* trans. G. W. Butterworth [New York: Harper & Row, 1966], p. 288).

68. See also *Homeric Problems* 21-22 on the attempted binding of Zeus: "There is only one remedy for this impiety: to show that the myth is an allegory"; see *Heraclitus: Homeric Problems,* Russell and Konstan, p. 41.

69. Philo, *On Mating with Preliminary Studies* 114-15.

70. Philo, *The Unchangeableness of God* 21-22, 51-52. Philo insists that God is not subject to irrational passions. On God's "regretting," see, for example, Genesis 6:6-7; Exodus 32:14; 1 Samuel 15:11, 35; Jeremiah 18:10; and Jonah 3:10. The Hebrew verb *nhm* in the Niphal stem can mean "regret," "be sorry," or "console oneself" (L. Koehler and W. Baumgartner, *The Hebrew and Aramaic Lexicon of the Old Testament,* vol. 2 [Leiden: Brill, 1995], p. 688).

71. Philo, *The Unchangeableness of God* 53-55.

72. See also Philo, *Allegorical Interpretation* 1.36-39; and *The Confusion of Tongues* 134-36, on the sentence "And the Lord came down to see the city and the tower" (Gen. 11:5).

73. *Clement Romance* 25-57; see Johannes Irmscher and Georg Strecker, "The Pseudo-Clementines," in *New Testament Apocrypha,* vol. 2, ed. W. Schneemelcher and trans. R. McL. Wilson, rev. ed. (Louisville: Westminster John Knox, 1992), pp. 513-16. Peter is portrayed as responding to objections made by a certain Simon, who was upsetting people with his teachings. Problematic texts mentioned in this discussion include Genesis 6:6-7; 8:21; 18:21; and 22:1.

74. Clement of Alexandria, *Miscellanies* 7.16.96 (*Alexandrian Christianity,* Oulton and Chadwick, p. 156; Ante-Nicene Fathers 2, p. 551).

75. Clement of Alexandria, *Miscellanies* 6.15.124.3 (Ante-Nicene Fathers 2, p. 509).

76. Origen, *On First Principles* 4.2.8-9. According to Origen, the Spirit placed these stumbling blocks into the text to make us recognize that a higher meaning lies hidden below the surface. When real events harmonized with the mystical meaning intended by Scripture, these events were recorded. But when no real events were found to be suitable for expressing the higher truth, "the scripture wove into the story something which did not happen, occasionally something which could not happen, and occasionally something that might have happened but in fact did not"; see *Origen: On First Principles,* Butterworth, pp. 284-87.

77. Origen, *Homilies on Joshua* 8.1; see *Origen: Homilies on Joshua,* trans. Barbara J. Bruce, ed. Cynthia White, Fathers of the Church (Washington: Catholic University of America Press, 2010), p. 85.

78. See Origen, *Homilies on Numbers* 27.12.

79. Origen, *Homilies on Joshua* 8.6.

80. Origen, *Homilies on Joshua* 8.7.

81. "Hebron" is being interpreted as if related to the Hebrew word *heber,* "union" or "association." See also Philo, *On the Posterity of Cain* 60; *Worse Attacks the Better* 15.

82. Origen, *Homilies on Joshua* 13.2.

83. See 1 Samuel 15:9-33.

84. Origen, *Homilies on Joshua* 8.7; see *Origen: Homilies on Joshua,* Bruce, p. 94. See also Origen, *Homilies on Joshua* 12.1-3.

85. Origen's theology of war is similar in some ways to the concept of the "greater *jihad*" in Islam. The term *jihad* in Arabic means "striving." In this line of thought, the "lesser *jihad*" refers to striving in physical battles that may be necessary, for example, because one is attacked. The "greater *jihad*" refers to striving within oneself in order to combat sin; see John Kaltner, *Introducing the Qur'an for Today's Reader* (Minneapolis: Fortress, 2011), pp. 168-70, 174-75.

86. Origen, *Homilies on Jeremiah* 20.1.

87. Origen, *Homilies on Jeremiah* 18.6 and 19.15.

88. Origen, *Homilies on Jeremiah* 20.1.

89. On this whole paragraph, see Origen, *On First Principles* 4.2.1-2. Origen continues: "Now the reason why all those we have mentioned hold false opinions and make impious or ignorant assertions about God appears to be nothing else but this, that scripture is not understood in its spiritual sense, but is interpreted according to the bare letter. On this account we must explain to those who believe that the sacred books are not the works of men, but that they were composed and come down to us as a result of the inspiration of the Holy Spirit by the will of the Father of the universe through Jesus Christ, what are the methods of interpretation that appear right to us, who keep to the rule of the heavenly Church of Jesus Christ through the succession from the apostles"; see *Origen: On First Principles,* Butterworth, pp. 271-72.

90. For other war texts in Joshua, see for example 10:28, 30, 33, 35, 37, 39, 40; 11:16-23; and 6:21: "Then they devoted all in the city to destruction, both men and women, young and old, oxen, sheep, and donkeys, with the edge of the sword." See also Numbers 21:34-35; 31:17-18; Deuteronomy 7:2; 13:6-15; 20:16-18; and 1 Samuel 15:3.

91. Eusebius, *Preparation for the Gospel* 8.10; see *Eusebius: Preparation for the Gospel,* vol. 1, trans. E. H. Gifford (Oxford: Clarendon, 1903), p. 407.

92. See *Didyme L'aveugle. Sur la Genèse,* vol. 1, trans. Pierre Nautin, Sources chrétiennes (Paris: Cerf, 1976), p. 46.

93. Gregory of Nyssa, *Life of Moses* 2.91; see *Gregory of Nyssa: The Life of Moses,* trans. A. J. Malherbe and E. Ferguson, Classics of Western Spirituality (New York: Paulist, 1978), p. 75. According to Gregory, this passage teaches that we as Christians must "destroy utterly the first birth of evil" within us. He quotes Ezekiel 18:20, "The soul who sins shall die. The son shall not suffer for the iniquity of the father," in order to demonstrate that God would not literally kill Pharaoh's son because of Pharaoh's sin. Gregory argues, "If such a one [an infant] now pays the penalty of his father's wickedness, where is justice? Where is piety? Where is holiness? . . . How can the history so contradict reason?" (*Gregory of Nyssa: The Life of Moses,* Malherbe and Ferguson, p. 75). See also *Gregory of Nyssa: Homilies on the Song of Songs,* trans. Richard A. Norris, Jr., Writings from the Greco-Roman World (Atlanta: Society of Biblical Literature, 2009), p. 169 (*Homily* 5).

94. On the hardening of Pharaoh's heart, see Exodus 3:19 and 4:21 (hardening an-

nounced); 7:13, 14, 22; 8:15, 19, 32; 9:7, 34, 35 (heart is hardened); 9:12; 10:1, 20, 27; 11:10; 14:8 (God hardens). See also Romans 9:6-29.

95. See *Philocalia* 21.1-23; 27.1-13. Ephrem the Syrian also emphasizes Pharaoh's free will and argues that Pharaoh alone was responsible for God's judgments against him (see *Commentary on Exodus* 5.1; 7.1; 10.1, 3-5).

96. Robert C. Hill, who translated many works of Chrysostom into English, preferred the translation "considerateness" for *synkatabasis*. I agree that sometimes this is a good translation, but I think that "condescension" does capture in many passages the right sense of God's lowering the presentation of his divine self to our understanding.

97. For "limitations," the Greek has *astheneia*, "weakness."

98. John Chrysostom, *Homilies on Genesis* 15.8. See also Chrysostom's *Homilies on Genesis* 58.7-13, on divine condescension in the story of Jacob wrestling with God in Genesis 32:24-32.

99. Theodoret of Cyrus, *Commentary on Jeremiah* 4:28; see *Theodoret of Cyrus: Commentaries on the Prophets*, vol. 1, trans. Robert C. Hill (Brookline: Holy Cross Orthodox, 2006), p. 42.

100. Theodoret of Cyrus, *Commentary on Jeremiah* 9:9; see *Theodoret of Cyrus: Commentaries on the Prophets*, vol. 1, Hill, p. 58. See also *Commentary on Jeremiah* 14:19.

101. On God's body parts as his various capacities, see Augustine, *Expositions of the Psalms* 9.33. On the necessity of not reading concrete depictions of God too literally, see *Expositions of the Psalms* 76.20.

102. Augustine, *On Christian Teaching* 3.11.17 (*On Christian Teaching*, Green, p. 77). See also 3.16.24: "But if [a statement in Scripture] appears to enjoin wickedness or wrongdoing or to forbid self-interest or kindness, it is figurative" (*On Christian Teaching*, Green, p. 80).

103. For example, see Paul Copan, *Is God a Moral Monster? Making Sense of the Old Testament God* (Grand Rapids: Baker, 2011), pp. 169-85.

Chapter Seven. Conclusions

1. Recent discussions of biblical inspiration that make positive contributions to our contemporary understanding of this doctrine include I. Howard Marshall, *Biblical Inspiration* (Grand Rapids: Eerdmans, 1982); Paul J. Achtemeier, *Inspiration and Authority: Nature and Function of Christian Scripture*, rev. ed. (Peabody: Hendrickson, 1999); and N. T. Wright, *Scripture and the Authority of God: How to Read the Bible Today* (New York: HarperCollins, 2011).

2. Of course, even with the examples given here the ancient views reflect kernels of truth; many proper names in Scripture are significant, many textual details do matter, and sometimes the specific historical context of a passage is not very important to the message, for example, in many Psalms. But as interpretive principles grounded in the nature of divine inspiration itself, the ancient perspectives on these topics are not very helpful.

3. John Barton, *The Nature of Biblical Criticism* (Louisville: Westminster John Knox, 2007), pp. 101-16, favors the term "plain sense" to describe the object of critical study of the Bible. Ideally, when biblical critics identify disharmony within a biblical book and posit multiple sources behind a document, this is a result of first having attempted to read the text holistically and having found significant problems with a holistic reading.

4. An important part of making a theological argument in favor of a particular interpretation of a biblical text is situating that text within a broader reading of Scripture as a whole. The best commentators from the patristic period regularly practiced this kind of theological biblical interpretation. It must be kept in mind, however, that even a "biblical theology," that is, a theology developed using biblical categories, is constructed by an individual interpreter and must be justified and explained both at the macro level and also in its application to specific biblical texts. There is no self-evident "biblical theology" that serves everyone as a universal guide for interpreting Scripture.

5. "Like the task of exegesis — and like real bridge building, I suspect — the application of scripture to our own age and world and lives means combining hard thinking with inspired intuition"; see John Goldingay, *Models for Interpretation of Scripture* (Grand Rapids: Eerdmans, 1995), p. 259.

6. In discussing the application of principles from the Bible to modern situations, I. H. Marshall rightly observes, "If it is objected that this method is somewhat subjective, it must be replied that this is inevitable, since there can be difference of opinion about how to apply biblical teaching to varying situations (just as there are differences of opinion about the mode of baptism)." See Marshall, *Biblical Inspiration*, p. 105.

7. For the U.S. Constitution, of course, the text itself, its tradition of legal interpretation, and its contemporary interpreters (that is, judges) are seen as possessing authority derived through a kind of social contract, not by divine right. The interpretive authority of the U.S. judicial system is therefore not a direct parallel to the divine right claim to authority put forth by certain churches.

8. The canons of these churches are not radically different from each other. The differences involve a small number of disputed books. For example, only the Syrian church recognizes the Prayer of Manasseh. Both the Syrian and Coptic churches recognize Psalm 151, while the Armenian church does not. The Ethiopian church has the fullest canon, recognizing books such as *Jubilees, Enoch*, and *4 Baruch*. Protestant thinking about the Old Testament canon follows the idea that Christians should only accept as canonical books that were regarded as canonical among Jews in the time of Jesus (that is, Jesus' "Scriptures"), applying Jerome's *hebraica veritas* ("Hebrew truth") concept as the criterion for determining this.

9. A well-written book on this topic is Christopher J. H. Wright, *Knowing Jesus through the Old Testament* (Downers Grove: InterVarsity, 1992).

10. N. T. Wright explains "scripture's authority" as "God's authority exercised through scripture" (Wright, *Scripture and the Authority of God*, e.g., pp. 118, 126, 128, 138).

11. See Willard M. Swartley, *Slavery, Sabbath, War and Women: Case Issues in Biblical Interpretation* (Scottdale: Herald, 1983), pp. 31-37. For Old Testament slavery texts, see Exodus 21:1-11, 20-21, 26-27; Leviticus 25:39-55; Numbers 31:7-12; Deuteronomy 15:12-18; 20:10-14. The New Testament letter of Philemon offers perhaps the most important biblical perspective that stands in direct criticism of slavery. Moreover, major Christian notions such as the unity of the body of Christ, love for one's neighbor, and doing good to all undercut slavery as an institution.

12. See Mishnah, *Eduyoth* 1:4-5; and Tosefta, *Eduyoth* 1:4, which suggest that one reason to preserve minority legal rulings (despite the fact that the majority ruling is followed in practice) is that a later court might need to go back and retrieve an older minority ruling.

13. For example, see Ambrose, *On the Duties of the Clergy* 1.28.135; 2.15.74; 1.27.129.

14. One result of pluralism in the modern world is that political states in the West,

which necessarily maintain law through force, have retreated from using scriptural revelation as the basis for civil law. This should not be seen as pushing religion out of the public realm, as if Christians can no longer be involved for good in society at large. Instead, Christians should welcome this modern situation as creating a non-coercive environment in which the gospel can prosper. The twentieth century witnessed terrible crimes against humanity that resulted from totalitarian governments that suppressed alternative viewpoints, including Christian viewpoints. The atrocities of the past century were not caused by modern pluralism but by ignorance, violence, and fanaticism. A key antidote against such evils is the freedom to express differing views. For Christians, a culture that allows multiple voices is a healthy environment in which to communicate the gospel.

Index of Ancient Authors, Works, and Figures

Index of Modern Authors

Index of Scripture References